First Daughters

First Daughters

LETTERS BETWEEN U.S. PRESIDENTS AND THEIR DAUGHTERS

Gerard W. Gawalt and Ann G. Gawalt

BLACK DOG
& LEVENTHAL
PUBLISHERS
NEW YORK

IN ASSOCIATION WITH THE LIBRARY OF CONGRESS

TO THOSE SPECIAL RELATIONSHIPS BETWEEN
DAUGHTERS AND FATHERS, ESPECIALLY IN THE
GAWALT, RUSHFORTH, BUNKER, FAGERSTEN,
AND CAVANAUGH FAMILIES.

Copyright © 2004 Library of Congress, Washington D.C.

All photos courtesy of the Library of Congress

All rights reserved. No part of this book may be reproduced in any form
or by any electronic or mechanical means, including information storage and retrieval
systems, without written permission from the publisher.

ISBN 1-57912-370-8

Library of Congress Cataloging-in-Publication Data

First daughters : letters between U.S. presidents and their daughters / [compiled by]
Gerard W. Gawalt and Ann G. Gawalt.
p. cm.
Collection of letters held by the Library of Congress.
1. Presidents—United States—Correspondence. 2. Children of presidents—United States—Correspondence. 3. Daughters—United States—Correspondence. 4. Fathers and daughters—United
States—Correspondence. 5. Presidents—United States—Family
relationships. I. Gawalt, Gerard W. II. Gawalt, Ann G. III. Library of Congress.

E176.1.F515 2004
973'.09'9—dc22

Jacket and interior design: Liz Driesbach

Manufactured in the U.S.A.

Published by
Black Dog & Leventhal Publishers, Inc.
151 West 19th Street
New York, New York 10011

Distributed by
Workman Publishing Company
708 Broadway
New York, New York 10003

b d f g e c a

CONTENTS

Foreword by James H. Billington, Librarian of Congress 7
Introduction by Gerard W. Gawalt and Ann G. Gawalt 9
The Correspondents 16

The Letters

 1 Just Friends: "your cheerful letter..." 37
 2 Advice: "by way of advice and admonition" 73
 3 Education: "real good lessons..." 93
 4 Marriage and Remarriage: "we are very much in love." 131
 5 Childbirth: "courage is as essential to triumph..." 157
 6 Encouragement: "your late success" 177
 7 Health and Consolation: "the sad, sad news" 193
 8 Politics: "the greatest victory of your life" 221
 9 Overseas Ventures: "some very decided step" 265
10 At Home: "those comforts which long habit has rendered necessary" . 291

Sources 307
Acknowledgments 314
Index 317

FOREWORD

"Will you please telephone out to the school and say that you want me to come home on the 2:10 bus as I think Quentin would like to have somebody to play with," wrote young Ethel Roosevelt to her father, President Theodore Roosevelt, at the White House, reflecting the very human side of the relationships between presidents of the United States and their daughters—even when the father is famous for being a "Rough Rider."

This letter is part of the Library of Congress's collection of the personal papers of twenty-three presidents of the United States. *First Daughters* draws upon the Library's magnificent and unparalleled holdings of manuscripts, books, microform, prints, and photographs —as well as those of other presidential libraries— to open a unique window into the special familial relationships of our first families.

First Daughters is the latest in a long list of Library of Congress publications of treasures from the personal papers of America's presidents, the most recent of which is an illustrated biography, *Thomas Jefferson: Genius of Liberty*. In addition, the Library's digital initiative is now making the papers of four presidents—George Washington, Thomas Jefferson, James Madison, and Abraham Lincoln—available free of charge to persons of all ages and nations through the Library's Web site at http://www.loc.gov.

First Daughters allows readers to explore the depth and range of familial relationships from the dual perspective of father and daughter. These private letters, many of which are published here for the first time, will surprise, entertain, enlighten, and occasionally sadden readers.

Thirty-one U.S. presidents of the United States have been the fathers of daughters. Their relationships were sometimes intense, sometimes distant, sometimes strictly personal, sometimes impersonal. The text and illustrations gathered here exhibit a wide range of sentiments, ideas, and plans.

The thematic groupings in the book allow readers to experience the evolution of parental relationships over two centuries as well as the increasing pressures of the ever more public presidency. Friendship, education, marriage, advice, encouragement, childbirth, health, consolation, home life, overseas adventures, and above all politics are the major themes.

First Daughters includes only a small number of the thousands of letters exchanged by presidents and their daughters. As the digital age moves forward, more institutions that have preserved these papers will want to follow the Library of Congress's lead and make them available through the Internet.

In today's world, as the personal lives of politicians and their families face the constant scrutiny of worldwide public view, private messages are increasingly expressed through secure but ephemeral electronic transmissions. This anthology of the written word from an earlier time documents the innermost thoughts, plans, and experiences of the nation's most public figures. *First Daughters: Letters Between U.S. Presidents and Their Daughters* is a book that continues the Library of Congress's tradition of providing ever increasing access to the richness and humanity of our cultural heritage.

James H. Billington
The Librarian of Congress

INTRODUCTION

Daughters and their fathers enjoy a special bond, no less so if they happen to be presidential fathers and daughters.

The personal letters of these leaders and their daughters reveal not only the ties that bound them inextricably together, but the efforts of all family members to achieve independence and fulfillment in full view of a national and sometimes international audience. *First Daughters* draws upon thousands of personal letters to allow readers to share in these special relationships. These letters, like poetry, speak directly to the reader without outside editorial or interpretive constraints.

Correspondence between presidents and their children often replaced the intimacy of presence. Because presidents tend to spend most of their time away from home—serving in the military, running for office, serving in office, traveling or fulfilling other demands—they often spend little time with their families. Because so little time is spent together, their letters become an important part of their relationship. Margaret Truman's father, for example, was gone for long periods of time, therefore "he tried to comfort himself, console me, and compensate for his absence by writing me some chatty letters."[1]

For many presidents and their daughters, the demands of public office had an opposite effect on their correspondence. For

---

[1] Margaret Truman, *Letters from Father: The Truman Family's Personal Correspondence* (New York: Arbor House, 1981), p. 11.

some, there are very few known written exchanges. In other cases, presidents dictated letters through their secretaries to their children or even, one suspects, had their secretaries simply compose such letters for their signature. Most of the extant letters are handwritten, but some, such as those of Lyndon Johnson, are initialed typescripts. Presidents Garfield, Hayes, Taft, F. D. Roosevelt, and Johnson all admitted to the pressures of time that occasionally forced them to dictate their letters to their children. The aides of one president claim to have written most of his letters to his own mother, including Mother's Day greetings.

Sometimes presidents indulged themselves by writing letters more for posterity than for their children. Theodore Roosevelt's children mused that he wrote some "posterity letters" in the form of pictographs. But the Rough Rider was not alone. Surely some of the letters of Truman, Taft, and Wilson fit this category.

Personal correspondence was often a means of expressing family members' emotions and innermost thoughts. Presidents and their daughters became experts at erecting a public façade to enhance their political aims and protect their private lives. Theodore Roosevelt's sentimental notes stand in stark contrast to his Rough Rider image, while the cool, aloof public images of Woodrow Wilson and George Washington disappear in their deeply personal letters. In some cases, the public façade is apparent in the private correspondence. Indeed, many of these letters are concerned with the various facets of maintaining a proper public facade. But this duality contributes to our interest in this collection of familial correspondence.

What shines forth from virtually all of these letters is the daughters' ideal of sacrifice in service of their fathers. They were constantly in the public eye, their activities constantly scrutinized and discussed by the news media of the time. Their personal lives were frequently sacrificed to the "public good" or simply the demands of their father's office. Opportunities for personal and parental glory or doom ever hovered overhead. From George Washington's time to the present, the situation faced by presidential offspring remains unchanged.

While the public persona of the fathers might first attract the reader to these letters, the intimate view, the real emotions and daily drama of the correspondents, are what will hold the readers' attention. Particularly before the use of the telephone and Internet as our primary means of communication, a personal letter was the preeminent and only practical means of communication across long distances. For this reason alone, the correspondence of our presidents remains fascinating to people interested in the lives of America's first families.

Presidential papers were first acquired by Congress in 1834 when it purchased the public papers of George Washington for $25,000. Subsequently, the Library of Congress became the repository of the personal papers of twenty-three presidents of the United States from George Washington to Calvin Coolidge. The Library has also published many books about presidents of the United States and made their papers available to researchers through microfilm and now the Internet. The many publications of presidential papers tend to focus on the political and professional activities of individual presidents, and sometimes on their spouses and sons. However, there is no work that focuses on the special relationships of presidents and their daughters. It is natural, then, that the institution that holds so many personal papers of presidents and has been a leader in providing access to them should provide the interested public with a book of the personal, private letters of presidents and their daughters.

First Daughters is structured to provide readers with the depth and range of sentiments, ideas, and plans expressed in the letters. Wherever possible, entire letters have been reproduced, to provide full access to the thoughts of their authors. This thematic approach enables readers to amply observe the correspondents' approaches to similar joys, sorrows, tensions, and pleasures of their respective private and public lives. The selection of letters was based on availability, readability, subject content, and contemporary interest.

Minimal editorial or interpretive intrusions have been made, so that the letters can speak directly as written. Letters transcribed by the editors from original manuscripts reflect the spelling and grammatical idiosyncracies of the authors of the letters, and the standards of the English their times. No attempt has been made by the editors of this volume to introduce modern/correct spelling or grammar. However, where text has been reproduced from previously printed sources, the letters may reflect earlier editorial efforts to normalize spelling and grammar.

Compiling the letters for this volume presented some unique challenges. Much of the correspondence is not available to the public. In some cases, presidents choose to keep it private for a variety of understandable reasons. In other cases, such as written communiqués between James Monroe or Millard Filmore and their daughters, such letters either were never written, were destroyed, or have simply become lost. In still another scenario, for example that of Ulysses S. Grant, only the letters of the presidents to their daughters have been found; the responses, if any, no longer exist.

Part of the problem is institutional. The papers at the Library of Congress were acquired by the government as the public papers of the presidents. As in the case of Thomas Jefferson, personal papers were deliberately excluded from those acquired by the federal government. Only after the creation of presidential libraries and presidential pyramids at the National Archives did the focus of the Library's collection shift to include personal papers.

Reinforcing this deliberate institutional selection process were private evaluations that placed family papers in the category of "too private" for public consumption or not important enough for public interest. Moreover, there was and is an overwhelming interest in the letters written by the president. Lurking in the background is the sexist bias that men's papers are important, women's are not. For example, there is with the Thomas Jefferson Papers a small volume containing some of Jefferson's pedestrian legal notes as well as the more interesting household accounts of Monticello maintained by Jefferson's wife, Martha, and then later by one of his granddaughters. The item is cataloged and indexed as being Jefferson's legal notes, without any mention of the household accounts. How many letters and documents of female members of presidential families have gone unidentified, due to such narrow views? How many personal letters have been secretly retained by well-meaning family members and subsequently lost to history? How many personal letters have been destroyed by well-meaning family members?

It is important to not try to rewrite history, to instead understand the style and content of these letters in the context in which they were written. The uses of slave labor and the treatment of individual slaves are routinely discussed in the letters of some pre-Civil War presidents and their daughters. Their everyday tone unfortunately reflects the everyday nature of their subject. Subjects that grate harshly on today's sensitive ears, such as the clashes of hunting dogs and cougars, were discussed without hesitation by Theodore Roosevelt in a friendly letter of January 18, 1901, to his young daughter Ethel.

On the other hand, presidential fathers offered great wisdom and common sense that still resonate despite the passage of time. George Washington advised his young granddaughter in a September 14, 1794, letter: "Love is a mighty pretty thing; but like all delicious things, it is cloying; and when the first transports of the passion begin to subside, which it assuredly will do, and yeild, oftentimes too late, to more sober reflections, it serves to evince, that love is too dainty a food to live upon *alone*."

The correspondents' raw emotions remain fresh through the years. Be it joy or fear or triumph or tragedy, feelings were openly bared to each other in so much of the correspondence of presidents and their daughters.

However, appearances were often as important as substance in the politically charged atmosphere of the presidential circle. Theodore Roosevelt, William Howard Taft, and Harry S. Truman were concerned about the impressions their daughters would make overseas. Taft worried that a proposed freelance writing project would appear improper or diminish his daughter's (read: his) standing in the community. Others fussed about their daughters' physical appearances, their clothing, their success at school, their friends, even their charitable works. For example, President Johnson's comments about his daughters' weight and grooming might be unsettling to some readers, though the subjects seem to have been simply comfortable, common ground for father and daughters. Now, these are all subjects that any parent might be concerned about, but the prism of the presidency magnifies every issue and distorts every view. The pressure on parent and child can lead to crumbling egos or explosive acting out. What is remarkable is the equanimity displayed by both presidents and their daughters in these letters throughout our history.

Presidents with more than one daughter often had different relationships with each child, as were often reflected in their letters. While Thomas Jefferson often discussed plantation problems with his elder daughter, Martha, these issues seldom appear in letters to his younger one, Mary. Woodrow Wilson's publicly available letters to his three daughters vary in style, content, and frequency: his correspondence with Jessie and Eleanor is fuller and more detailed, filled with concerns and ideas of public/political events, than that with Margaret—but all demonstrated close emotional ties. Theodore Roosevelt's seems to have written no letters to his daughter Alice when she was a child, while those to young Ethel are frequent and charming. On the other hand, his later letters to the adult Alice reflect their deep mutual interest in politics.

Some letters reflect breakdowns in familial relations. The death of a wife and mother and subsequent remarriage of the father often caused family crises. When Presidents John Tyler and Benjamin Harrison married younger women after the deaths of their first wives (the mothers of their daughters), their writings—or lack thereof—captures their turmoil: Tyler's letters beg for acceptance. Harrison's correspondence with his daughter ends. On the other hand, Woodrow Wilson's and his daughters' letters show an uptick in emotion as the family comes to grips with his remarriage. Theodore Roosevelt's failure to correspond regularly with his daughter Alice during her childhood was perhaps as a reaction to the death of his first wife and Alice's mother, just as he failed to include that part of his life in his autobiography. President Jefferson has often been viewed as a very controlling parent, issuing detailed instructions to his daughters and demanding unfettered love. But this may have simply been the concerned reaction of a single parent who was away from home for long periods, leaving his children under the supervision of another person. All are natural behaviors that would resonate with any parent.

There is an irresistible attraction to historical, personal letters, whether they are between presidents and their daughters, soldiers and their families, or migrant workers and theirs. They provide windows into the private thoughts and intimate feelings of people who, however famous, are otherwise strangers to us. Sometimes the view is clear and clean, sometimes opaque and cloudy, sometimes distorted, but always it is interesting. This selection of letters provides a unique perspective into the lives of the most public of America's families.

THE CORRESPONDENTS

GEORGE WASHINGTON (1732-99) was born in West-moreland County, Virginia, the son of Augustine Washington (1694–1743) and Mary Ball (1708–89). After a distinguished career as a commander of Virginia troops during the French and Indian War, Washington settled down as a planter and politician in Fairfax County, Virginia. In 1759 he married Martha Dandridge Custis (1731–1802), a wealthy widow. A leader of the revolutionary movement against Great Britain in Virginia, Washington was appointed commander-in-chief of the American revolutionary forces in 1775. After leading the Americans to victory, he was the unanimous choice in 1789 to serve as president of the United States under the newly adopted federal constitution. After serving two terms as the nation's first federal president, he retired to his home, Mount Vernon. President Washington served from 1798–99 as head of the federal army raised to fight a feared French invasion.

Washington had no direct descendants, but he reared Martha's two children as his own. At the death of his stepson, John Parke Custis (1755–81), Washington and his wife took in John's four children, including Martha Parke Custis, Elizabeth Parke Custis, and Eleanor Parke Custis, who spent much of their young lives with George and Martha at Mount Vernon and the nation's capitals. Although Martha, Elizabeth, and Eleanor were not technically Washington's daughters, their unusual circumstances justify their inclusion here.

ELIZABETH PARKE CUSTIS (1776–1832) was born at Mt. Airy, Maryland. "She has a double Chinn . . . in Point of Fatness with fine black Hair, & Eyes, upon the whole I think It is as pretty & fine a Baba as ever I saw," wrote John Parke Custis to his mother, Martha, on Elizabeth's birthdate, August 21, 1776. Despite President Washington's cautionary advice to Elizabeth in 1794, just two years later she married Thomas Law (1759–1834), a native of England and son of Edmund Law, bishop of Carlisle. Although Martha described Thomas as "a man of fortune from the East Indies and Brother of the Bishop of Carlyle" (Martha Washington to Sally Cary Fairfax, May 17, 1798), Eliza and Thomas's marriage had dissolved by 1811. In August, 1804, Elizabeth and Thomas signed a separation agreement, granting her an annual $1,500 payment and her husband custody of their daughter.

ELEANOR (NELLY) PARKE CUSTIS (1779–1852) lived with her grandparents after the remarriage of her widowed mother (née Eleanor Calvert) to Dr. David Stuart in 1783. Educated by private tutors and her grandparents, Eleanor spent her teenage years in Washington's presidential household. Washington became Eleanor's legal guardian in 1799 to facilitate her marriage to Lawrence Lewis (1767–1839), a nephew of Washington's, on February 22, 1799. The couple had eight children and built their house, Woodlawn, on lands given to Eleanor by President Washington.

Like her older sisters, **MARTHA PARKE CUSTIS** (1777–1854) spent a considerable amount of time with her grandparents after the death of her father in 1781. In 1795 she married Thomas Peter (1769–1834). The couple spent most of their married life in Georgetown in the new District of Columbia. She was the mother of six children and a grand dame of the Washington social scene.

JOHN ADAMS (1735–1826), born in Braintree, Massachusetts, the son of John Adams (1691–1761) and Susanna Boylston (1699–1797), graduated from Harvard College, and practiced law before becoming immersed in revolutionary politics. In 1764 he married Abigail Smith (1744–1818), who became his confidant, political advisor, and business manager. Adams was a member of the Continental

Congress, where he helped write the Declaration of Independence before becoming American minister in Paris and London. After serving eight years as President Washington's vice president, Adams was elected to the presidency in 1796. An undeclared war with France and numerous political battles marked his presidency.

ABIGAIL (AMELIA, EMMY, NABBY) ADAMS (1765–1813), the first-born child of John and Abigail Smith Adams, was born in Braintree, Massachusetts. Educated at home, Nabby prepared for a traditional role as daughter, wife, and mother.

Nabby became engaged at seventeen to a young Boston lawyer, Royall Tyler. John and Abigail believed that Nabby was too young to marry and discouraged the alliance. When Mrs. Adams traveled to France to join John, then one of America's ministers at Paris, Nabby went with her. As her parents had hoped, her relationship with Royall Tyler foundered on the broad Atlantic.

In 1785 John Adams became the first American minister to Great Britain, and Nabby and her mother went with him to London. Discouraged by Royall Tyler's lack of attentions to her and encouraged by the presence of an older, handsome veteran of the American Revolution, Nabby broke her engagement to Tyler and quickly married New Yorker William Stephen Smith, her father's secretary at the American legation, on June 26, 1786.

Nabby's marriage proved unfortunate, her husband absent for long periods as he pursued various ventures in the American West and attended an insurrection in Venezuela. Her brother, John Quincy, later described her as "an innocent victim of fortune's treacherous game."

Nabby's and her father's letters, however, reveal a deep personal relationship between them; indeed, she became a close political advisor to her father. Like her mother, she served as a sounding board for her father in his hours of trouble and triumph, and again like her mother, offered him sound advice.

THOMAS JEFFERSON (1743–1826), son of Peter Jefferson (1708–57) and Jane Randolph (1720–76), was born in Albemarle County, Virginia, graduated from the College of William and Mary, and practiced law while running a large plantation. In 1772 he married Martha Wayles Skelton and the couple had six children. A political leader in revolutionary Virginia, Jefferson drafted the Declaration of Independence and served as a wartime governor of Virginia and American minister to France. Upon his return to the United States in 1789, he became Secretary of State, and then vice president in 1797, before being elected president in 1800. Jefferson's two presidential terms were highlighted by the acquisition of the Louisiana Territory, the Lewis and Clark Expedition, and deteriorating relations with Great Britain and France over boundaries and maritime rights.

MARTHA JEFFERSON (1772–1836), Thomas's eldest child, was educated by tutors and at Abbaye Royale de Panthemont, a Roman Catholic convent school in Paris. Almost immediately after their return from Paris, she married her cousin, Thomas Mann Randolph (1768–1828). They settled at Edgehill, near Jefferson's home plantation, Monticello, where, despite the responsibilities of her own plantation and large family, Martha always stood ready to assist her father with advice or active assistance. Her second of twelve children, James Madison Randolph (b. January 17, 1806), was the first child born at the President's House.

MARY (MARIA) JEFFERSON (1778–1804) was the younger of Jefferson's two daughters to reach adulthood. Educated by tutors and at Abbaye Royale de Panthemont, a Roman Catholic convent school in Paris, she married her cousin John Wayles Eppes (1773–1823) in 1797. Mary inherited a weak constitution from her mother and, like her, died at a young age from the effects of childbirth. Her correspondence with her father reflects the confining closeness of their personal relationship.

JAMES MONROE (1758–1831), the eldest son of Spence Monroe and Elizabeth Jones, graduated from the College of William and Mary (1776) and was wounded in the battle of Trenton, New Jersey. Monroe practiced law in Virginia where he became a protégé of Thomas Jefferson. He served in the Continental Congress, in the U.S. Senate, as American minister to France, England, and Spain, and as Secretary of State in the administration of James Madison. Elected to the presidency in 1816, Monroe served two terms, marked by peace at home and abroad. Monroe married Elizabeth Kortright (1768–1830), and the couple had three children. President and Mrs. Monroe are credited with the restoration of the President's House after it was burned during the War of 1812.

Born in Virginia, ELIZA KORTRIGHT MONROE (1786–1835) was reared in a sophisticated world of European and American capitals. Accompanying her parents to Paris when Monroe became American minister to France, Eliza was educated at Madame Campan's school for girls in Paris. There she acquired a lifelong love for the French aristocratic life style, and developed a firm friendship with Hortense Beauharnais, the daughter of Josephine Bonaparte, a future queen of Holland and the mother of Napoleon III of France. Before reaching her majority, Eliza had spent nearly a decade in European capitals, while her father served multiple terms as minister to France, Spain, and Great Britain.

A year after the family's return from Europe, in September 1808, Eliza married a Richmond lawyer and politician, George Hay, who was twenty years older and best known for prosecuting Aaron Burr for treason. Eliza and George Hay settled near Richmond, Virginia, and had a single child, Hortensia. When Monroe became president in 1817, Hay became his secretary and Eliza began assisting her mother Elizabeth as hostess at the president's house.

After James Monroe died on July 4, 1831, Eliza returned to France to visit her friend Hortense Beauharnais and became a Roman Catholic. She lived until her death in Paris, where she was buried.

Born in Paris shortly after Monroe helped negotiate the purchase of the Louisiana Territory, MARIA HESTER MONROE (1803–50) was the first presidential child born overseas. She was a trendsetter from the time she returned to the United States in 1807 wearing pantalettes! Educated in private schools in Washington, Maria was a teenager during her years in the President's House. Like her mother, Maria was only seventeen in 1820 when she married her cousin, Samuel Lawrence Gouverneur, a junior secretary to the president. Their marriage in a private ceremony was the first wedding of a president's daughter at the President's House. The couple had three children who survived infancy: James, Elizabeth, and Samuel, Jr.

Maria and Samuel Gouverneur moved to his home city of New York after the Monroe presidency. There, Samuel became postmaster of New York City and the Gouverneurs lived in comfort. James Monroe spent the last few years of his life with Maria in New York, where he died and was buried.

JOHN TYLER (1790–1862), the son of John and Mary Armistead, was born in Charles City County into a Virginia plantation family with a long tradition of public service. A graduate of the College of William and Mary, Tyler successively married Letitia Christian (1791–1842) and Julia Gardiner (1820–89) and was the father of fourteen children who lived to maturity—the most of any president. His second marriage to the youthful Julia caused vibrations within the family, but most of his children were eventually reconciled to the relationship. After long service as a U.S. representative and senator, Vice President Tyler became president on April 5, 1841, when President Harrison died of pneumonia. Tyler later had the distinction of being the only former U.S. president to serve in the Confederate government.

MARY TYLER (1815–48), Letitia and John Tyler's oldest child , was born in Charles City County, Virginia. Raised in the comforts of the Tylers' Virginia plantation home, she married Henry Lightfoot Jones, a North Carolina plantation owner, in December, 1835.

Mary went to the White House, when her mother became ill, and remained there to help her father after Letitia's death, until his second, secret marriage to Julia Gardiner, a New York woman of only twenty-four. Needless to say Tyler's remarriage to a woman five years younger than his eldest daughter caused a sensation, not only among the immediate family but across the nation.

ELIZABETH (LIZZIE) TYLER (1823–50) was born in Charles City County, Virginia, to John and Letitia Tyler. Throughout her mother's illness and until Tyler's remarriage in 1844, Elizabeth assisted her sister Mary in running the White House family and social affairs; with her mother, Letitia, barely able to leave her deathbed to attend the wedding, Elizabeth had married William N. Waller in a White House ceremony in 1842. At first resentful of her stepmother, Elizabeth later befriended the woman who was only a year her senior. Elizabeth died from a childbirth-related illness, leaving five young children.

ANDREW JOHNSON (1808–75) was born in Raleigh, North Carolina, and trained as a tailor. He married Eliza McCardle (1810–66) in 1827. When he was fifteen, Johnson ran away from his apprenticeship to a tailor, and traveled to South Carolina, Alabama, and then Tennessee. He never attended school and was largely self-educated. Finally settling in Greenville, Tennessee, he operated a tailor shop, prospered, and invested in real estate. Johnson entered politics in Greenville, serving as alderman, U.S. representative, Tennessee governor, and U.S. senator. His valiant effort to keep Tennessee in the Union brought him the appointment as military governor of Tennessee and, in 1864, the nomination for vice president on the ticket with Abraham Lincoln.

Like Harry S. Truman nearly a hundred years later, Johnson became president near the end of a major war and after barely one month in office. Johnson's term in office was marked by the triumphant end of the Civil War for the North and his own tumultuous relations with Congress. Seeking a harsher treatment of the Southern states than the president desired, the Radical Republicans secured the impeachment of Johnson but failed by one vote to convict him and remove him from office. The year his presidency terminated, in 1869, Johnson ran unsuccessfully for the U.S. Senate, then became the first former president elected to the senate in 1875. He served only five months in the senate—with twelve senators who had voted "guilty" in his impeachment trial.

MARTHA JOHNSON (1828–91), Johnson's eldest of five children, was born in Greenville, Tennessee. She was educated at public and private schools, including Miss S. L. English's Female Seminary in Georgetown. Martha married David T. Patterson (1818–91) of Greenville, Tennessee, who served in the U.S. Senate from 1866 to1869, while Johnson was president. (Patterson may have been the only man in history to have a chance to vote against his own father-in-law's impeachment.) When her mother, who suffered from consumption, was unable to fulfill her role as White House hostess, Martha, then married and the mother of two children, stepped into the breach. Credited with restoring order and elegance to the White House after the Civil War, Martha was even able to secure funds in 1866 from Congress for interior renovation and refurbishing. She also maintained several dairy cows at the White House. Martha and her sister Mary (mother of Mary Belle and Andrew J.), held the first official children's "soiree" at the White House on December 29, 1868. Martha's and her father's letters indicate a close personal and political relationship.

HIRAM ULYSSES S. GRANT (1822–85), the son of a prosperous tanner and store owner, graduated from West Point in 1843. After serving in the army until 1854, including service in the Mexican War, he operated a farm in Missouri and then went to work for his father in Galena, Illinois. In 1848 Grant married Julia Boggs Dent, daughter of a slave-holding Missouri planter. Grant's commanding service in the Civil War led to the defeat of the Confederacy and his subsequent election as president of the United States in 1868. Grant was the last president to have owned a slave, whom he had freed in 1859. After two terms in the White House marked by "reconstruction" of the former Confederacy— and corruption—he went on an extended global tour. Grant was nearly nominated for president again at the 1880 Republican Convention in Chicago, but James Garfield was beat him out on the 36th ballot. In 1884, facing a bleak financial future after the failure of his son's brokerage firm and a bleaker medical future with throat cancer, Grant wrote his memoirs, at the urging of Mark Twain, before his death in 1885.

ELLEN (B. JULIA) WRENSHALL GRANT (1855–1922), Grant's only daughter, was born fittingly enough on July 4 at Wish-ton-wish, a family farm near St. Louis, Missouri. Ellen, or Nellie as she was usually called, was educated at home and public school before she briefly attended Miss Sarah Porter's School for Girls in Farmington, Connecticut, during Grant's first presidential term. When her father became president in 1869, the teenaged Ellen threw herself into the Washington social whirl. There, despite her father's initial opposition, she married a British citizen and a nephew of the actress Fanny Kemble, Algernon Sartoris (1851–93), whom she met on a Grand Tour in 1873. After a well-publicized and some might say extravagant White House wedding on May 21, 1874, she moved to Southampton, England, where she remained until her husband's death. Ellen and Algernon Sartoris had four children—Grant Grenville, Algernon, Vivien, and Rosemary. In 1912 Ellen married Frank H. Jones (1857–1922), and she resided in Chicago, Illinois, until her death.

RUTHERFORD B. HAYES (1822–93), the son of Rutherford Hayes and Sophia Birchard, was born and raised in Delaware, Ohio, by his mother and uncle, Sardis Birchard. Educated at Kenyon College and Harvard Law School, Hayes practiced law in Cincinnati, Ohio, where he married Lucy Ware Webb (1831–89) in 1852.

After serving as a Union major general in the Civil War and having a long political career in Ohio, Hayes became president in 1877 after one of the nation's most disputatious elections that was only settled by a special electoral commission. Despite Hayes's positive attempts at government reform, his reputation is forever sourly linked to the election of 1876 and the settlement that apparently brought him to the White House in dubious exchange for ending the Federal military occupation of the Southern States.

FRANCES (FANNY) HAYES (1867–1950) was the Hayes's only daughter. As a ten-year-old in the White House, Fanny was described by her father in his diary, as "very sensible, does not take jokes, defends her absent friends, is like Mother Hayes." Frances was educated by tutors (for a time in an improvised schoolroom in the White House) and at Miss Augusta Mittleberger's School in Cleveland, Ohio, as well as at Miss Sarah Porter's School for Girls in Farmington, Connecticut, from 1885 to 1887 (where Mollie Garfield was a classmate). Despite the times when they were physically apart, Frances maintained a close relationship with her father; hostessing the first Easter Egg Roll on the lawn of the White House in 1879 after the annual event was barred from the Capitol grounds and, returning to Ohio a decade after his single presidential term, acting as Hayes's hostess and traveling companion following the death of her mother in 1889. After Hayes's death, Frances worked with the residents of the Reformatory Prison for Women in Framingham, Massachusetts, before marrying Ensign Harry Eaton Smith of Fremont, Ohio, in 1897. The couple had one child, Dalton.

JAMES A. GARFIELD (1831–81) was born on an Ohio farm, the son of Abram and Eliza Ballou Garfield. Educated at local schools and Williams College, he taught at the Eclectic Academy in Hiram, Ohio, and studied law before the Civil War propelled him to the rank of major general and a future political career in the U.S. House of Representatives. Securing the Republican presidential nomination over Ulysses S. Grant in 1880, Garfield had just begun his first year in office when he was shot at the Baltimore and Potomac Railroad Station in Washington, D.C., and died two months later.

MARY (MOLLY OR MOLLIE) GARFIELD (1867–1947), the second daughter of Garfield and Lucretia Rudolph (1832–1918), was instructed by a governess at home and attended Miss Augusta Mittleberger's School in Cleveland, Ohio, and Miss Sarah Porter's School for Girls in Farmington, Connecticut, as did Fanny Hayes, who was also from Ohio. A teenager when her father became president, she fell in love with Garfield's private secretary, Joseph Stanley Brown, but did not marry him until 1888. The couple lived in New York and Pasadena, California.

GROVER (B. STEPHEN GROVER) CLEVELAND (1837–1908) was the only president to be elected to nonconsecutive terms of office(1885–89, 1893–97). Born in New Jersey—the son of Richard Cleveland, a Presbyterian minister, and Ann Neal—he graduated from the local academy in Fayetteville, New York, and became a lawyer in Buffalo, New York. Despite having purchased a substitute soldier for service in the Civil War (then an acceptable practice), Cleveland became governor of New York in 1883 and president in 1885. He was the first president to be wed in the White House, where he married his niece and ward, Frances Folsom (1864–1947). The couple had five children, including **RUTH** (1891–1904) and **ESTHER** (1893–1980).

Ruth, Cleveland's eldest child, was almost two years old when her father became president for the second time in 1893. "Baby

Ruth" died as a youngster of diphtheria, but she was immortalized by the Curtiss Candy Company's marketing of the "Baby Ruth" candy bar.

Esther was the only presidential child physically born in the White House. She married English Captain William Bonsanquet at Westminster Abbey. After a long, private life, Esther died in Tamworth, New Hampshire.

BENJAMIN HARRISON (1833–1901), the son of John Scott Harrison and Elizabeth Irwin, was born in North Bend, Ohio, the home of his grandfather, former president William Henry Harrison. Educated at Miami University in Ohio, Harrison became a lawyer in Indianapolis, Indiana. After military service in the Civil War, he became a U.S. senator before winning the Republican nomination for the presidency and defeating Grover Cleveland in 1888. His presidency is known for the first billion-dollar federal budget, the Sherman Anti-Trust Act, and the admission of the most (six) states to the federal union during a single presidential term. They were the first to erect a Christmas tree at the White House, and electricity was installed at the White House during a renovation overseen by them.

Harrison married Lavina Scott (1832–92) in 1853. The couple had two children, one of whom was **MARY (MAMIE) SCOTT** (1858–1930).

In 1876 Mamie graduated from Chestnut Street Female Seminary in Philadelphia. She married James Robert McKee (1857–1942) of Indianapolis in 1884, and the couple had two children, Benjamin and Mary Lodge, who lived at the White House with their mother and grandfather. When her father became president, Mamie and her children moved to Washington to assist her often ill mother, who became the second presidential wife to die in the White House. Mamie later campaigned with the president in 1892.

After the death of Lavina, despite the disapproval of his grown children, in 1896 Harrison married Mary Scott Lord Dimmick (1858–1948), his ward and Mamie's blood cousin. Their child, **ELIZABETH HARRISON WALKER** (1897–1955), was the first daughter of a president to become a lawyer.

THEODORE ROOSEVELT (1858–1919), the son of Theodore Roosevelt and Martha Bulloch, was born in New York City, graduated from Harvard College, and in 1882 embarked on a long career of public service. He first married Alice Hathaway Lee (1861–84) in 1880 and then Edith Kermit Carow (1861–1948) in 1886. First a New York state assemblyman, Roosevelt held various state offices, rising to governor in 1898, and led a regiment of "Rough Riders" to victory in the Spanish-American War. After serving only six months as William McKinley's vice president, he became the youngest U.S. president when McKinley was assassinated, and served until 1909. Roosevelt is best known for sending the American naval fleet around the world, the building of the Panama Canal, and his motto, "Speak softly and carry a big stick."

ALICE LEE ROOSEVELT (1884–1980) was the only child of Roosevelt and his first wife. Alice was raised by her Aunt Bamie after her mother's death, until her father remarried. Alice was educated at schools in New York and Washington, D.C., until her exuberant participation in sports with boys was labeled "tomboyish"; thereafter she was taught by private tutors, until her society debut in 1902. Four years later, she married Nicholas Longworth, a U.S. representative from Ohio who later became Speaker of the House of Representatives. More than one thousand guests attended Alice's White House wedding on February 17, 1906. Nelly Grant Sartoris, who was herself married at the White House, attended the East Room ceremony. Alice and Nicholas had one child, Paulina, in 1925. Always an independent person, Alice was long known as a sharp-witted and outspoken "grande dame" of Washington society.

ETHEL CAROW ROOSEVELT (1891–1977), the only daughter among the five children of Theodore and Edith Roosevelt, was just ten when her father became president. Educated privately as well as at the National Cathedral School in Washington, D.C., where she flourished, her personality and life paled in comparison to her sister's. Ethel was considered the "sane center" of the family and was often given the responsibility of supervising her siblings. She was reportedly fluent in French and German and accomplished in horsemanship and the piano; she often accompanied her father on long horseback rides. In 1914, she and her husband, Dr. Richard Derby, successfully served in the American Ambulance Hospital in Paris; her parents cared for six-month-old Richard Derby, Jr., during their volunteer service.

WILLIAM HOWARD TAFT (1857–1930), was the son of Alphonso Taft, who served as President Grant's U.S. Attorney General and Secretary of War, and his second wife, Louise Maria Torrey. Raised in Cincinnati, Ohio, he was educated at Yale University and the University of Cincinnati Law School. Long service as a federal judge and Commissioner General of the Philippines brought him an appointment as Theodore Roosevelt's Secretary of War and was Roosevelt's choice to succeed him in 1909. However, after one term as president, he was defeated by Woodrow Wilson, who was helped by Taft's own mentor, Theodore Roosevelt, a third-party candidate. Taft later served as Chief Justice of the United States, 1921–30.

Taft married Helen Herron (1861–1943) in 1886. The couple had three children, including their only daughter, **HELEN HERRON TAFT** (1891–1987), who attended a series of public and private schools before attending the Baldwin School at Bryn Mawr, Pennsylvania, and was attending Bryn Mawr College when her father became president. After Mrs. Taft suffered a stroke in 1909, young Helen served as hostess for many White House functions. In 1920 she married Frederick J. Manning, a fellow history instructor. Despite her father's fears that marriage would end her career and curb her drive to obtain her doctorate in American History, Helen obtained her doctoral degree from Yale, writing a dissertation entitled "British Colonial Government after the American Revolution, 1782–1820," and had a long career as a professor, dean, and president at Bryn Mawr. She had two children, Helen (b. 1921) and Caroline (b. 1925).

(THOMAS) WOODROW WILSON (1856–1924) was born in Staunton, Virginia, to Joseph R. Wilson and Jessie Janet Woodrow. Educated at Princeton University and Johns Hopkins University (Ph.D. 1886), Wilson taught at Bryn Mawr College and Princeton before becoming president of Princeton and then governor of

New Jersey in 1911. In 1912, he was the first person with a doctorate to be elected president. Wilson's two terms in office were marked by victory in World War I and his failure to secure U.S. ratification of the Versailles Treaty and entrance into the League of Nations. His presidency saw the passage of three Constitutional Amendments, including the nineteenth, which provided for women's right to vote.

Wilson and his first wife, Ellen Louise Axson (1860–1914) had three daughters. In 1915, following the death of Ellen during his first term in the White House, he married Edith Bolling Galt (1872–1961). After Wilson suffered debilitating strokes in 1919, Edith, nearly the only person to have daily contact with the president, screened his official messages and relayed his responses to members of the government. Many people considered her an unconstitutional *de facto* president.

Wilson's children were already adults when he first entered the White House. It has been said by one family biographer, Frances W. Saunders, that Eleanor (Nell) was "the closest" to their father, while Jessie had "the greatest rapport" with her mother.

MARGARET WOODROW WILSON (1886–1944) was educated at the Woman's College of Baltimore (Goucher College) and the Peabody Institute of Music in Baltimore, Maryland. She debuted as a singer with the Chicago Symphony Orchestra in 1915 and later became an advertising consultant, writer, and stock investor. After the death of her mother in 1914, Margaret acted as official hostess for several White House events because of the pregnancy of Jessie and the busy life of Eleanor.

ELEANOR (NELL) RANDOLPH WILSON (1889–1967) was born in Middletown, Connecticut, and attended St. Mary's School in Raleigh, North Carolina. She married William McAdoo, Wilson's Secretary of the Treasury, at the White House in 1914. After McAdoo's defeat for the Democratic presidential nomination in 1920, the couple moved from New York to California in 1922 in hopes of furthering McAdoo's presidential quest, but he was again defeated for the Democratic Party nomination in 1924.

JESSIE WOODROW WILSON (1887–1933) also attended the Woman's College of Baltimore, where she was elected Phi

Beta Kappa in 1908. Jessie worked in a settlement house before marrying Francis Bowes Sayre, an expert in international relations and law, at the White House in 1913. Jessie returned to the White House for the birth of her first child, Francis Sayre, Jr. on January 17, 1915.While her husband taught at Williams College and then the Harvard Law School, Jessie was active in national organizations, such as the YMCA, and state Democratic Party organizations.

FRANKLIN DELANO ROOSEVELT (1882–1945) was born at Hyde Park, New York, the second child and only son of James Roosevelt and Sara Delano. After graduating from the Groton School and Harvard College, Franklin married Anna Eleanor Roosevelt (1884–1962) in 1905. Franklin Roosevelt attended Columbia Law School and practiced law in New York City before entering the political lists as a Democrat (his cousin Theodore was a Republican). After serving in the New York Senate (1911–13), as Assistant Secretary of the Navy (1913–20), and as New York governor (1929–32), Roosevelt was elected president in 1932 in the midst of the Great Depression and reelected three more times. (Amendment XXII, which limited presidents to two elected terms in office, was not added to the Constitution until 1951.) His New Deal, including the Social Security Act, and the successful campaigns of World War II highlighted his presidency, the longest in American history.

ANNA (SIS) ELEANOR ROOSEVELT (1906–75) was Roosevelt's eldest child and only daughter. She attended Cornell University before marrying, in 1926, a stockbroker, Curtis B. Dall, whom she divorced in 1934. In 1935, she married Clarence John Boettiger, a news reporter for the *Chicago Tribune*, whom she had met while campaigning with her father. Anna and John then moved to Seattle, Washington, where John became editor of the *Seattle Post Intelligencer*. When her husband went into military service school in Charlottesville, Virginia, in 1943, Anna became the acting editor of the newspaper, but early in 1944 moved into the White House. For nearly two years, she assumed a role of personal assistant to her father, and accompanied him to the Yalta Conference in 1945. Despite a lifetime of closeness to her mother, Anna now became very attached to her father, even conspiring with him to arrange for his mistress, Lucy P. Mercer, to visit him at the White House. After attempting to start their own newspaper in Phoenix, Arizona following Roosevelt's death, Anna and John divorced. In 1952, Anna married James A. Halsted. In all, she had three children—Anna E. Dall, Curtis R. Dall, and John R. Boettiger.

HARRY S. TRUMAN (1884–1972) was born in Lamar, Missouri, the son of John A. Truman and Martha Ellen Young. Raised in Independence, Missouri, where he attended public schools, he held a number of clerical jobs before returning to the family farm. He served in the U.S. Artillery in France and attended Kansas City Law School, 1923–25. Married in 1919 to Elizabeth (Bess) Virginia Wallace, Truman pursued a political career beginning as a judge in Jackson County in 1922. In 1835, he was elected to the U.S. Senate, where he served until he became vice president of the United States in 1945. President Roosevelt's death, just one month after Truman took office, propelled him into the presidency on April 12, 1945. Although actually elected president only once, in 1948, Truman served nearly two full terms before declining to run for reelection in 1952. The end of World War II, the reconstruction of Europe, and the onset of the Cold War were highlights of his presidency. As president, Truman strongly supported Amendment XXII that limited a president to two full terms in office.

MARY MARGARET (MARGIE) TRUMAN (1924–) was born at home in Independence, Missouri. When her father became president in 1945, she moved into the White House and finished her degree at George Washington University (1946). Interested in acting and singing since childhood, Margaret embarked on a career as a professional concert singer in 1947, appearing on the *Ed Sullivan Show* in 1950. She later became a prolific author of mysteries and family histories. In 1956 she married Elbert Clifton Daniel, Jr., a foreign news editor for the New York Times, and the couple had four children—Clifton, William, Harrison, and Thomas.

LYNDON B. JOHNSON (1908–73), the son of Sam E. Johnson, Jr. and Rebekah Baines, was educated at public schools in

Johnson City, Texas, and Southwest Texas State College. After a brief teaching career, he went to Washington as a congressional aide. Johnson became a U.S. congressman in 1937, serving until his switch to the U.S. Senate in 1948. After becoming Majority Leader of the Senate, he was elected vice president in 1960. When President Kennedy was assassinated on November 22, 1963, Johnson became president, and was elected to continue in office in 1964. The passage of a strong Civil Rights Act and the escalation of the war in Vietnam marked his presidency. In 1934 Johnson married Claudia Alta (Lady Bird) Taylor (1912–), a graduate of the University of Texas, and the couple had two daughters who would share the same initials as their father, LBJ.

LYNDA BIRD JOHNSON (1944–) was a student at the University of Texas when her father entered the White House and grew to maturity as the president's daughter. Johnson admired her intelligence and political acumen, often consulting her about his public speeches. Lynda married Charles S. Robb (1939–), a Marine Corps aide stationed at the White House, in a 1967 White House wedding, and the couple have three children—Lucinda, Catherine, and Jennifer. Robb served as Virginia governor (1986–1990) and U.S. senator (1990–2002); Lynda has worked as a journalist for *McCall's* and *Ladies' Home Journal*, and more recently has made literacy and youth advocacy her priorities.

LUCY (LUCI) BAINES JOHNSON (1947–) graduated from the Episcopalian National Cathedral School in Washington, D.C., and attended the Georgetown University School of Nursing and the University of Texas. Luci, who had converted to Roman Catholicism during her father's presidency, married Patrick L. Nugent (1943–) at Washington's National Catholic Shrine in 1966, and the couple had four children before their divorce in 1979. She later married Ian J. Turpin (1944–). She is chair of the LBJ Holding Company.

RICHARD M. NIXON (1913–94) was born in Yorba Linda, California, the second of five sons of Frank A. Nixon and Hannah Milhous. After graduating from Whittier College in 1934, Nixon received his law degree from Duke University Law School in 1937. In 1940 he married Thelma (Pat) C. Ryan (1912–93) and served from 1942 to 1946 in the U.S. Navy. He began his long political career in 1946 by winning a seat in the U.S. Congress, where he served as representative and then a senator until 1953. Elected vice president as Dwight D. Eisenhower's running mate in 1952, he was narrowly defeated by John F. Kennedy in his 1960 presidential bid. Staging a remarkable political comeback, Nixon was elected president in 1968, only to be impeached and then forced to resign on August 9, 1974, in the culmination of the Watergate scandals. He was later pardoned by President Gerald R. Ford and in his retirement wrote and traveled extensively, once again reviving his career and reputation. During Nixon's presidency, his diplomatic mission to the People's Republic of China, commemorated in the John Adams opera, *Nixon in China*, virtually reopened that nation to the West.

PATRICIA (TRICIA) NIXON (1946–), the eldest daughter of Richard Nixon and Thelma (Pat) Ryan, graduated from Finch College. Patricia grew up in the public spotlight and married Edward F. Cox in a White House wedding in 1971; the couple has one son.

JULIE NIXON (1948–) graduated from Smith College before her 1968 marriage to David Eisenhower, grandson of Dwight D. Eisenhower. The couple has two daughters and a son. Julie is the author/editor of ten books, including a biography of her mother, *Pat Nixon: The Untold Story*, and a photographic study of her father and family, *Eye on Nixon*.

GERALD R. FORD, JR. (1913–) was born Leslie Lynch King, Jr., the son of Leslie Lynch King and Dorothy A. Gardner. He became Gerald R. Ford after his mother divorced King and married Gerald Rudolph Ford, who adopted her young son and changed his name. Ford graduated from the University of Michigan, coached football at Yale University, and graduated from Yale Law School in 1941. After Navy service in World War II, he practiced law in Grand Rapids, Michigan. He was elected to the U.S. Congress in 1948 and that same year was married to Elizabeth Bloomer Warren (1918–), a graduate of the Bennington School of Dance and a professional dancer with Martha Graham's company in New York. He was a congressman until 1973, when he became vice president in 1973 to replace Spiro Agnew, who resigned at the height of the Watergate scandals. When President Nixon was forced to resign on August 9, 1974, Ford was sworn into office; he and his appointed vice president, Nelson Rockefeller, were thus the first presidential team to serve without a national election. The pardoning of former president Nixon, the American evacuation of South Vietnam, and the celebration of the Bicentennial of American Independence marked Ford's term in office.

SUSAN ELIZABETH FORD (1957–), Ford's youngest child and only daughter, was educated at Holton-Arms School, Mount Vernon College, and the University of Kansas. Susan married Charles F. Vance in 1979, then Vaden Bales in 1989. The mother of two daughters, Tyne (1980–) and Heather (1983–), she worked as a professional photographer. She is now a national spokesperson for breast cancer awareness and the Betty Ford Center, and a regular on the public-speaking circuit; and is the author of mystery books, including *Sharp Focus*.

RONALD WILSON REAGAN (1911–2004) was born in Tampico, Illinois, the son of John E. Reagan and Nelle Wilson. After spending an active youth in Dixon, Illinois, he graduated from Eureka College, then embarked on a successful career as a film actor. He married Jane Wyman (1914–), actress, in 1940, and the couple had two children, Maureen (1941–2001) and Christine (1947, who lived only one day) and adopted a son, Michael (1945–). Reagan's marriage to Nancy Davis (b. 1921–), a graduate of Smith College and an actress, in 1952 produced two children, Patricia (1952–) and Ronald (1958–). Reagan served as Republican governor of California, from 1967 to 1975, prior to his election to the first of two presidential terms in 1980. After the end of his second term in 1989, he retired to California.

PATRICIA (PATTI) ANN REAGAN attended a series of public and private schools, then Northwestern University, before pursuing careers in acting and writing. In 1984 she married Paul Grilley. Known professionally as Patti Davis, she has written several novels, including *Deadfall, Home Front,* and *Bondage,* as well as her autobiography, *The Way I See It.* Although she was not very active in Reagan's political campaigns, Patti, an advocate of more liberal political causes than her father's, became known for her opposition to nuclear weapons.

GEORGE H. W. BUSH (1924–), born at the family home in Milton, Massachusetts, the son of Prescott S. Bush and Dorothy Walker, graduated from Yale University after service in the U.S. Navy during World War II. In 1945 he married Barbara Pierce (1925–) and the couple had six children. Bush was the founder and CEO of an oil exploration and drilling company before his 1966 election to the U.S. Congress. After serving as U.S. ambassador to the United Nations and director of the CIA, he was elected vice president in 1980, serving two terms with President Ronald Reagan. Bush was then elected president in 1988. His term in office saw the breakup of the Soviet Union, ending the cold war, and America's participation in the Gulf War.

DOROTHY (DORO) W. BUSH (1959–), the youngest child of George and Barbara Bush, was born six years after the death of their first-born daughter, Pauline (Robin) Bush (b. 1949), who died of leukemia in 1953. A graduate of Boston College, Dorothy has had various professional positions that include travel agent and bookkeeper. After working at the National Rehabilitation Hospital in Washington, D.C., she married William LeBlond (1957–), a contractor, in 1981, and then Robert P. Koch, a lobbyist, at Camp David in 1992. Dorothy is the mother of four children. Her father reports in his book, *All the Best,* that "our only daughter is particularly close to her dad."

Mentor. May 14th 79.

My dear Papa.

You don't know
how happy I am. now the
piano has come.
Moses was very busy
ploughing so that he
could not go for it, and the
other men were busy, Mr Dilz
happened to be over here.
& he kindly offered to go down
to get it. When it got up
by the front porch, all
and every man on the
farm, came to help
unbox it, we had so
much fun watching them

CHAPTER 1

JUST FRIENDS:
"YOUR CHEERFUL LETTER..."

> *"It is delightful,*
> *dear Girlie, to read your cheerful letter."*
> —Woodrow Wilson to Jesse W. Wilson,
> August 2, 1918

> *"If you knew how happy your daddy was*
> *to get your nice long letter you'd write him oftener."*
> —Harry S. Truman to Margaret Truman,
> January 14, 1937

FRIENDLY letters—those simply exchanging family news, without overtones of advice or a focused theme, such as a daughter's education or pending marriage—became very common after the Civil War. Although in the preceding century many presidents and their daughters were assuredly friends as well as close relations, their letters reveal a more formal pattern of concern for health, education, and politics.

JOHN ADAMS
TO
ABIGAIL ADAMS

*A*dams was a delegate to the Continental Congress in Philadelphia during the Revolutionary War when he wrote this letter to his only surviving daughter, who was about to turn twelve. In it, he vividly describes the jubilation and the distinctly military tone of Philadelphians' celebration of the first anniversary of the Fourth of July, commemorating the date of the signing of the Declaration of Independence.

Philadelphia, July 5th, 1777

My Dear Daughter

Yesterday being the anniversary of American Independence, was celebrated here with a festivity and ceremony becoming the occasion.

I am too old to delight in pretty descriptions, if I had a talent for them, otherwise a picture might be drawn, which would please the fancy of a Whig, at least.

The thought of taking any notice of this day, was not conceived, until the second of this month, and it was not mentioned until the third. It was too late to have a sermon, as every one wished, so this must be deferred another year.

Congress determined to adjourn over that day, and to dine together. The general officers and others in town were invited, after the President and Council, and Board of War of this State.

In the morning the Delaware frigate, several large gallies, and other continental armed vessels, the Pennsylvania ship and row gallies and guard boats, were all hawled off in the river, and several of them beautifully dressed in the colours of all nations, displayed about upon the masts, yards, and rigging.

At one o'clock the ships were all manned, that is, the men were all ordered aloft, and arranged upon the tops, yards, and shrowds, making a striking appearance—of companies of men drawn up in order, in the air.

Then I went on board the Delaware, with the President and several gentlemen of the Marine Committee, soon after which we were saluted with a discharge of thirteen guns, which was followed by thirteen others, from each other armed vessel in the river; then the gallies followed the fire, and after them the guard boats. Then the President and company returned in the barge to the shore, and were saluted with three cheers, from every ship, galley, and boat in the river. The wharves and shores, were lined with a vast concourse of people, all shouting and huzzaing, in a manner which gave great joy to every friend to this country, and the utmost terror and dismay to every lurking tory.

At three we went to dinner, and were very agreeably entertained with excellent company, good cheer, fine music from the band of Hessians taken at Trenton, and continual vollies between every toast, from a company of soldiers drawn up in Second-street before the city tavern, where we dined. The toasts were in honour of our country, and the heroes who have fallen in their pious efforts to defend her. After this two troops of light-horse, raised in Maryland, accidentally here in their way to camp were paraded through Second-street, after them a train of artillery, and then about a thousand infantry, now in this city on their march to camp, from North Carolina. All these marched into the common, where they went through their firings and maneuvres; but I did not follow them. In the evening, I was walking about the streets for a little fresh air and exercise, and was surprised to find the whole city lighting up their candles at the windows. I walked most of the evening, and I think it was the most splendid illumination I ever saw; a few surly houses were dark; but the lights were very universal. Considering the lateness of the design and the suddenness of the execution, I was amazed at the universal joy and alacrity that was discovered, and at the brilliancy and splendour of every part of this joyful exhibition. I had forgot the ringing of the bells all day and evening, and the bonfires in the streets, and the fireworks played off.

Had General Howe been here in disguise, or his master, this show would have given them the heart-ache.

I am your affectionate father, John Adams

ULYSSES S. GRANT
TO
ELLEN GRANT

*A*t the conclusion of his second presidential term, Grant and his wife, Julia, set off on an around-the-world tour. The Grants were entertained royally wherever they went, and their children joined them at various stops in their travels. Ellen was living in England with her husband, Algernon C. Sartoris, and their infant son, when she received the following newsy letter from her father:

Hotel Bristol, Paris. Nov. 22d, 77

Dear Daughter:

I received a very nice letter from you day before yesterday, which we were all glad to receive. we like to hear from you just as often as you will write. The only point to answer specially is in regard to the sale of your Adams & Co. Express stock, and converting it into Pullman. If Buck has done so you may be sure it is right. He is where he sees, and knows. It may be that Adam's is about to reduce the dividend from 8 to 6 pr. ct. Pullman pays the latter is bought for 75 cts. or thereabouts on the dollar, while the latter sells for one hundred. I have trusted Buck with a Power of Attorney for me in all I have.

We have abandoned all idea of going to Spain from here. Every one tells me that it is an impropitious season of the year, and that the travel would be most uncomfortable, specially for a lady. We will leave here for Nice on Saturday week, the 1st of Dec. and will probably remain in the Soritto of Flaisia for as much as ten days. From Nice we will take a Man of War—a United States vessel and sail along the Mediterranean stopping at all points of interest, going up to Constantinople, possible and certainly going up to the Nile, and up that—but not in the Man of War. We will no doubt meet you in Italy in our return from the Nile.

Your Ma and I will express to you to-morrow a cloak as a New Year's present—a little early, but we do not know that an opportunity will present itself later. To night we go out to dine with the Marquis de Tellerand. It will be our first dinner with—exclusively—French people since we have been here except the dinner immediately after our arrival, given by the President, at which his Cabinet was present. We have accepted invitations for every evening but two up to the close of the month. Otherwise I should insist on leaving here earlyer.

Give our love to Algy and the babe, to Mr. & Mrs. Sartoris and write just as often as you can to some one of us.

Yours affectionately, U.S. Grant

MARY (MOLLY) GARFIELD
TO
JAMES GARFIELD

*G*arfield was a U.S. congressman living in Washington, D.C., with his two oldest boys, Harry and James, for a congressional session, when he and his daughter exchanged these two informal letters about the new piano and other general news of the family back home, including Garfield's gentle breaking of some bad news to twelve-year-old Molly. The exchange subtly details the realities of nineteenth-century life, when travel difficulties and the need to care for ill or elderly family members often led to geographically divided families.

Mentor. May 14th. 79

My dear Papa
You don't know how happy I am, now the piano has come.

Moses was very busy ploughing so that he could not go for it, and the other men were busy. Mr. Dilley happened to be over here & he kindly offered to go down to get it. When it got up by the front porch, all and every man on the farm, came to help

unbox it, we had so much fun watching them. At last it was in its place in the parlor, then the men came in and sat down asked me to play for them. I had forgotten nearly every-thing I knew, but, played anything that came into my head. it is a lovely piano, and I thank you ever and ever so much for it. I don't mean that it is all mine, but nevertheless it is part mine. Mary Aldrich, her cousin, & Mrs. Tyler came in the evening and we all had a splendid time. Mr. Dilly is going to paper the kitchen today. Mamma will be here Saturday for a few days, then she will have to go right back and stay until Aunt Nellie comes.

Tell Hal & Jim I thank them very much for their letters and will answer them soon. I will be glad to see "Veto" when he comes, had he grown any since we came away? I hope you and the boys injoyed the "Pinafore." Will you please send my music, if it is bound? I have nothing to practise from.

I must close now and study my lessons.

Give my love to the boys Mr. Harber, the girls, and everybody in the house.

Ever your loving Molly

[P.S] We four got weighed the other night. Miss Mays weighed 115 lbs, Orv 66 lbs, Abe 52 lbs and I 100 lbs. Molly

MARY (MOLLIE) GARFIELD POSED WITH HER FOUR BROTHERS,
HARRY, JAMES, IRVING AND ABRAM, IN THE LATE 1870S
FOR THIS BRADY-HANDY PHOTOGRAPH.

JAMES GARFIELD
TO
MARY (MOLLY) GARFIELD

House of Representatives,
Washington, D.C. May 22nd, 1879.

Dear Molly:

I believe I have not answered your good letter of the 14th inst. and I am so busy now that I must answer by dictating it to Mr. Brown.

I hope you are pleased with the piano and that its tone will improve, as I think it will. I believe a piano is made sea sick by a long journey, even though it be a land journey.

We received a letter from Mamma this morning, written from Hiram after her return from Mentor. Poor grandma seems to be failing and I fear she can not live long.

We all regret this separation of the family into three parts, and hope we may before long, all assemble at Mentor. We will try to get your music as soon as possible. The binder is very slow.

I note your weight and that of the two boys. You come within two pounds of Jim.

Tell me if you have had rain lately for I fear the crops are suffering for want of it.

Give my love to the little boys and thank them for their good letters, which are highly appreciated by their batchelor friends here at 1227 "I" St. We also all send love to Miss Mays (a.m.) and hope she will keep me informed of farm affairs. Harry says he will answer your letter soon.

With much love I am affectionately Your Father, JA Garfield

RUTH AND ESTHER CLEVELAND
TO
GROVER CLEVELAND

*R*uth and Esther's mother, Frances Folsom Cleveland, undoubtedly penned this cute Christmas gift tag from their children, Ruth and Esther, to their father, President Cleveland. Ruth was just three and Esther a year old for this Christmas in the White House. Baby Ruth and Esther, the only presidential child born in the White House, were favorites of the national press and public, as well as their parents.

Christmas 1894

For Papa
For his little room at Gay Gables from Ruth & Esther

THEODORE ROOSEVELT
TO
ALICE LEE ROOSEVELT

*A*lthough Alice and her father often did not see eye to eye on family relations, this particular letter shows no such discord.

1810 N. St. Feb. 27th '98

Darling Alice
Mother is about the same; Ted is very much better; he still has headaches, at which I do'nt wonder, considering the extraordinary antics he cuts as soon as he feels well. He and Kermit have been absorbed in three little flying squirrels which I let them get. At first there were two; but Ted's became very sick, which produced in Ted

a marked increase of headache, and general look of patient-suffering; so I gave him 50 cents to buy another, which acted like a tonic on his general health. Then the sick one, under careful nursing from Molly, Ted and Kermit, recovered; so now Ted is one flying squirrel ahead! The convalescent lives by himself in a pasteboard box, and is developing a most social and friendly nature. At the animal store there is a little chubby coon, which the two small boys were wild to have me buy, so that they "might keep it for sister"! But I was Spartan like in declining.

Last Sunday, Dr. Wood, Mr. Homans and I took a splendid scramble down the other side of the Potomac, from Cabin John bridge back. Poor Mr. Homans was done out.

Walter Tuckerman told me to tell you that they all missed you dreadfully.

Ethel and Archie are very much at home at the Tuckermans.

Your loving father.

ALICE LEE ROOSEVELT, DAUGHTER OF THEODORE ROOSEVELT, DURING HIS FIRST YEAR IN THE WHITE HOUSE.

THEODORE ROOSEVELT
TO
ETHEL CAROW ROOSEVELT

*R*oosevelt's sentimental pre-battle note to seven-year-old Ethel belies his tough "Rough Rider" image. Colonel Roosevelt and other soldiers were waiting aboard ship off Santiago to engage the Spanish Army in Cuba when he first wrote. After only 133 days of mobilization, Roosevelt resigned his commission in the U.S. Army and was soon elected governor of New York.

Off Santiago, [c. June 20] 1898.

Darling Ethel:

We are near shore and everything is in a bustle, for we may have to disembark to-night, and I do not know when I shall have another chance to write to my three blessed children, whose little notes please me so. This is only a line to tell you all how much father loves you. The Pawnee Indian drew you the picture of the little dog which runs everywhere round the ship, and now and then howls a little when the band plays.

THEODORE ROOSEVELT
TO
ETHEL CAROW ROOSEVELT

Camp near Santiago, July 15, 1898.

Darling Ethel:

When it rains here—and it's very apt to rain here every day—it comes down just as if it was a torrent of water. The other night I hung up my hammock in my tent and in the middle of the night there was a terrific storm, and my tent and hammock came down with a run. The water was running over the ground in a sheet, and the mud was knee-deep; so I was a drenched and muddy object when I got to a neighboring tent, where I was given a blanket, in which I rolled up and went to sleep.

There is a funny little lizard that comes into my tent and is quite tame now; he jumps about like a little frog and puffs his throat out. There are ground-doves no bigger than big sparrows, and cuckoos almost as large as crows.

THEODORE ROOSEVELT
TO
ETHEL CAROW ROOSEVELT

---

*T*he second daughter of Theodore Roosevelt was nearly ten years old when she received this almost too vivid letter from her father about hunting dogs in Colorado, written while Vice President—elect Roosevelt was on one of his frequent hunting expeditions in the American West. Although she was overshadowed in the public eye by her older sister Alice and her brothers, the letters between Ethel, who was about to begin her education at the Cathedral School in Washington, D.C., and her father reveal an especially friendly as well as familial relationship.

Keystone Ranch, Colorado, January 18, 1901

Darling Little Ethel:

I have had great fun. Most of the trip neither you nor Mother nor Sister would enjoy; but you would all of you be immensely amused with the dogs. There are eleven all told, but really only eight do very much hunting. These eight are all scarred with the wounds they have received this week in battling with the cougars and lynxes, and they are always threatening to fight one another; but they are as affectionate toward men (and especially toward me, as I pet them) as our own house dogs. At this moment a large hound and a small half-breed bull-dog, both of whom were quite badly wounded this morning by a cougar, are shoving their noses into my lap to be petted, and humming defiance to one another. They are on excellent terms with the ranch cat and kittens. The three chief fighting dogs, who do not follow the trail, are the most affectionate of all, and, moreover, they climb trees! Yesterday we got a big lynx in the top of a pinon tree—a low, spreading kind of pine—about thirty feet tall. Turk, the bloodhound followed him up, and after much sprawling actually got to the very top, within a couple of feet of him. Then, when the lynx was shot out of the tree, Turk after a short scramble, took a header down through the branches, landing with a bounce on his back. Tony, one of the half-breed bulldogs, takes such headers on an average at least once for every animal we put up a tree. We have nice little horses which climb the most extraordinary places you can imagine. Get Mother to show you some of Gustave Dorf's trees; the trees on these mountains look just like them.

THEODORE ROOSEVELT
TO
ETHEL CAROW ROOSEVELT

---

*R*oosevelt was in the middle of his second term as president, when he told Ethel, then a teenager, this sweet story of rescuing a kitten from two dogs. He signed the letter with his current nickname, "The Tyrant," and attached a cute little illustration—a frequent habit of the president.

Washington, June 24, 1906

Darling Ethel:
Mother is torn by conflicting emotions—regret at leaving me and longing to see all of you. She is too cunning and pretty for anything, and seems at the moment to be really well and enjoys the

rides that we take almost every afternoon. She has just disciplined me with deserved severity. Except when the weather forbids we breakfast and lunch on the portico and take dinner on the west terrace, which is really lovely. This afternoon we spent an hour sitting under the apple tree by the fountain.

You will love Audrey; but I do not want Mother to ride until you have thoroughly tried her, for gentle though she is, she is a high-spirited mare, and if she has not had much exercise will kick and buck a little from mere playfulness.

Tell Archie that the other day as Mother and I were driving out to the horses we passed a large pile of fine sand on Sixteenth Street. There were several boys on it, two of them already buried up to their waists, while the others were industriously shoveling the sand still higher around them. The two bowed with eager friendliness, and then we saw that they were the Newberry twins. Today as I was marching to church with Sloan some twenty-five yards behind, I suddenly saw two terriers racing to attack a kitten which was walking down the sidewalk. I bounced forward with my umbrella, and after some active work put to flight the dogs while Sloan captured the kitten, which was a friendly, helpless little thing, evidently too well accustomed to being taken care of to know how to shift for itself. I inquired of all the bystanders and of people on the neighboring porches to know if they knew who owned it; but as they all disclaimed, with many grins, any knowledge of it, I marched ahead with it in my arms for about a half a block. Then I saw a very nice colored woman and little colored girl looking out of the window of a small house with on the door a dressmaker's advertisement, and I turned and walked up the steps and asked them if they did not want the kitten. They said they did, and the little girl welcomed it lovingly; so I felt I had gotten it a house and continued toward church.

Am concerned to hear that Phil got into a scrape and was bounced from St. Marks. I hope it is only temporary. I am very sorry to learn that poor Jack is still having hard work with his studies. It is not his fault at all.

There is nothing in Kermit's school record to have warranted him in trying to compress the last two years in one. Has the lordly Ted turned up yet? Is his loving sister able, unassisted, to reduce the size of his head, or does she need any assistance from her male parent?

Your affectionate father, The Tyrant Chorus of offspring (led by daughter) "For he is a tyrant king"!]

THEODORE ROOSEVELT DREW THIS CUTE CARTOON AT THE BOTTOM OF THIS JUNE 24, 1906, LETTER TO HIS YOUNGEST DAUGHTER, ETHEL. ROOSEVELT'S CARTOONS AND NICKNAMES FOR HIS CHILDREN AND HIMSELF WERE REGULAR PARTS OF HIS LETTERS.

ETHEL CAROW ROOSEVELT
TO
THEODORE ROOSEVELT

*I*t is believed that Ethel wrote this undated, gossipy letter to her father, whom she addresses as "Fado," around 1906.

Sagamore Hill. Oyster Bay, Long Island, N.Y.

Dear Fado:

When do you think that you will be able to come here?

Quentin and Mame have just come up from the beach and told me that Hector [who is a perfect beauty] and Jack have just had a fight, and that Jack got the worst of it. Mame said that Quentin cried and he also gave Hector an awful whack with a stick and that Hector ran under the bathing house.

Quentin told me to "give Fado a hug and a great big kiss."

Lorraine's boat got loose and Alfred Mills saw it and tied it to the Swans dock. Where she has just found it.

I am riding astride and am going to go out riding every other day, it is awfully nice and I can get off and get on again, Mr. Proctor is riding Texas, And every other day we go out Mr. Proctor, Archie (very cunning on the pony) and I on Diomand I have found an awfully nice saddle.

Did Mother tell you that Nicholas has the mumphs so that I can not go down to see Lorraine atall, she has to come up here. It is perfectly beautiful here, this morning especially you can almost see the houses in Connecticut, and it is very nice and cool.

The telephone has been put up and its comes right across the field and looks awfully.

There are ever so many nests I have just found such a cunning robins one it is right on the roof under Archies window.

You need not answer this letter because I suppose that you are too busy.

Lots and lots of love from Ethelylykins

HELEN HERRON TAFT
TO
WILLIAM HOWARD TAFT

---

*H*elen turned fourteen on the day that she wrote this letter to Taft, who was then serving as President Roosevelt's Secretary of War. She was on a holiday in England with her mother. Let's hope her "darling Papa" remembered Helen's birthday.

Oxford England. August 1, 1905

My darling Papa:
You may have forgotten so I think I shall write you to remind you that today is my birthday. Mama gave five pairs of gloves and Aunt Agnes and Katharine gave me a purse.

I like Oxford very well. We generally go in bathing in the morning and out on the river in the afternoon. I only wish that we knew a few more children and could play tennis.

Mama and Aunt Agnes came back from their trip in Devonshire two days ago. They had a very good time.

We hear from Rob almost every other day. He writes long descriptions of the scenery about which he is enthusiastic.

Frederick and I go out in the canoe together a good deal and when there is any wind we sail with an umbrella. Our one ambition is to turn over and we have come pretty near it once or twice. The river is so narrow that we couldn't drown if we tried.

Mama and Charlie send their love and I send lots of love and kisses.

Your loving daughter Helen

WOODROW WILSON
TO
JESSIE WOODROW WILSON

$\mathcal{W}$ilson wrote this friendly but concerned letter to his youngest daughter in the midst of American participation in World War I. Her husband, Francis Bowes Sayre, was then serving in France and Italy for the YMCA, and Jessie was expecting the couple's second child.

The White House. 2 August, 1918

My precious little Girl,

My heart has been specially full of you since Frank left. If you can in any way feel conscious of the loving thoughts I am constantly sending your way, you can, I am sure, never be very lonely. You are so brave and fine that I know you never allow yourself to admit that you are lonely, but I know that the absence of dear Frank must every day make a deep difference, even when you do not allow it to go the length of unhappiness, and I want you to feel all the time how my thoughts keep you company, how full my heart is of you and the dear little ones. I am so glad that Frankie is proving such good company for you. That makes an immense difference. But if at any time you need any of us do not hesitate to say so and we will come! Edith joins me in sending a heartful of love.

No, indeed, I do not share the idea that there is any real danger to Nantucket or to those who come and go to and from the island from the submarines. Those are dangerous waters for the submarine, both because they are comparatively shallow and because they are so constantly under observation and so hard to get away from if you are once observed. If the stupid submarine commanders should seek to create terror anywhere, it would be some crowded coast like that of New Jersey, not on remote Nantucket. I should not feel in the least uneasy there myself, although at present the naval people think it might be taking unnecessary risks for me to cross the open waters opening from Long Island

WOODROW AND ELLEN WILSON AND THEIR DAUGHTERS, MARGARET, ELEANOR, AND JESSIE, IN A PHOTOGRAPH TAKEN CIRCA 1912.

Sound, if I did so in the slow and easily reconizable Mayflower. I do not share their uneasiness about such a trip, but everybody there threatens to raise a row if I insist upon it at present.

It is delightful, dear Girlie, to read your cheerful letter, God bless you! Please give our dearest love to Frank whenever you write; and tell us what you learn of his work and movements when you can. We are always hungry for letters from you. My warm regards to Mrs. Sayre and my thanks and best wishes to the young friend who is staying with you till Nevin comes. Margaret sends heeps of loving messages. Helen is away, at York Harbor.

Your loving Father

ELEANOR RANDOLPH WILSON
TO
WOODROW WILSON

---

*E*leanor and her husband were moving to California when she wrote this emotional letter to her father.

March 2nd 1922

Darling, darling Father,

I couldn't do down to Washington to tell you good-bye—not because there wasn't time, but because I couldn't bear to say good-bye to you. This is the only way that I can stand it at all—going so far away from you. It isn't as if we won't be back before long on a little visit—we'll probably be here in the fall, but I feel as if I were chopping a great big piece off of my heart when I put four days, instead of five hours between you and us. I don't see how I'm going to stand it. Father darling, I love you more than I have ever been able to tell you and I owe you so much in every, every way that I shall never, never be able to repay it all. I wish I knew how to tell you what you and your love mean to me.

I can't write very much—for I am too sad—this is just a little note to tell you that I love you and that we'll be back soon.

Will you give dear, dear Edith a big hug and kiss for me and ask her to hug you for me?

Ellen sends her heart full and so does Mac—to you both.

With oh so much love darling darling Father
from Your adoring daughter Nell

We are leaving to-morrow—Friday—and our address will be Hotel Huntington, Pasadena, California

---

ANNA ROOSEVELT

TO

FRANKLIN D. ROOSEVELT

---

*A*nna was living in New York with her second husband and two children by her first marriage when she wrote this letter tinged by political humor, typical of correspondence between presidents and their daughters.

2 West 53rd Street New York City
Jan. 29th, '36

Dearest Pa,

I wish I could see you tomorrow & give you a great birthday hug—and the kids are terribly disappointed to miss out on the spanks! But, as we can't be where you are, all four of us send you loads of love, plenty of mental spanks, and the wish that you may have a great many really happy birthdays before you.

Everybody and his brother seem to be going to your Birthday Ball here tomorrow night—including of course, Granny, Jimmy, Bets and us. Why don't you break up the dignity of the occasion by ending your broadcast with a ditti such as "Where was Moses when the Light went out?" I started to suggest your singing "The

Old Gray Mare, she ain't what she used to be" but decided that your political opponents might capitalize!

Do you realize you've never seen our flat? If you can possibly do it, won't you try to plan to have a meal here on your way back to Washington from Hyde Park in February. It's very easy to get in here—I don't mean by that that we have no thugs, g..men and speak-easy trap doors, but that there is only one step and that is in the entrance hall.

Lots of love, and a Happy Birthday tomorrow! Anna

FRANKLIN D. ROOSEVELT
TO
ANNA ROOSEVELT

---

*I*n the midst of frantic efforts to ship "surplus arms" to Great Britain after the Dunkirk evacuation, Roosevelt, who loved the ocean and sailing, wrote this jocular letter to his daughter about her husband John's boating accident. Anna and her family were living in Seattle, Washington, where John was the editor of the Seattle Post Intelligencer. The hope of a future visit is standard fare for presidents and daughters, as indeed for virtually all fathers and daughters separated by long distances.

The White House June 1, 1940

Dearest Sis:

It was grand to get your note the other day which came just at the time that John was reputed to have tried to lift a lifeboat or two into the water or out of it, with the result of a broken arm. John ought to realize by this time that his heavyweight ring career is over—that the old days of giants have passed into mythology, and that no newspaper publisher can be a H.A. sailorman at the same time. If John does not know what H.A. means, I will instruct him in private!

I am distressed that the trip is off. I have not even been able to get away to Hyde Park for weeks and weeks—in fact,

I am hitting on all cylinders about seventeen hours a day.

The Coast seems the most peaceful spot in the world from this long range—nevertheless, I do hope that somehow you will be able to come this way this Summer.

I miss all five of you lots and lots.

Ever affectionately,

P.S. I am dictating this to Grace because I am leaving this afternoon late for one night of sleep on U.S.S. Potomac—running down the river and straight back again.

HARRY S. TRUMAN
TO
MARGARET TRUMAN

---

*M*argaret was just three years old when her father wrote this affectionate letter to her. Truman, the presiding judge of Jackson County, Missouri, was serving in the U.S. Army summer camp at Fort Riley, Kansas, as a reserve officer in the Field Artillery, and Margaret was home in Independence, Missouri, with her mother and grandmother.

Ft. Riley, Kans. Saturday. 16. July '27

Dear Little Daughter:

I recieved your letter this noon along with your mothers and it was very fine. I was glad to get it because another gentleman at my table had just recieved one just like it from his little girl. There are two little yellow haired girls in this same barrack. One of them is four and the other is two and they have a fine time playing together. The four year old ran across the porch yesterday and fell down. She bumped her nose just like you do when you fall and she cried just like you do. Her father is a nice looking cavalry captain. He picked her up and swore at the government for having him live where the boards in his front porch are loose so his little girl would fall. I told him that my little girl always picked a gravel road to fall on. These little girls have dolls and tea tables and scooters. You'd have a fine time with them.

Kiss your Mother and write me again. Your daddy

HARRY S. TRUMAN
TO
MARGARET TRUMAN

---

*M*argaret was thirteen, but already a budding pianist and singer, when Truman wrote this letter during his first term as U.S. senator. Music and events in Washington were nearly constant topics of their exchanges.

Washington D.C. Jan. 14 1937.

Dear Daughter:

If you knew how happy your daddy was to get your nice long letter you'd write him oftener. I am so sorry you have had the Flu but I'm most happy to hear that everyone else is out of danger. We haven't had any snow and it hasn't been cold. You must have had a real winter out there. I wish I was with you. I'll keep on trying to find an apartment and when I do you and your mother will be here right soon afterwards.

You should have been here night before last to hear Rachmaninoff. He directed the Symphony here and played some of his own pieces on the piano. I didn't go but I read about it in the papers.

It sure was too bad I was in Baltimore last night when you all called up. I'll never go again so I'll be sure and be here when you call again.

The inauguration is going to be some stunt. They have the whole front of the Capitol covered with seats have some on top of the Senate office building and have the front of the white House completely covered up.

Wish you and Mamma were here.

Give her a big Kiss for me and take several yourself.

Love to you from Dad

HARRY S. TRUMAN

TO

MARGARET TRUMAN

---

*T*ruman makes one of his many apologies for his long absences from home as a U.S. senator on the eve of America's involvement in World War II, in this letter to fifteen-year-old Margaret. Although he was a frequent correspondent, Margaret seldom returned the favor.

Washington, D.C. June 16, 1941

My dear Daughter:

Your old dad was most highly pleased when he came in this morning and found your telegram. There was a note on the apartment door saying Mr. Vaughan had called me up to tell me it had arrived. You see I went out there about two o'clock and went to bed turned the phone on down stairs and told Mrs. Rickets to take all calls— and she did it literally so I didn't Know about the nice wire until this morning.

I wish that I could be a real nice dad but you Know with all this terrible emergency and the awful political fights your dad has had to make ever since you were born, there hasn't been much chance to be the right Kind of a dad.

I am most happy however with a sensible, beautiful young lady for a daughter—and that's because she had the right sort of mother.

Now you can help square me with your Independence Grandmother. I went off without saying goodbye an awful thing to do. See what she thinks about it and tell me.

Kiss your mamma for me. I'm sending you some funny papers.

Much love, Dad XXXXXXX

RONALD REAGAN
TO
PATRICIA REAGAN

---

*P*atricia was just twenty-one months old when her father wrote to her at length from Glacier National Park in Montana where he was filming Cattle Queen of Montana. The letter seems to be directed more to Patti's mother, Nancy Davis Reagan, than to a small child.

July 12, 1954

Dear Patti:

I thought I'd better write and explain why you aren't finding me in the usual place these mornings. I had to come way up here to a beautiful place called "Glacier Park" in order to keep alive the myth that I'm a working man. This won't take too long and then I'll be home saying "Boo Patti" to you and "Deedee and Teddy and Saing."

This place is beautiful with granite peaks and lakes and glaciers—and contrary to what the studio told me it is rather cool. Therefore unless the weather changes I have all the wrong clothes with me. That isn't serious however because by tonight the wardrobe man will be here with my picture clothes and I'll wear them most of the time.

Incidentally we are way up on the continental divide near the Canadian border and they tell us it is not uncommon to see the northern lights. The altitude is such that if you walk and talk at

the same time (a thing not entirely foreign to my nature) you have to pause for a few deep breaths.

There were no "Northern lights" last night but there was a big moon and a sky full of stars shining down on the glaciers and snow covered peaks. It was a beautiful night with a constant breeze that seems to have come from out among the stars and it seems that if you listen very carefully it will whisper secrets as old as time.

Pretty soon the moon and the stars and this breeze got together and filled me with a longing so great that it seemed I'd die of pain if I couldn't reach out and touch your Mommie. You aren't old enough to really understand what I mean but you will someday. Right now just imagine what you feel like when you want "num num" real bad and it isn't in sight and when you want to hold Teddy real tight—put this all together, double it and it is just a faint hint of how I feel.

Maybe it is a good thing to be apart now and then. Not that I have to be away from your Mommie to know how much I love her but a thirst now and then makes you know and remember how really sweet the water is.

I'm counting on you to take care of Mommie and keep her safe for me because there wouldn't be any moon or stars in the sky without her. The breeze would whisper no secrets and the warmth would go out of the sun. So you guard her very carefully and then you'll always have a pair of footsteps to follow, and if you follow her footsteps you'll grow up to be a sweet, lovely person just made for love.

This love is why we are apart right now. You see we want you to always be surrounded with love so you'll know how important it is. So now we taste of loneliness in order to share some of our love with you. We are happy to do this because you are very much a part of our love.

Just guard her and keep her safe till I come home—because I love her and you very much.

Daddy

P.S. My address here is St. Marys
Browning, Montana

LYNDON B. JOHNSON
TO
LYNDA BIRD JOHNSON

*L*ynda, thirteen, was attending summer camp at Camp Mystic when her father wrote this newsy note.

June 10, 1957

Dear Lynda:
The Cains will get to the LBJ Ranch about the 14th—next Friday—and they are going to spend the night. When they go to Fort

Clark they may stop by Camp Mystic and I thought I would let you know to be looking for them about next Saturday or Sunday.

We had a good trip to New York and got home yesterday evening. Mr. and Mrs. George Brown are here for a visit and we had them out to the house last night after we got back.

Willie Day stayed with Lucy Saturday night and Sunday, and Lucy cried because she wouldn't stay again last night. She said she didn't have anybody to sleep with her now that you are gone, but Willie Day was real firm that she didn't want to be kicked out of bed two nights in a row.

Beagle says he wishes he was in the Hill Country too and would like to see you, but I'll have to confess he said he would like to see a big jack rabbit even more!

Send me the Mystic Murmurs so I will know what's going on—who is the best camper and who catches a beau from Camp Stewart and who is eating cookies and who isn't—you know, just a lot of little things that I am interested in keeping up with.

A heart full of love to my beautiful daughter.

Your Daddy, Lyndon B. Johnson

DOROTHY BUSH
TO
GEORGE H. W. BUSH

---

*D*orothy was only nine when she wrote these two amusing "camp" letters to her father, then a U.S. congressman.

[undated, c. July 1968]

Dear Dad

I miss you very much. Thank you for your nice letter. This camp is very fun. I want to come next year. My Best friend is Koko. She is from a faren contry.

I love you, Doro

July 1, 1968

Dear Mom and Dad,

Today we played on the blob, that was so much fun.

I got 1 demeret by slaming the door by axadent—it is a screen but I got a meret by being nice and caching a hen that got out of wild life.

Love XXXX0000 Doro

LUCI JOHNSON
TO
LYNDON B. JOHNSON

---

*L*uci was married to Patrick Nugent when she wrote this enthusiastic letter to her father about their appearance on the Merv Griffin Show. Luci's letters and cards always seem to reflect her exuberant personality, while her father's response reveals the close emotional ties between the correspondents.

November 10, 1970

Dearest Daddy

Patrick and I want to thank you from the bottom of our hearts for the many thoughtful expressions that you have shown us lately. The goodie package that you sent Mr. Griffin was such a big plus for our interview—although I fear I did not do you justice, I'm sure Patrick did.

Most of all, of course, I want to thank you for the most overwhelming and exciting note I've ever received—that one that you sent with the goodie package for Mr. Griffin! Please know how deeply touched and well plain elated we were!!

We had the most exciting time. Mr. Wasserman gave us the most thrilling tour of Universal that one could imagine. We dined with the Wassermans, the Host and several other friends. And everyone we met asked about you and said they missed you.

All in all our trip was a little bit of Heaven.

We love you, your Luci

LYNDON B. JOHNSON
TO
LUCI JOHNSON

November 19, 1970

Dear Luci:

Nobody but a Luci could write such a dear letter. I'm so proud of it as I am of you. We watched and listened to you and Pat with more love than you know. And, you gave us even more to be proud of Tuesday night.

Stay as sweet as you are, Love, Daddy

GEORGE H. W. BUSH
TO
DOROTHY BUSH

*B*ush was director of the CIA when he wrote this friendly letter to Dorothy, then a student at Boston College in Massachusetts, who was touring Great Britain.

Wednesday. July 7th [1976]

Dear Doro,

It's July 7th at about 8 am. I'm at the office. Yesterday was George's 30th birthday. I called him and he didn't sound any older at all.

We got your three England cards—sounds like a great trip so far, though I worry a little about your reference with less than full enthusiasm about at least one of your travelling companions. Hang in!

The last weekend, a long one Thursday night til Monday nite, we spent at K'port. I turned down being on the Forrestal and seeing the tall ships and we also turned down fireworks on the White House lawn on the 4th; but we made the right choice. We had 4 perfect Maine days—lots of short boat (opposite of tall ship) the Fidelity is running good—parked in her corner behind Herby's boat. Marv has taken the Fidelity out some, and he handles it OK. It runs fast.

Some mackerel were caught. Mum and I went out one evening alone and grabbed 10 of em at about 6–7 P.M. a great quiet time. They were Holy Mackerel being caught between the church and the black can.

The Scarboroughs are there in force. David drove us to the airport Monday at Sandford. I had to fly down to see Jimmy Carter at Hershey Penna. So Dave took us over there. Katie is working a lot and looks just great. The other sister (the one you also like) came by the house. Fred gets along great with Jessica.

Barker has 2 dogs—one looks like a lobo (wolf that is) and looks tough but he proves to be a cowardly and friendly wolf and after much sniffing and pawing the dirt he and Fred are AOK together. The black female that Barker's family has looks fierce but is O.K. so Fred is happy up there. He stayed up for the week with Paula and Marvin. Mum came back with me though we hope to go up this coming weekend again.

Fred loves the ocean, ball chasing etc. He just charges in all alone when he gets near the ocean. He likes the boat a lot too—closing his eyes and sleeping when we go fast.

Tennis—not so hot. Marv and I lost two close ones to Hemenway and Boardman. Marv and I beat Bucky and Hemenway. Marv and I lost to Buck and some pro friend from South Carolina.

Nottman is there not Pierce. Mrs. ONeil is there with new husband and a bunch of kids—5 I think.

Billy Scarb is working hard at the boat club as is long haired Dwight who is great with the Fidelity.

Not much other news. Ganny had a 75th birthday on July one but she sounds 35. Louisa and Scott are the same. Louisa is so cute—a non stop talker. Scott is Mr. Clean.

The Veto is not in the water—no users though Scott may use it.

I better run now. Just know that your old Dad loves you

GEORGE H. W. BUSH AND HIS INFANT DAUGHTER, DOROTHY (DORO), IN THE FALL OF 1959.

very much and misses you. I will be glad when you are back in Maine. They are all waiting for you up there. One forgets the beauty and the peace of that place. Sitting out on our deck looking over the ocean, or the great sound sleeps in the salt air—it's great.

Have a great and wonderful trip. Learn a lot, but don't forget to love your Dad.

Devotedly Dad

GERALD R. FORD
TO
SUSAN ELIZABETH FORD

*S*usan, clearly the doting daughter, received these brief but charming notes from her father on her birthdays and holidays.

[April 12, 1998]

Dearest Susan,
You are a very special, wonderful daughter. We are so very proud of you in every way. You do so many & thoughtful things for others.

LOVE, Dad

[undated]

Dearest Susan,
You are very special in our heart. We are so proud of all you do for all of us.

With all of our LOVE. Dad.

[undated]

Dearest Susan,
We congratulate you on another birthday and we know you will have many more of the best.

We are so very proud of you as our daughter. Mom and I are so grateful for all the good things you do for our family.

LOVE, Dad

SUSAN FORD, DAUGHTER OF GERALD FORD, DANCES WITH HER ESCORT, WILLIAM PIFER,
DURING THE 1975 HOLTON ARMS SCHOOL SENIOR PROM IN THE EAST ROOM OF
THE WHITE HOUSE, MAY 31, 1975.

GEORGE H. W. BUSH
TO
DOROTHY BUSH

*F*ormer president Bush was living in Texas when he wrote to his daughter about her four children—Sam, Ellie, Robert, and Gigi—after a happy holiday visit.

Undated [c. Christmas 1996]

Dear Doro,

A crisis—the Secret Service are desolate, for no one is there to stand guard with them. No blazer clad little guy with a tie on and a pin in his lapel. It is not the same around here any more.

Gigi is gone away. That dampens my spirits, for no more when I wake up is there a gentle cooing sound coming from the most lovely baby in the whole world. No beautiful Ellie to brighten my life either. No wonderful Sam to take me back to those happy teen age sports oriented years of the days of yore. What a treat you and Bobby gave us by coming here and making Christmas really come alive.

Here, dear Doro, are a couple of pairs of Size 11 Shoes, one old brown pair of tasseled loafers and one quite new pair of black loafers—fit for a fussy Italian. When he was here Sam tried on the blacks and they were a little large.

But he's growing fast. As I watched him try them on I would have sworn his feet grew 1/5th of an inch. Stand by and they'll soon fit. If not give them a hand off to some worthy homeless guy up there or to one of those demonstrators in front of the White House who could maybe use a nice stylish loafer.

I love you, Doro Koch.

My dear Patsy   Annapolis. Dec. 11. 1783

I wrote you by the post this day fortnight, since which
I have received two letters from you. I am afraid that you may
not have sent to the post office, wherefore this letter may
be still lying there this day sennight hence. I will let me
write to you every week, yet it will not be amiss for you
to enquire at the office every week. I wrote to mrs house by
the last post, perhaps her letter may still be in her office.
I hope you will have good sense enough to disregard those foolish
predictions that the world is to be at an end soon. the almighty
has never made known to any body at what time he created
it, nor will he tell any body when he means to put an end
to it. if ever he means to do it. as to preparations for that
event, the best way is for you to be always prepared for it.
the only way to be so is never to do nor say a bad thing. if
ever you are about to say any thing amiss or to do any thing
wrong, consider before hand. you will feel something within you
which will tell you it is wrong & ought not to be said or done.
this is your conscience, & be sure to obey it. our maker has
given us all, this faithful internal Monitor, and if you
always obey it, you will always be prepared for the end of the
world: or for a much more certain event which is death.
this must happen to all. it puts an end to the world as to
us, & the way to be ready for it is never to do a wrong act.

1551

CHAPTER 2

ADVICE:
"BY WAY OF ADVICE AND ADMONITION..."

*"Will try that your
advise shall not be thrown away"*
—Mary (Maria) Jefferson to Thomas Jefferson,
May 23, 1790

*"You must meet contingencies
as they arise and face them squarely."*
—Harry S. Truman to Margaret Truman,
February 15, 1944

JOHN ADAMS
TO
ABIGAIL ADAMS

Abigail was just nine years old when her father wrote this charming letter of advice from Philadelphia, while attending the First Continental Congress—the initial national step on the long road to American independence from Great Britain. She was to receive many such letters as he traveled to distant places during the next decade.

Philadelphia Sept. 19. 1774

My dear Child
I have received your pretty Letter, and it has given me a great
deal of Pleasure, both as it is a Token of your Duty and Affection to me and as it is a Proof of your Improvement in your
hand Writing and in the faculties of the Mind. I am very sorry
to hear of your Grand Mamma's Indisposition: but I hope soon
to hear of her Recovery. Present my love to your Mamma, and
to your Brothers, Johnny, Charly and Tommy. Tell them they
must be good Children and mind their Books, and listen to the
Advice of their excellent Mamma, whose Instructions will do
them good as long as they live, and after they shall be no more
in this World.

Tell them, they must all strive to qualify themselves to be good
and usefull Men—that so they may be Blessings to their Parents,
and to Mankind, as well as qualified to be Blessings to those who
shall come after them.

Remember me to Mr. Brackett, and Copeland, and to Patty
Field, Molly Marsh, Jonathan Bass and Patty Curtis. I am my dear
little Nabby, with continual Prayers for your Happiness and Prosperity, your affectionate Father, John Adams

---

THOMAS JEFFERSON
TO
MARTHA JEFFERSON

---

*J*efferson was in Annapolis, Maryland, for a session of the Continental Congress, when
he wrote this advisory missive to eleven-year-old Martha (Patsy). Advice and admoni-
tions were staples of his letters to his daughters Mary and Martha, whose feelings of
love and guilt led them to dedicate their lives to helping their father as plantation mis-
tresses and social hostesses.

Annapolis Dec. 11, 1783

My Dear Patsy

I wrote you by the post this day fortnight, since which I have received two letters from you. I am afraid that you may not have sent to the post office & therefore that my letter may be still lying there. tho' my business here may not let me write to you every week yet it will not be amiss for you to enquire at the office every week. I wrote to Mr. House by the last post. perhaps his letter may still be in the office. I hope you will have good sense enough to disregard those foolish predictions that the world is to be at an end soon. the almighty has never made known to any body at what time he created it, nor will he tell any body when he means to put an end to it. if ever he means to do it. as to preparations for that event, the best way is for you to be always prepared for it. the only way to be so is never to do nor say a bad thing. if ever you are about to say anything amiss or to do any thing wrong, consider before hand, you will feel something within you which will tell you it is wrong & ought not to be said or done. this is your conscience, & be sure to obey it. our maker has given us all, this faithful internal Monitor, and if you Always obey it, you will always be prepared for the end of the world; or for a much more certain event which is death! This must happen to all. it puts an end to the world as to us, & the way to be ready for it is never to do a wrong act.

I am glad you are proceeding regularly under your tutors. you must not let the sickness of your French master interrupt your reading French because you are able to do that with the help of your dictionary. remember I desired you to send me the best copy you should make of every lesson Mr. Cimitiere should set you. in this I hope you will be punctual, because it will let me see how you are going on. always let me know too what tunes you play. present my compliments to Mrs. Hopkinson, Mrs. House & Mrs. Trist. I had a letter from your uncle Eppes last week informing me that Polly is very well, & Lucy recovered from an indisposition. I am my dear Patsy.

Your affectionate father Th. Jefferson

MARY (MARIA) JEFFERSON
TO
THOMAS JEFFERSON

*J*efferson and his younger daughter corresponded frequently during his regular trips from Monticello to the nation's capital. In this typical exchange, Mary tries to mollify her father by explaining her regular study routine. In return, Jefferson chides her for owing him a letter, but then praises her work and domestic skills, and provides lively news about local flora and fauna.

Eppington May 23 [1790]

Dear Papa

I received your affectionate letter when I was at presqu'isle but was not able to answer it before I came here as the next day we went to uncle Bolings and then came here. I thank you for the pictures you was so kind as to send me and will try that your advise shall not be thrown away. I read in don quixote every day to my aunt and say my grammar in spanish and english and write and read in robertson's america. After I am done that I work till dinner and a little more after. It did not snow all last month. My cousin Boling and myself made a pudding the other day. My aunt has given us a hen and chickens. Adieu my Dear papa. Believe me to be your ever dutiful and affectionate daughter, Maria Jefferson

THOMAS JEFFERSON
TO
MARY (MARIA) JEFFERSON

New York June 13. 1790

My dear Maria

I have recieved your letter of May 23 which was in answer to mine of May 2. but I wrote you also on the 23d of May, so that you still owe me an answer to that, which I hope is now on the road. in matters of correspondence as well as of money you must never be in debt. I am much pleased with the account you give me of your occupations, and the making of pudding is as good an article of them as any. when I come to Virginia I shall insist on eating a pudding of your own making, as well as on trying other specimens of your skill. you must make the most of your time while you are with so good an aunt who can learn you every thing. we had not yet pease nor strawberries here till the 8th day of this month. on the same day I heard the first Whip-poor-will whistle. swallows and martins appeared here on the 21st of April. when they appear with you? and when had you peas, strawberries, & whip-poor-wills in Virginia? take notice hence after whether the whip-poor-wills always come with the strawberries & peas. send me a copy of the maxims I gave you, also a list of the books I promised you. I have had a long touch of my periodical head-ack, but a very moderate one. it has not quite left me yet. Adieu, my dear, love your uncle, aunt & cousins, and me more than all.

Your's affectionately Th. Jefferson

GEORGE WASHINGTON
TO
ELEANOR PARKE CUSTIS

Washington, in the midst of his second presidential term, sent this letter to his seventeen-year-old granddaughter. He warmed to his task by correcting her writing skills, and then launched into some direct, fatherly advice about love and passion. Three years later in 1799, he became her legal guardian to facilitate her marriage to his nephew, Lawrence Lewis.

Philadelphia 21st Mar. 1796

My dear Nelly,

In one respect, I have complied fully with my promise to you, in another I have deviated from it in a small degree. I have given you letter for letter, but not with the promptitude I intended;

ELEANOR (NELLY) PARKE CUSTIS WAS RAISED AT MOUNT VERNON BY HER GRANDPARENTS, GEORGE AND MARTHA WASHINGTON, AFTER THE 1781 DEATH OF HER FATHER, JOHN PARKE CUSTIS.

your last of the 29th ult. having lain by me several days unacknowledged. This, however might reasonably have been expected from the multiplicity of my business.

Your letter, the receipt of which I am now acknowledging, is written correctly, and in fair characters; which is an evidence that you command, when you please, a fair hand. Possessed of these advantages, it will be your own fault if you do not avail yourself of them: and attention being paid to the choice of your subjects, you can have nothing to fear from the malignancy of criticism, as your ideas are lively, and your descriptions agreeable. Your sentences are pretty well pointed; but you do not as is proper begin a new paragraph when you change your subject. Attend to these hints and you will deserve more credit from a few lines well adjusted and written in a fair hand, then for a whole sheet scribbled over as if to fill or . . . the bottom of the paper, was the principal . . . or design of the letter.

I make these remarks not from your letter to me, but because many of those to your Grandmama appear to have been written in too much haste; and because this is the time to form your character, improve your diction.

This much by way of advice and admonition. Let me touch a little now, on your George Town Ball; and happy, thrice happy, for the fair who were assembled on the occasion, that there was a man to spare; for had there been seventy nine Ladies & only seventy eight Gentlemen, there might, in the course of the evening, have been some disorder among the caps; notwithstanding the apathy which one of the company entertains for the "youth of the present day, and her determination never to give herself a moments uneasiness on account of any of them.": A hint here; men & women feel the same inclinations towards each other now that they always have done, and which they will continue to do until there is a new order of things. And you, as others have done, may find perhaps, that the passions of your sex are easier roused than allayed. Do not therefore boast too soon, nor too strongly, of your insensibility to, or resistance of its powers.

In the composition of the human frame there is a good deal of inflaminable matter; however dormant it may be for a while, and, like an intimate acquaintance of yours, when the torch is put to it, that which is within you may burst into a blaze; for which reason, and especially too, as I have entered on the chapter of advices I will read you a lecture drawn from this text.

Love is said to be an involuntary passion and it is therefore contended that it cannot be resisted. This is true, in part only; for like all things else when nourished and supplied plentifully with ailment it is rapid in its progress; but let these be withdrawn and it may be stifled in his birth or much stunted in its growth.

For example—a woman (the same with the other sex) all beautiful & accomplished will, while her hand & heart are undispared of the heads, and set the Circle in which she moves on him.

Let her marry, and what is the consequence? The madness ceases and all is quiet again; Why? Not because there is any diminuation in the charm of the lady but because there is an end of hope. Hence it follows that love may and therefore that it ought to be under the guidance of reason. For although we cannot avoid first impressions, we may assuredly place them under guard; and my motives in treating on this subject are to show you "whilst you remain Eleanor Custis Spinster, and retain the resolution to love with moderation" the propriety of adhering to the latter; at least until you have secured your game, and the way by which it is to be accomplished.

When the fire is beginning to kindle, and your heart growing warm, propound these questions to it. Who is the invader? Have I competent knowledge of him? Is he a man of good character? A man of sense? For be assured a sensible woman can never be happy with a fool. What has been his walk in life? Is he a gambler? a spendthrift, a drunkard? Is his fortune sufficient to maintain me in the manner I have been accustomed to live, and my sisters do live? and is he one to whom my friends can have no reasonable objection? If these interrogations can be satisfactorily answered there will remain but one more to be asked; that however is an important one. Have I sufficient ground to conclude that his affections are enjoyed by me? Without this, the heart of sensibility will struggle against a passion that is not reciprocated; delicacy, custom, or call it by what epithet you will having precluded all advances on your part, the declaration without the most indirect invitation on yours must proceed from the man to

GEORGE AND MARTHA WASHINGTON WITH GEORGE
WASHINGTON CUSTIS AND ELEANOR (NELLY) PARKE CUSTIS,
TWO OF THEIR GRANDCHILDREN.

render it permanent & valuable. And nothing short of good sense, and an easy unaffected conduct can draw the line between prudery & coquetry; both of which are equally despised by men of understanding; and soon or late, will recoil upon the actor.

Flirting is hardly a degree removed from the latter and both are punished by the counter game of men, who see this the case & act accordingly. In a word it would be no great departure from truth to say that it rarely happens otherwise, than that a thorough coquette dies in celibacy, as a punishment for her attempts [to] mislead others; by encouraging looks, words, or actions, given for no purpose than to draw men on to make overtures that they may be rejected.

This day according to our information gives a husband to your dear sister; and . . . it is presumed her fondest desires.

The dawn (with us) is bright, and propitious I hope, of her future happiness; for a full measure of which she and Mr. Law have my earnest wishes. Compliments & congratulations on this occasion, and best regards are presented to your Mama, Dr. Stuart & family, and every blessing among which a good husband when you want & deserve one, is bestowed on you by Your affectionate Go. Washington

RUTHERFORD B. HAYES
TO
FANNY HAYES

*H*ayes, who had recently completed his presidential term, wrote to his daughter urging her to "curb your rebellious spirit." It is not known what effect this letter had on Fanny's "wild oats."

Spiegel Grove Fremont, Ohio.
1 June 1883 Columbus, O.

My Darling Daughter:
We came from the Grove to Lauras Tuesday. Lizzie accompanies your mother and is very helpful. Wednesday I went to Piqua, and had a part in very agreeable Decoration Day Ceremonies, both afternoon and Evening. Yesterday I returned here. Your mother seems very happy meeting old friends and acquaintances. We shall probably remain until Monday, and then visit Mr. & Mrs. Herron during the most of next week in Cincinnati.

I am made a little uneasy—not seriously however, by the mysterious intimations of your last letter to your mother. You must curb your rebellious spirit. You inherit I know, Enterprise and daring from a long line of Scotch borderers—the Scotts, the Rutherfords and the Hayes. There are, I must tell you, a basketful of reasons why a demure and subdued line of conduct is most becoming in you. Your immediate ancestors, maternal especially have a place in the good opinion of good people not to be imperilled by their children's wild oats without misgiving and perhaps tears. Think of it Darling, and makes us all happy by your Considerate and discreet conduct.

We found the dear ones here all just as we could wish them. More of happiness and less of the opposite in their several Cups than often falls to the lot of mortals. Three better and more promising and admirable children than Laura's are under few roofs.

Fanny Fullerton is quietly blessed also, in the same way. Aunt
Hatty (Mrs. Solis) is here from Detroit. The new home in D. has
made most agreeable impressions on her.

No more now, from your loving father
R. B. H.

THEODORE ROOSEVELT
TO
ALICE ROOSEVELT

---

*T*hen-president Roosevelt was clearly worried that the actions of nineteen-year-old
Alice would reflect badly on their respective public images. In time, Alice would attain
the reputation of being politically savvy and outspoken.

Washington, November 19, 1903

Do not like the advertisements of your appearing at portrait show. They distinctly convey the impression that any person who wishes to pay five dollars may be served tea by you and Ethel Barrymore. I cannot consent to such use of your name and must ask you not to serve tea. In my opinion managers have shown poor taste in making this use of your name, and they should in some way withdraw it so that no one will come with the expectation of seeing you serve tea.

HARRY S. TRUMAN
TO
MARGARET TRUMAN

---

*T*ruman was at Army summer camp in Minnesota when he penned this letter to eight-year-old Margaret. His advice was to bear fruit in her eventual careers as a singer and author.

Camp Ripley, Minn. July 20, 1932

Dear Daughter:
Your fine letter came this morning and your dad was surely glad to get it. I do wish you and your mother were here in spite of cannons. A little boy about your age came out to the firing point yesterday, and when the big guns went off he almost climbed the flagpole. I think he was more scared than you'd have been. Someday I hope you don't mind them and will come and watch your daddy shoot, and see how it is done.

I am glad you are practicing because I would be disappointed if someone should say that the reason Margaret Truman can't play is because her daddy is trying to teach her and he doesn't know how. I want you to know how, but I can't do it for you.

You have to work for yourself if you expect to accomplish anything. And I surely want you to be as good as the best in everything you undertake except smoking cigarettes, and I hope you'll never do that. I've never yet seen a smoking woman that I'd have around me for a minute.

I am glad you are walking everywhere and I hope you'll be entirely well when I get home next Sunday.

Kiss your mamma for me and tell her I still look for letters.

Your loving Dad

[P.S.] Here are two more pictures of your dad.

MARGARET TRUMAN
TO
HARRY S. TRUMAN

In this typical exchange between them, Margaret offers her father assurances that she is diligently studying her music and thanks him for his support. For his part, Truman offers his daughter advice about controlling her temperament in the pursuit of a career.

Monday [13 August 1946]

Dear Daddy,

Thank you very much for the very nice letter. Thank you also for the big piece of green lettuce. I'll use it sparingly. I have been singing all afternoon with Mrs. Strickler, Mrs. Shaw at the piano and Mr. Letson, Rose Conway's uncle, is Rigoletto in that opera. We're getting it polished up so I'll be able if I get the chance to stand on the Met stage and sing it as if I'd always been there singing opera. It's not so hard when you get the hang of it, and it's loads of fun. We're going to work every day this week.

Went to a picnic at Louise Duke's last night. Tish and her husband and Wiley Mitchell, one of Louise's cousins. We had a lot of

MARGARET WAS JUST A BABY WHEN THIS PICTURE WAS TAKEN
WITH HER FATHER, HARRY S. TRUMAN, IN 1924.

fun. I guess I was a bad girl, because I made the date last week and
Cousin Ethel didn't know about the family gathering until Sunday morning. Aunt Louella never did call us so I felt I had to go
to Tish's. Mother said they had a good time seeing the Texas cousins.
We took Aunt Mary's presents to her all right so don't worry.

Wednesday night the Stricklers are coming for dinner. It's
her birthday.

Nothing much has happened since you left. The town has
been sleeping off all the excitement you caused. Did you see Time
this week about George Allen. It's a riot.

Pete says dinner is ready so guess I'd better go. After singing
all afternoon, I'm so hungry. Bet I'll get fat now, and I don't want
to. Be good and sleep lots on the boat.

Loads of love, "Sistie" XXXXXOOOOO

Bermuda, August 23, 1946

My dear Daughter:
Your letter was a nice one and highly appreciated by your old
dad. I am glad you are working hard at your music. If you love
it enough to give it all you have nothing can stop you. There is
only one thing I ask—please don't become a temperamental case.
It is hard to keep from it. I know—and no one knows better than
I. But it is not necessary nor does it help in your public relations.
It makes no friends and to succeed at anything you must have
friends on whom you can rely. that is just as true of a musical
career as it is of a political one or a business career.

Now that's out of my mind I wish you and your mother were
here. This is a paradise you dream about but hardly ever see. I
don't think I'd want it as a steady diet but for my purpose it is
ideal. This island is a coral one 22 miles long in the shape of a
fish hook. Look at the map in the encyclopedia. All the houses
are built of coral with coral roofs as white as snow.

They saw the coral out with a hand saw and it hardens and
then they paint it with concrete and whitewash it or paint it. The
houses are pink, white, red, tan, and most other colors.

The sea is blue as the sky and it is 84 degrees. I take a walk on
shore every morning and then have breakfast, take a sunbath on
deck and a swim alongside the ship, have lunch, a nap and this
afternoon I'm going deep sea fishing! Beat that if you can. Called
on the Governor General yesterday. He met me at the dock in an
open carriage with a coachman & footman up. drawn by two
spanking grey horses. We rode through Hamilton in truly royal
state, to Government House on top of a hill overlooking the town.
Then we rode back to the boat in the same style and back to the
yacht. It was a pleasant experience. There are 33,000 people on

the islands, ten thousand white and the rest colored. It is funny as can be to hear these blacks talk with an Oxford accent.

Well, I went fishing southwest of the Islands about five miles over a coral reef. Caught three very beautiful fish weighing from four to about ten pounds. One of them, the smallest, was red, one was tan with white spots and the other was a bright yellow with white stripes on him. You never saw anything prettier but they don't stay that way. After they are out a while they turn dark fast but they say they are good to eat. We'll try my catch tomorrow. Ted caught a big brown fish and Capt. Foskett caught four not so large as mine. The rest caught none. Clifford almost fell overboard, Vaughan got seasick and Allen told me how good he is with fish but they didn't take to him.

Here's a piece about you from the Sunday Post-Dispatch, also some expense money. Kiss mommy for me. Tell all the rest hello.

Lost of Love Dad XXXX OOOOO

RONALD REAGAN
TO
PATRICIA REAGAN

---

*P*atricia was fifteen and a student at the Orme School in Arizona when she received this long letter from her father, then governor of California, after she had reported herself for smoking. In addition to the advice on honesty and smoking, the letter contains a charming section on "the pleasure of remembering" childhood experiences.

March 5, 1968

Dear Patti:

Yes—turning yourself in was the right thing to do and I'm sure you feel better for having done it. I'm sure you realize also that it was proper for the school to impose a punishment as they did.

If we could pay for rule breaking just by confessing it there wouldn't be much law and order. In the Bible we can read where Jesus heard confessions and promised forgiveness but on the condition that we would go forth and not commit the sin again.

These are two issues here Dear Patti. One is the fact that for two years you broke not only school rules but family rules and to do this you had to resort to tricks and deception. Why is this of such concern to the school or to me and your mother? The answer is very simple. We are concerned that you can establish a pattern of living wherein you accept dishonesty as a way of life.

Let's turn from you and translate it into someone else. Would you be happy if you weren't sure that I was quite honest? Would you be comfortable if you had to wonder whether you could believe things I said? Or if perhaps now you had to worry that maybe I was being dishonest in this job—that some day the paper would carry a story exposing me as a lawbreaker? You know the answer of course. But don't you see—compromising with truth no matter how trivial does something to us. The next time it serves our purpose we do it again and one day we find ourselves in trouble and we're not quite sure why or how.

Now issue number two—smoking itself. I'm sure I don't have to repeat all the reasons why it's bad for you. Science leaves us very little doubt about it anymore. Yes I know many adults continue to smoke but I don't know any who don't wish they could quit. That alone should tell you something—if they want to quit and can't that's pretty good proof that tobacco is capable of forming a habit stronger than human will power. Unfortunately women are more susceptible to habits than men and find them much harder to break or change. How many I've seen (among our friends) pregnant and told by the doctor that smoking during pregnancy would harm their baby—but the habit was too strong. You see it's very hard to do something wrong and just hurt yourself.

I enjoyed your poem although I read a touch of nostalgia. There is nothing wrong with that all our lives we build memories and the important thing is to build happy ones. I too will remember the ranch with nostalgia but with great warmth for the happy days spent there. You'll be part of those memories—sitting up on a big black horse (Baby) in front of my saddle–splashing in the pool (without bathing suit) at age three and getting your own first horse.

What keeps the memory from haunting us with unhappiness is if we have moved on to some things equally or more enjoyable. For example I built and loved a small ranch in the valley before you were born. I remember it happily but then came the ranch you knew–now there will be another ranch and so it goes. There was Baby, then Nancy D. and now it will be "Little Man." Life is to remember with pleasure and look forward with anticipation. Your poem will add to the pleasure of remembering when we must leave this ranch and thank you for it.

I must go now. I hope you'll accept and work out your hours without bitterness and with the intention of not repeating the act that brought them about. I hope too you'll continue to improve in your studies.

We are all looking forward to Easter vacation together at Bama Deedees and Bapas. They were over here for our wedding anniversary yesterday. You'll probably quit writing poems if you think each one will bring on a four page letter from me. I promise not to do this often. Love, Dad

---

GERALD FORD
TO
SUSAN ELIZABETH FORD

Ford wrote this generic "Personal Reflection" in preparation for writing his memoirs, *A Time to Heal.* There is no evidence that he had given this "reflection" directly to his daughter Susan.

Advice to a teenage daughter
In today's confusing & complex society a teenage daughter needs to know that there are certain century old fundamental

principles which if adhered to are the best path to future good health & happiness.

She should reciprocate the love of her parents with her love. She should respond to the friendship of others with her own in return. She must realize the respect & admiration are a two way street. She must understand that her mind & body are a priceless heritage, once given, that she must use wisely for health & happiness. She must recognize that what she does today will have an impact on the future.

A teenage daughter must be taught thru example, not just words, that happiness & success depend on unselfishness, giving more than receiving. It makes one secure & confident. She must be guided to believe there are certain intangibles—love, integrity, God—are the anchor in adversity and the best insurance for a better life.

SUSAN FORD, DAUGHTER OF GERALD FORD, IS PRESENTED A BOOK ON TRANSCENDENTAL MEDITATION BY MIKE LOVE OF THE BEACH BOYS AT THE WHITE HOUSE ON JUNE 25, 1975.

Mentor, May 7th "79

My dear Papa.

You said we
must write and tell you
what kind of lessons we had
each day. I am glad to say
that I had very good lessons
yesterday. I feel just like
studying now I am in
Mentor. I saw in the Herald
a piece about you. it said that
you had come here with your
family. and then at last it

CHAPTER 3

EDUCATION:
"REAL GOOD LESSONS..."

"I had real good lessons yesterday."
—Mary (Mollie) Garfield to James Garfield,
May 7, 1879

*"You may have some desire to know
how your daughter's education is progressing."*
—Frances (Fanny) Hayes to Rutherford B. Hayes,
January 20, 1886

NO SUBJECT, with the possible exception of politics, found
its way into the letters of presidents and their daughters more
than did education, be it formal schooling or simple at-home
instruction. Success in one's studies was seen as a precursor of
success in later life, an attitude that has not changed in the more
than two hundred years of the nation's history.

JOHN ADAMS
TO
ABIGAIL ADAMS

*A*dams was one of the most intellectual of U.S. presidents, and his correspondence with his daughter quite naturally reflects his approach to life. In this letter to eleven-year-old Abigail, Adams, then a member of the Continental Congress, took the time to discuss many facets of education.

Philadelphia, March 17th, 1777

My Dear Daughter

I hope, by this time, you can write an handsome hand; but I wish you would, now and then, send a specimen of it to Philadelphia, to your papa, and he may have the pleasure of observing the proficiency you make, not only in your handwriting, but in your turn of thinking, and in your faculty of expressing your thoughts.

You have discovered in your childhood a remarkable modesty, discretion, and reserve. I hope these great and amiable virtues will rather improve in your riper years. you are now, I think, far advanced in your twelfth year; a time when the understanding generally opens, and the youth begin to look abroad into that world, among whom they are to live. To be good, and to do good, is all we have to do.

I have seen, in the progress of my last journey, a remarkable Institution for the education of young ladies, at the town of Bethlehem, in the commonwealth of Pennsylvania. About one hundred and twenty of them live together, under the same roof; they sleep all together, in the same garret, every night. I saw one hundred and twenty beds, in two long rows in the same room, with a ventilator, about the middle of the ceiling, to make a circulation of the air, in order to purify it of those gross vapours with which the perspiration of so many persons would otherwise fill it. The beds and bed-clothes were all of them of excellent quality, and extremely neat. How should you like to live in such a nunnery? I wish you had an opportunity to see and learn the various needle work and other manufactures, in flax, cotton, silk, silver, and gold, which are carried on there; but I would not wish you to live there. The young misses keep themselves too warm with Dutch stoves, and they take too little exercise and fresh air to be healthy. Remember me with the tenderest affection to your mamma and your brothers. I am with inexpressible affection,

Your father, John Adams

JOHN ADAMS
TO
ABIGAIL ADAMS

---

*O*ne striking aspect of Adams's letters to his daughter was the absence of the gender limitations so typical of the late eighteenth century. In this letter, written while he was an American minister in Paris, he encourages Abigail to study French in the very same manner successfully pursued by her brother.

Passy, December 2d, 1778

My Dear Daughter

In your letter to your brother, which is a very pretty one, you express a wish that you understood French. At your age, it is not difficult to learn that language; patience and perseverance is all that is wanting.

There are two ways, which are sure. One is to transcribe, every day, some passages from the best authors. Another is to conjugate the verbs, in writing, through all the modes and tenses and persons, both of the active and passive voice. If you are resolute to practise this every day, you are sure of the language in no long time. I have made your brother do this, and write the English in every person against the French, so that he has sometimes filled two sheets of paper in conjugating one verb. In this practice he has had great success.

I shall not lay down any rules for your behaviour in life, because I know the steadiness of your mind, your modesty and discretion; and you cannot find in this world, in my opinion, a better preceptor than your mamma, both in her precepts and examples.

I have so many things to do, and so many cares upon my mind, that I cannot write to you so often as I wish: but I should take great pleasure in receiving letters from you. I am, with the tenderest affection, my dear daughter, Your father, John Adams

---

THOMAS JEFFERSON
TO
MARTHA JEFFERSON

---

*W*hile a member of the Continental Congress meeting in Annapolis, Jefferson worked out a detailed plan of education for his eldest daughter in the absence of her deceased mother. Ever the controlling parent, he warned his daughter that following his instructions "will render you more worthy of my love." On the one hand, Jefferson wanted his daughters to be well schooled; on the other, he was preparing them to dutifully serve as wives to masters of upper-class plantation households.

Annapolis Nov. 28. 1783

My Dear Patsy

After four days journey I arrived here without any accident and in as good health as when I left Philadelphia. The conviction that you would be more improved in the situation I have placed you than if still with me, has solaced me on my parting with you, which my love for you has rendered a difficult thing. The acquirements which I hope you will make under the tutors I have provided for you will render you more worthy of my love, and if they cannot increase it they will prevent it's diminution.

Consider the good lady who has taken you under her roof, who has undertaken to see that you perform all your exercises, and to admonish you in all those wanderings from what is right or what is clever to which your inexperience would expose you, consider her I say as your mother, as the only person to whom, since the loss with which heaven has been pleased to afflict you, you can now look up; and that her displeasure or disapprobation on any occasion will be an immense misfortune which should you be so unhappy as to incur by any unguarded act, think no concession too much to regain her good will. With respect to the distribution of your time the following is what I should approve.

from 8. to 10 o'clock practice music.
from 10 to 1. dance one day and draw another
from 1. to 2. draw on the day you dance, and write a letter the next day.
from 3. to 4. read French
from 4. to 5. exercise yourself in music.
from 5. to bedtime read English, write &c.

Communicate this plan to Mrs. Hopkinson and if she approves of it pursue it. As long as Mrs. Trist remains in Philadelphia cultivate her affections. She has been a valuable friend to you and her good sense and good heart make her valued by all who know her and by nobody on earth more than by me. I expect you will write to me by every post. Inform me what books you read, what tunes you learn, and inclose me your best copy of every lesson in drawing. Write also one letter every week either to your aunt Eppes, your aunt Skipwith, your aunt Carr, or the little lady from whom I now inclose a letter, and always put the letter you so write under cover to me. Take care that you never spell a word wrong. Always before you write a word consider how it is spelt, and if you do not remember it, turn to a dictionary. It produces great praise to a lady to spell well. I have placed my happiness on seeing you good and accomplished, and no distress which this world can now bring on me could equal that of your disappointing my hopes. If you love me then, strive to be good under every situation and to all living creatures, and to acquire those accomplishments which I have put in your power, and which will go far towards ensuring you the warmest love of your affectionate father.

Th. Jefferson

P.S. Keep my letters and read them at times that you may always have present in your mind those things which will endear you to me.

MARTHA JEFFERSON
TO
THOMAS JEFFERSON

---

*W*hen Martha went to France with her father, she was placed in the Roman Catholic Convent School, Abbaye Royale de Panthemont. Following some initial misgivings, she adapted, if anything, too well to convent life. Despite his satisfaction with the more secular teachings of the school, Jefferson immediately removed his daughters in April 1789, when Martha voiced an interest in coverting to Catholicism and becoming a nun.

March 25th 1787

My Dear Papa

Though the knowledge of your health gave me the greatest pleasure, yet I own I was not a little disappointed in not receiving a letter from you. However, I console myself with the thought of having one very soon, as you promised to write to me every week. Until now you have not kept your word the least in the world, but I hope you will make up for your silence by writing me a fine, long letter by the first opportunity. Titus Livius puts me out of my wits. I can not read a word by myself, and I read of it very seldom with my master; however, I hope I shall soon be able to take it up again. All my other masters go on much the same, perhaps better. Every body here is very well, particularly Madame

MARTHA JEFFERSON RANDOLPH, DAUGHTER OF THOMAS JEFFERSON.

L'Abbesse, who has visited almost a quarter of the new building, a thing that she had not done for two or three years before now. I have not heard any thing of my harpsichord, and I am afraid it will not come before your arrival. They make every day some new history on the Assemblée des Notables. I will not tell you any, for fear of taking a trip to the Bastile for my pains, which I am by no means disposed to do at this moment. I go on pretty well with Thucydides, and hope I shall very soon finish it. I expect Mr. Short every instant for my letter, therefore, I must leave you.

Adieu, my dear papa; be assured you are never a moment absent from my thoughts, and believe me to be, your most affectionate child, M. Jefferson

---

THOMAS JEFFERSON
TO
MARTHA JEFFERSON

While America's minister to France, Jefferson addressed another educational matter in this communiqué to his eldest daughter: his expectation that she mentor her younger sister when the girl arrived in France. Above all she was to teach her to "be good" and learn "useful pursuits." However, even with Martha's aid, Mary did not adapt well to her removal from the Jefferson/Randolph family circle back in Virginia.

Toulon April 7. 1787

My dear Patsy
I received yesterday at Marseilles your letter of March 25 and I received it with pleasure because it announced to me that you were well. Experience learns us to be always anxious about the health of those whom we love, I have not been able to write to you so often as I expected, because I am generally on the road;

& when I stop any where, I am occupied in seeing what is to be seen. it will be some time now, perhaps three weeks before I shall be able to write to you again. but this need not slacken your writing to me, because you have leisure, & your letters come regularly to me. I have received letters which inform me that our dear Polly will certainly come to us this summer. by the time I return it will be time to expect her. when she arrives, she will become a precious charge on your hands. the difference of your age, and your common loss of a mother, will put that office on you. teach her above all things to be good: because without that we can neither be valued by others, nor set any value on ourselves. teach her to be always true. no vice is so mean as the want of truth, and at the same time so useless. teach her never to be angry. anger only serves to torment ourselves, to divert others and alienate their esteem. and teach her industry and application to useful pursuits. I will venture to assure you that if you inculcate this in her mind you will make her happy being in herself, a most inestimable friend to you, and precious to all the world. In teaching her these dispositions of mind, you will be more fixed in them yourself, and render yourself dear to all your acquaintance. practice them then, my dear, without ceasing. if ever you find yourself in difficulty and doubt how to extricate yourself, do what is right, & you will find it the easiest way of getting out of the difficulty. do it for the additional incitement of increasing the happiness of him who loves you infinitely, and who is my dear Patsy your's affectionately, Th. Jefferson

---

JAMES MONROE
TO
ELIZA MONROE

---

*M*onroe's eldest daughter attended Madame Campan's fashionable school for girls near Paris at St. Germain-en-Laye during her father's two periods of service as American minister to France and Spain. Madame Campan was a former lady-in-waiting to Marie Antoinette. Like Jefferson's daughter Martha, Eliza became interested in the Roman Catholic religion and—after the death of her father and her husband, George Hay—she returned to France, converted to Catholicism, and died in a convent.

Aranjuez March 1, 1805

My dear child
As Mr. Preble will present you this, who has a daughter with Mdme Campan I wod. Not suffer so favorable an opportunity to pass, without informing you of my health & inquiring after yours. I hope you have intirely got rid of your toothache, & of every other complaint and are making such a progress in all things as merits the perfect approbation of Mdme. Campan. Don't forget among all yr. Useful acquirements the comparatively trivial one of playing & singing several airs on the harp; I will get you one at Paris. That is an accomplishment that will be really useful to you. I have written so much on other points that I have little to add at present even

THIS PORTRAIT OF ELIZABETH KORTRIGHT MONROE,
THE ELDER DAUGHTER OF JAMES MONROE, WAS DONE BY AN
UNKNOWN FRENCH ARTIST, CIRCA 1803.

had I time, which indeed I have not, having much to write by this opportunity; I have also dropped a line to your mama, to inform her that I still enjoy good health. I hope you will have recd. Mine by Captn. Dulton, make my best respects to Mdme. Campan. Most affecy. I am my dear child yours, Jas. Monroe

---

JAMES MONROE
TO
ELIZA MONROE

---

*H*ere, Monroe, as U.S. Minister to Great Britain, urged his daughter to broaden her education via travel.

London Jany. 28. 1806

I have my dear child received two lettrs from you since I left you, the last today wch. Gives me concern to find that you had been indisposed. I perfectly agree with your mother & yourself that there is no motive for you to remain longer at Bath. You have derived all the advantage from the waters wch. They can give. It depends here-after on exercise, and animal diet, for you to prepare your health. Too long a use of the water instead of strengthening will I am per-suaded weaken your stomach. As soon as it has gained its proper tone, & been confirmed in it, the use of the water shod. Be dis-continued. You shod. then rely on nature, & it would be hard, with a constitution wch. is really good and strong, if you could not at your time of life preserve it so. To your mother the water has been of no use, and therefore on her accot. there is no motive for your remaining there. I agree with you also that the amusements of the place must soon cease to be interesting. I am satisfied that you have seen enough of Bath, & that it will be better for you to return here without delay, that is, after the term for wch. the house was taken expires. I think that will be about the 6th of next month, tho it

JAMES MONROE, FIFTH PRESIDENT OF THE UNITED STATES
AND FATHER OF ELIZA AND MARIA, SEATED AT THE WHITE HOUSE
WITH A VIEW OF THE CAPITOL IN THE BACKGROUND IN THIS 1817
STIPPLE ENGRAVING AFTER A PAINTING BY CHARLES B. KING.

ought to certainty, & arrangements made not to remain one day longer than the term expires. I have put an advertisement in the papers, & have several friends looking out for a house in the neighborhood of the city, so that I hope to get one soon. I have so little doubt of this that my wish is that your Mama, be prepared to set out on the return at the time above mentioned, if she hears nothing from me to the contrary. I shall give her notice in time of the place she will stop at, & send sufficient money to pay house rent & bring you all up. I hope Mrs. Purviance will be able to accompany you, & will take the trouble to see that all matters are properly adjusted. There is a place in the neighborhood called Stone Henge, an antient Druidical building & I wished you have seen, also Bristol, I requested your Mama to write her old friend & companion Mrs. Church, to advise her being so near her, & the pleasure she wod. have to see her. It is not yet too late to do it, wch. I hope she will. I hope you will have recd. before this your muff & tippet, &

your Mama hers, & approve them. I have nothing new from America. Ld. Grenville & Mr. Fox are to be in the ministry & their friends. It seems to be improper at such a time for me to leave this. I hope your Mama will approve the above plan. To her & Maria make my affectionate regards & be assured of them yourself. Jas. Monroe

If my coming down is necessary to bring you up I will certainly do it. On enquiry if the distance is not too great & you could visit Stone Henge & Bristol I shod. be glad of it.

JOHN TYLER
TO
MARY TYLER

---

*K*nowledge of the literary arts and especially an ability to write elegant letters were valuable skills for politicians'daughters in the eighteenth and nineteenth centuries, as can be seen in this letter from then-Senator Tyler to his eldest daughter, fifteen-year-old Mary.

Washington March 4. 1830

My dear daughter
I owe you a letter for yours of the 18th February and pay it with the more pleasure as I percieve an obvious improvement in your writing in all respects. A little attention will bring you to write very well but without that nothing can be done. Your style is also more flowing than formerly. To write any thing well it is necessary to overcome all constraint. to feel perfectly at ease and to give the mind full play. By reading Pope, Addison, Johnson and especially the Spectator, you will acquire an easy and happy diction. Nothing can surpass their epistolary style.

You do the Duke of Marlborugh injustice by comparing him to Charles XII. The Duke was a man of the most exalted endowments both of mind and person. A soldier and a gentleman. He possessed all the courage of Charles without his rashness, the able minister and accomplished soldier. It was nevertheless said of him that he was the creature of avarice, and this overshadow'd all his good qualities. The lines which were said to be true in regard to the celebrated Lord Verulam, who was Francis Bacon, that he was "the brightest, greatest, meanest of mankind" are said to have been in some measure true in regard to the Duke. He was charged with prolonging the war merely to receive his pay, and as being the first man in England who sold commissions in the army pocketing himself the proceeds. (Now all commissions in the army in England are bought and sold, not so here) These charges were made by his enemies and no doubt were carried further than they deserv'd. Charles XIIth was possess'd of the most invincible courage...but after all he was little better than a madman. The Duke of Marlborough after being idoliz'd by England, was turned adrift hated and despised. This teaches us not to place our hopes of happiness on others, and least of all to rest it upon popular favor. The purest and the best of men have been neglected and abus'd. Aristides was banished and Socrates was poison'd. We should rather rely upon ourselves, and howsoever the world may deal with us, we shall by having securd our own innocence and virtue, learn to be happy and contended even in poverty and obscurity. Our creator will then be our friend, as he is always our great and good benefactor. It will be a safe rule of action through all your life, before you do any act, to enquire of yourself whether it be proper and virtuous that it should be done. If your heart and judgement do not concur in approving it, do not do it. for you may then rest assured that it is wrong to move. I could not hold up to you a better pattern for your imitation than is constantly presented you by your dear mother. You never see her course mark'd with precipitation, but on the contrary every thing is brought before the tribunal of her judgement, and her actions are all founded in prudence. Follow her example my dear daughter, and you will be, as you always have been a great source of comfort to us.

JOHN TYLER, THE ONLY FORMER PRESIDENT TO SERVE IN THE CONFEDERATE GOVERNMENT, IS SEEN IN THIS CIVIL WAR–ERA PHOTOGRAPH BY BRADY–HANDY.

The course you have mark'd out for your future reading I am satisfied with—reflection on what you have read is as necessary, nay
more necessary than mere reading—learn to descriminate between
the character with which history presents you. The newspapers are
the history of the present day—read them as you would any othr
history and remember what you read.

Old Mrs. [erased] has not yet reachd the city. She is a worth-
less old woman who does not deserve to be countenanc'd, but
when she comes I will get her book. I shall much regret however if she introduces you and your mother into it. Write to me
often & assist your mother in all that you can. Your Aunt Waggaman and all are well except Mr. W. who has been confind by
imprudent use of medicine, but is recovering.

God bless you and all the children. Yr. Father J.Tyler

ULYSSES S. GRANT
TO
ELLEN WRENSHALL GRANT

---

*T*he day after one of the bloodiest single battles of the war, Grant—then commanding
general of the Union army—still found the time and lightness of heart to write this
homey letter to nine-year-old Ellen.

Cold Harbor Va. June 4th 1864

My Dear Little Nelly,
I received your pretty well written letter more than a week ago.
You do not know how happy it made me feel to see how well my
little girl not yet nine years old could write. I expect by the end
of the year you and Buck will be able to speak German and then
I will have to buy you those nice gold watches I promised. I see
in the papers, and also from Mamas letter, that you have been
representing "The Old Woman that lived in a Shoe" at the Fair!

I know you must have enjoyed it very much. You must send me one of your photographs taken at the Fair.

We have been fighting now for thirty days and have every prospect of still more fighting to do before we get into Richmond. When we do get there I shall go home to see you and Ma, Fred, Buck and Jess. I expect Jess rides Little Rebel every day! I think when I go home I will get a buggy to work Rebel in so that you and Jess can ride about the country during vacation. Tell Ma to let Fred learn French as soon as she thinks he is able to study it. It will be a great help to him when he goes to West Point. You must send this letter to Ma to read because I will not write her to-day. Kiss Ma, Cousin Louisa and all the young ladies for pa. Be a good little girl as you have always been, study your lessons and you will be contented and happy. From Papa

ELLEN (NELLIE) GRANT, DAUGHTER OF ULYSSES S. GRANT, PLAYING
THE OLD WOMAN IN THE SHOE TO RAISE MONEY BY SELLING DOLLS
AND PHOTOGRAPHS AT THE SANITARY FAIR IN ST. LOUIS IN 1864.

*G*arfield and Mary (Mollie), then eight, exchanged letters about her progress as a beginning Latin student. She proved a model student as a youngster, studying hard and reporting dutifully to her father while he served as a member of the U.S. House of Representatives.

Washington D.C. Oct 12. 1875

Dear Papa.
I am beginning Latin today I have learned four words. First I learned Mensa a Table. Next Columba A Dove. I can decline them both. I wrote them on the black board for Mamma. I will begin music tomorrow morning. We got your letter this morning. And was glad to get it. Irvins foot is most well.

I think it is lonesome here with out you. Jennie has not come home. Irvin has been learning his lessons this morning. I cant think of any more. So good by your daughter Mollie Garfield

JAMES GARFIELD

TO

MARY GARFIELD

Cleveland. O. Oct 14, 1875

My Dear Mollie.
I received your letter of the 12th, & was very glad to know that you had begun Latin. I feel quite sure you will do well. But you know it will take a good deal of real close hard study to be a good Latin Scholar. But think how nice it will be, to write papa a nice letter in Latin. So that I can answer in this way.

Maria Carissima

Bona epistola tua, mihi gaudu maximus dat. Est bonae filiae stud-
ise librum Latinum, at amare parentis. Vale, Votre Pater Amicus

Our friends in Hiram are well and would send love to little
Mollie if they knew I was writing to you. I shall hope to see my
little girl next week. Your Affectionate Papa, J. A. Garfield

JAMES GARFIELD, WHILE SERVING AS A U.S. REPRESENTATIVE,
AND HIS ONLY DAUGHTER, MARY (MOLLIE), BY MATHEW B. BRADY CIRCA
1870, A DECADE BEFORE HIS ELECTION TO THE PRESIDENCY.

MARY GARFIELD
TO
JAMES GARFIELD

*W*hen Mary was twelve she sent this brief letter to her father. She later continued her studies at Miss Augusta Mittleberger's School in Cleveland, Ohio, and Miss Sarah Porter's School in Farmington, Connecticut.

Mentor, May 7th. '79

My dear Papa.

You said we must write and tell you what kind of lessons we had each day. I am glad to say that I had very good lessons yesterday. I feel just like studying now I am in Mentor. I saw in the Herald a piece about you. it said that you had come here with your family and then at last it said you were slightly pale from overwork. if you could come here you would be just the opposite from pale.

I must close now and study my other lessons.

Give my love to the boys & Ethel.

Ever your loving little Molly

RUTHERFORD B. HAYES
TO
FANNY HAYES

*I*n 1883 Frances (Fanny) was a student at Miss Augusta Mittleberger's School in Cleveland, Ohio. Hayes tried to give his daughter advice about friends and studies, while Fanny replied in disarmingly charming schoolgirl notes. Mary (Mollie) Garfield was a classmate of Fanny's at both Miss Mittleberger's School and at Miss Sarah Porter's School in Farmington, Connecticut. Despite her expressed fears of examinations, Fanny was an excellent student.

My Dear Daughter:

Your nice letter, received this Morning, makes our hearts glad. I hope you will be very Considerate and Cordial with your new roommate, and that she will prove in all respects an acceptable Chum. Chum may not be the proper word for a female, but you know what I mean. Lizzie has not returned, but Sophy and Adda were mindful to send you a reminder of our Grand Army Reception.

You have perhaps heard of our G.A.R. Reception. It was a happy and beautiful affair. Miss. Sherman and the Glee Club enlivened the occasion with old Soldiers' Songs—the Band gave us their best music, and all passed off as we would have wished.

Adda left the next morning, Thursday, and Maggie Came in the afternoon—so we keep our number good.

We missed you at the reception. Scott and his friend Harry Smith were very efficient. Mary Miller, Miss. Haynes and others assisted, and I think all were attended generously. We suppose the number was two hundred, making it the largest party with full entertainment we have had.

The good Sleighing lasted until today. The snow is now melting with a strong South wind. "The January thaw" has probably come. We have had, including today, thirty-six (36) days of sleighing. Some days it was very poor, but a great part of the time it could hardly have been better.

Your mother has still occasional attacks lasting an hour or two, which cause her much suffering. I suppose they are fits of indigestion, or dyspepsia. She is now taking medicines which it is hoped will bring relief.

Your letter is well written. You do not always use periods at the end of a sentence, and you sometimes begin a sentence without a capital letter. I will give you one example of this mistake. You say "I have a new roommate, Lizzie Allen, from Hillsdale, Michigan, she is very bright, etc." The period should be a distinct point (.) after the word Michigan. The next sentence should have begun with a large S. But your letter is so good and has so few faults that on the whole I must compliment you on its Excellence.

I will write Miss. Mittleberger not to worry you too much with Examinations or Severe Studies.

With love from all, Affectionately, R. B. Hayes

FRANCES (FANNY) HAYES, DAUGHTER OF RUTHERFORD B. HAYES, POSES IN HER MARTHA WASHINGTON COSTUME IN 1880.

Jan. 16th 1883.
1020 Prospect St., Cleveland, O.

Dear Papa:

I received your letter Monday, and was very glad to hear from you. I feel very much relieved that I do not have to take all the examinations, Mabel says that they are very severe. I do not feel very uncomfortable as regards the examinations in U.S. History, but Grammar, Arithmetic, French, Bible, Definitions and Reading are dreadful nightmares.

Today is Mollie Garfield's birthday, she invited Nellie Moss, Carrie Hogan and myself to dine and spend the evening with her, but we were not allowed to go.

I went to Auntie Austin's this afternoon, Uncle Austin's health is not good, he has a very severe cold, and is confined to the house.

Enclosed you will find Prof. Brainard's bill for my music.

The first bell for supper has rung, so good-bye, Papa.

Your loving daughter
Fanny Hayes.

P.S. Mollie has just sent a bunch of lovely roses to Nellie, Carrie and myself, also a box of candy. I think it was very sweet of her, don't you?

I have not spent any of the money you gave me, yet.

Give a great deal of love to Mamma, and a kiss.

Give my love to Rud, Scott and Cousin Mag.

Lovingly, Fanny Hayes

FANNY HAYES
TO
RUTHERFORD B. HAYES

*F*anny was a student at Miss Sarah Porter's School for Girls when she and her father exchanged these two letters, concerning her desire to drop some of her classes.

Farmington, Conn. Jan. 20th 1886.

My dear Papa:

I have not heard from any member of the family, except Scott, since I left but as "no news is good news" I am not anxious at all.

I am rather, no decidedly, busy this term. You may have some desire to know how your daughter's education is progressing so I will tell you what I am studying. I recite in French, Greecian

History, Literature, Physics and Astronomy every day, have "Gen. Ex." with Miss Porter twice a week, music lessons twice a week and Harmony once a week. I find that I am kept hurrying to an uncomfortable degree, my brain being rather slow at working, so don't you think that I might stop my music for this term if no longer?

That would give me two divisions more for study so that I need not study during walking hour.

I enjoy Astronomy, as far as I have got, very much. The teacher is excellent, talks well, and is fond of the study which is, I think, a very necessary thing.

A good many of the girls went coasting this afternoon but I had to go to the "Harmony" class, much to my disgust. You see all the music scholars have to be in the old class whether they wish or no.

Our new girl came today. I think we shall like her very much as she seems to be pleasant and is quite pretty.

Give my best love to all the family and advise some of them to write.

Your affectionate daughter
Fanny Hayes.

RUTHERFORD B. HAYES
TO
FANNY HAYES

Spiegel 24 Jany 1886

My Darling:
You shall have more letters. I will not neglect you. As to your studies I agree with you. There are too many of them. The only question is which to drop. My decided preference is that you drop either Grecian History, Physics, or Astronomy. You will have another year at F. I hope. I don't know what "harmony" means. You may drop that if you prefer. Music, you know, is the pet of both your mother and Father. But if you can't manage it

why do as you Suggest. You are "wisest discreetest best". Who said that? Of whom was it said?

All the boys are now here. The weather is charming. We only need you with your "Oho!" to be one of the happiest families on the Continent.

I am glad the new girl is a favorite.

If you stay another year, you Must go into the Main building that is if you want to do so.

How can you be assured of that?

With all love, Ever
Rutherford B. Hayes

THEODORE ROOSEVELT
TO
ALICE LEE ROOSEVELT

---

*H*igher education is not only about books and studying, as can be seen in this letter from Roosevelt to his eldest daughter, who was being educated by private tutors. Football games were a major interest at the start of the twentieth as well as twenty-first centuries.

Washington, November 29, 1901

Darling Alice:

We were very much relieved to get your letter today, and though we know how wretched you felt, still the letter was so bright and amusing that we were all cheered by it. It was awfully hard luck not to see the football game, especially as it proved such a smashing triumph for Harvard. Tomorrow morning we start to see Annapolis and West Point play.

Blestein is still tender in the nigh forefoot, and I am riding the long-tailed sheep—a health-giving rather than an exhilarating occupation.

Mother had a very successful musical entertainment and an equally successful Thanksgiving dinner, and looked more than ever like the Colonel's niece on both occasions. Her dress was very pretty, and she looked so young and well. I play bear with the children almost every night, and some child is invariably fearfully damaged in the play; but this does not seem to affect the ardor of their enjoyment. Poor Quentin still has a little asthma and cannot play, and I tell him stories and hum songs in a hoarse murmur until my brain fairly reels. Uncle Douglas and Auntie Corinne have been with us—just as nice as possible; and Auntie Bye is as dear as ever and oversees the entire nation.

Give my love to all the long-suffering Lee family. Your affectionate father

---

ETHEL CAROW ROOSEVELT
TO
THEODORE ROOSEVELT

---

*R*oosevelt's youngest daughter may have written this amusing letter to her father in 1904 while attending the Cathedral School. Young Ethel was clearly confident that she could charm and manipulate her doting dad.

Thursday 04

Dearest Father
Will you please telephone out to the school and say that you want me to come home on the 2:10 bus as I think Quentin would like to have somebody to play with and I have done most of my lessons.
Your loving Ethel

[P.S.] This was written in the carriage. Ethel C. Roosevelt

HELEN HERRON TAFT
TO
WILLIAM HOWARD TAFT

*F*ifteen-year-old Helen complained to her father, then Secretary of War, that "we have to work awfully hard" at the Baldwin School, Bryn Mawr, Pennsylvania. Despite her complaints, Helen excelled at the Baldwin School in such sports as field hockey and basketball, as well as in academic subjects.

The Baldwin School
November 18, 1906

Dearest Papa:

Mama told me that you had been off on a trip so I haven't written you before. I love it here, but we have to work awfully hard. You mustn't be disappointed if my marks seem very low for they have a way here of marking every body extremely low. Last year I thought I was doing poorly if I didn't get ninety in every thing. Mama will be disappointed when she sees that I got only "passed" in exercise. The trouble was that I forgot to sign on the exercise blank several times. Yesterday we went for a long walk. We walked three miles to a river crossed in a boat and took a train for four miles. Then we crossed again and walked about four miles home. I was all mud up to my knees when I got back for the snow is just melting. I am afraid I ruined my poor tan skirt but we had a splendid time.

Wasn't it fine about Rob's taking the prize in his entrance exams? He will soon be able to make his living at earning prizes.

My room-mate here is Anne Ward and she says you know her uncle Mr. Woodruff. We have a quite respectable looking room now what with the things Mama sent me and the things Anne has acquired. Aren't you coming up here to see me pretty soon? can't you just stop in on one of your many trips.

Your loving Helen

WILLIAM HOWARD TAFT
TO
HELEN HERRON TAFT

*A*fter his daughter's marriage to Frederick J. Manning, Chief Justice Taft continued to urge the completion of her doctoral thesis at Yale. The following exchange between Helen and her father reflect their mutual satisfaction as she neared the completion of her doctoral dissertation, "British Colonial Government after the American Revolution, 1782–1820."

Supreme Court of the United States.
May 11, 1924

My dear Helen:

I suppose that in spite of the fact that you have got your thesis into the hands of the printer, you are very busy correcting proof and gathering up the threads and getting ready for your examination. You haven't told me what kind of an examination it is you are to pass.

I think I am getting slowly into normal condition, but I have to be quiet and try to be, and I am not at all certain how much progress I make. I feel all right and the Doctor says I look all right. It is the irregularity of the heart that gives uneasiness. I send you your mother's letters, which I wish you would return to me— one from Grenada and one from Cordova. The cable I had from the Ambassador was after they had returned from Madrid and its later than these letters. So far as I can see, she hasn't received any of my letters, although I have written her one every day.

The Corporation has asked me to ask President Coolidge whether he would accept a Doctorate of Letters from Yale this year, and I must go down to see him. I should think he might do so. It will be after he is nominated and before the democratic Convention, and it will give him a kind of eclat among the college men that will be quite in the spirit which they feel toward him.

I have written two opinions this week, and hope to deliver them tomorrow. It looks to me now as if I could get through easily by

the time of the adjournment, so that I shall have nothing to bother me in vacation in the way of judicial opinions. I have succeeded I think in getting two sisters who are nice looking girls, who will go up with Maggie and Annie and Tom that will be enough during the first part of the summer before the other children come, and then we shall have to get somebody as parlor maid to help out. You know that Eleanor More and John and Catherine will go up with you to Murray Bay from New Haven. The girls will be up there and I shall go around by way of Montreal, reaching Murray Bay the day before you leave. But I must go to church. Love to Fred and the baby. Your loving father, Wm. H. Taft

---

HELEN HERRON TAFT

TO

WILLIAM HOWARD TAFT

May 29, 1924

Dear Papa.
The thesis went to the binder this morning so I suppose that all is well. We had to sit up all last night to get the bibliography

into shape so I am feeling rather groggy and can't do more than write a line.

I am terribly upset to hear that you have not been well. If you should continue to feel under the weather I will come down and pay you a visit for you must be rather lonely. But I hope that you are better by this time. Please let me know.

I had a letter from Aunt Maria which I enclose as I think you may not have heard from her except by cable. She sounds as if she had not intended to stay in Spain, but I hope Mama can persuade her to. Every one tells me that they have seen in the paper that I accompanied Mama—because of the scene we made on the dock I suppose.

I have a long exam to take just before June 1st but if that passes off I shall be your loving daughter H. T. Manning P.h.D.

HARRY S. TRUMAN
TO
MARGARET TRUMAN

---

*E*ducation and politics were the subjects of this brief letter from Truman, serving as a U.S. Senator from Missouri, to thirteen-year-old Margaret, back home in Independence, Missouri.

Washington, D.C. Feb. 23, 1937

My Dear Daughter:

I hope you passed all your tests with flying colors. You have to work very hard now trying to get a lot of information into your head so you can be perfectly at home with educated people and can be tolerant with the uneducated ones. It seems very hard while you are doing it, but you'll be very glad that you can play the piano, speak French, talk intelligently about Agrippa and Genghis Khan, and reasonably understand geography and math.

So keep right at it and in six or eight years you'll have a fine foundation for a practical education.

Politics is a great game. Your dad has been playing at it for some twenty-five years. It is a game of people and how they act under certain conditions. You never can tell, but you can sometimes guess, and I've been a good guesser. You must be able to tell the facts too, and to believe them yourself.

I'm going to look for my next letter on time, and if I get it, then maybe I'll tell you something you want to hear when I write again.

The office force all say hello.

Lots of love to my sweet Margie. Dad

LYNDON B. JOHNSON
TO
LYNDA BIRD AND
LUCY (LUCI) BAINES JOHNSON

---

*J*ohnson, then a U.S. senator from Texas, wrote this encouraging letter to his young daughters, Lynda (fourteen) and Luci (eleven).

September 24, 1958

Dearest Lynda and Lucy:

Last night while I couldn't sleep, I lay awake and started to thinking about all the things I have to be thankful for. I have a good job, a lot of friends who love me, a certain amount of success, a certain amount of financial security and a certain amount of prestige. But the things that I am most grateful for are that I have two sweet and lovely daughters who always make me very proud of them and who always reflect more credit on me than I deserve. When you add everything up, nothing really matters in the world except the people who love you and the people that you love.

Lucy, I couldn't be more proud than to hear that you are doing so well in school. You must be an awfully smart little girl to make such wonderful ratings in your classwork. It is very important that you learn everything you can so that you will be an intelligent, well-informed young woman. And it is just as important to be interested in the world about you and to be alert to the happenings around you. You remember how she was interested in what was going on. She was not content to just live within herself but instead she was concerned with others.

And, Lynda the best news I have had all week is that you have lost eight pounds! I bet you look like a movie star and I can't wait until I get to see you for myself.

I have to be in Washington for a meeting on October 16th so I'm coming up there for a nice long visit with you. By that time you should both be real pretty and slim and maybe I'll take you out on the town with me!

Love,

LYNDA BIRD JOHNSON, DAUGHTER OF LYNDON B. JOHNSON, AND HER HUSBAND CHARLES ROBB STAND UNDER A PICTURE OF GEORGE WASHINGTON AFTER THEIR WHITE HOUSE WEDDING IN 1967.

LYNDA BIRD JOHNSON
TO
LYNDON B. JOHNSON

*W*hen her husband, Charles Robb, was deeply involved in his legal studies at the University of Virginia Law School in Charlottesville, Lynda and her father exchanged these candid letters about the sometimes difficult demands of raising a family while one spouse is still pursuing a professional education. The former president provided parental support and morale for both Lynda and Charles.

[April 1972]

Dear Boppa

Lucinda started a thank you letter to you for the darling yellow dresses you and Nana sent but Cathy kept fighting her for the pencil so it is messy. The dresses are darling. They wore them to church and got only a minimum of chocolate on them.

Cathy has reached the terrible twos early. She has been beating on Cindy lately and getting into trouble every minute with me. I was making some cookies for Law Wives and she grabbed a fist full right out of the center of the pan. How can I offer cookies with finger holes? She also has a terrible habit of throwing things. She is very strong and has hit me with her thrown objects. She doesn't mean to hurt but rather than hand something to me, she throws it at me!

I have been trying to spring clean this week and I am a failure. This cleaning is for the birds—the dodos! It took me hours to get 2 rooms done. So much dust and guff accumulates under the beds on shelves and on ledges.

Nothing new with Chuck he just studies all the time. Last night I tried to wait up for him. Finally I turned out my light at 1 a.m. I don't know what time he got in bed. He sends me off to get new tax forms every few days but that is all the communication I get from him. Go to the courthouse and get me state corporation tax information etc.!

Next week I am going to New York. I will take Carolyn to Molly's and get a dress for her from you. I bought her theatre tickets with the money you gave me. I know she will be very appreciative, You are such a dear man. It will be such fun for me too.

We all love you so much. Get well quick so Cindy can come to ride with you. She talks about Boppa all the time. Even Cathy mentions Boppa and Nana in her prayers.

You have a lot of grandfathering to do. Love your 3D girl

PS When I mentioned to Cindy that she should send you a letter, she immediately cut a letter (A,B, C etc) out of a book. Do you like A better than K?

LYNDON B. JOHNSON
TO
LYNDA BIRD JOHNSON

April 28, 1972

Dear Lynda:
Tell Cindy and Cathy not to outgrow the yellow dresses before I can see them wearing them.

I feel that I have improved even more since reaching the ranch Wednesday afternoon. Although it has rained cats and dogs, that too is a cheering sight as we need it so badly.

Why don't you just hire someone to do a spring cleaning job on the house? After all, every housekeeper should have that treat once a year.

We are so proud of everything Chuck has done in law school. Please congratulate him on his election to membership on the Student Legal Forum, and President of it besides! And we congratulate you too for being an understanding wife while he studies most of the time these three years. Great benefits from this will soon follow.

I will be interested to hear about the New York trip with Carolyn. I hope you will both have great fun. I know you will make it memorable for her.

We are looking forward to summer and hope you all can spend some of it with us. Meanwhile tell Cindy to write me more letters. I don't necessarily like "A" better than "K" but I do love "LJR" and everybody under her roof.

Your father, Lbj

RONALD REAGAN
TO
PATRICIA REAGAN

Reagan wrote this letter to fifteen-year-old Patricia to try to convince her to study at the Orme School in Arizona, where she had been a student for two years. She had already tried to run away from the boarding school on at least one occasion, and later left Northwestern University before obtaining her degree. Although none of Reagan's four surviving children received a college diploma, Patti later became a successful author of both fiction and nonfiction.

April 2, 1968

Dear Patti:

I know we'll be seeing you soon, so this won't be too much of a letter, but I did want to tell you your grades came, and not only were we thrilled and very proud of you, but even more so at the things your teachers wrote about your attitude towards your studies and about your ability and participation. We're very happy.

I've enclosed this page of the paper on Bonnie and Clyde, and I'm sure your reaction is going to be that I did it as a kind of "I told you so," but it isn't that at all. Knowing your interest in writing I thought that here was a great example of how a screen writer, wanting to make a successful and entertaining picture, used some of the truth and then used dramatic license where necessary to make his story successful. You can compare that to this story, where the author's purpose was completely different in that he wanted to write a factual account.

You'll see passages in here and recognize how, in some instances, they were truthful in the picture, but in others they altered the facts for dramatic purposes. You can even see the possibilities that they wanted to go in another direction. For example, suppose they wanted to make a hero of the Texas Ranger. Then he would have been the central figure, with a story written about his almost ruined career and his effort to reestablish himself, and then, of course, Bonnie and Clyde would have appeared as the villains.

At any rate, I think you'll find this most interesting now that you've seen the picture.

Again, though, we're very proud of you. Love, Dad

PATTI REAGAN DAVIS IS SHOWN VISITING HER FATHER, RONALD REAGAN, IN THE OVAL OFFICE OF THE WHITE HOUSE ON FEBRUARY 21, 1981.

Sunday, Jan. 11.
1920

PEN-Y-GROES
BRYN MAWR

Dear Papa —

I meant to have
a conversation, or consultation rather, with you
during the Christmas
holidays, on the subject
of my private affairs —
But I had planned it
for the end of the vacation
and you went away so
often that I missed out.
You will be sorry to hear, I am
afraid, that I spent the
~~vacation~~ persuading Fred
to marry me this summer.

CHAPTER 4

MARRIAGE
AND REMARRIAGE:
"WE ARE VERY MUCH
IN LOVE."

"We are very much in love."
—Helen Taft to William Howard Taft,
January 11, 1920

"Will not my dear child rejoice in my happiness!"
—John Tyler to Mary Tyler Jones,
June 28, 1844

FEW EVENTS can exceed the emotions surrounding the marriage of a daughter or the remarriage of a father. This selection of letters reveals the joys and pains experienced by presidents and their daughters at these defining moments in their lives.

JOHN ADAMS
TO
ABIGAIL ADAMS

*A*bigail was in the midst of a romance with Royall Tyler, which her parents opposed. At one point during the conflict, Adams wrote angrily to his wife, "My Child . . . is not to be the Prize, I hope of any, even reformed Rake." Even after the couple had an understanding to be married, her father arranged for Abigail to postpone the wedding until her return from a long trip abroad. It worked: after her arrival in Europe, Abigail broke off with Tyler and married William Smith, Adams's secretary.

Paris, April 14th, 1783

My Dear Daughter:

By this time, I hope, your inclination to travel has abated, and the prospect of peace has made you more contented with your native country. You little know the difficulties of a voyage to Europe, even in time of profound peace. The elements are as unstable in peace as in war, and a sea life is never at first agreeable, nor ever without danger. In foreign countries few persons preserve their health; the difference of climate, of air, of manner of life, seldom fail to occasion revolutions in the constitution and produce disorders, very often violent, dangerous and fatal ones. Those who escape have a seasoning. Besides, the polite life in Europe is such an insipid round of head-dressing and play, as I hope will never be agreeable to you—or rather I hope you will detest it as beneath the character of a rational being, and inconsistent with the indispensable duties of life, those of a daughter, wife, or mother, and even those of a sister, friend, or neighbour.

Policy, which is but another word for imposture in these countries, encourages every species of frivolity and dissipation on purpose to divert people from reading and thinking. But in our country every encouragement ought to be given to reading and thinking, and, therefore, diversions should be very sparingly indulged.

You are now of an age, my dear, to think of your future prospects in life, and your disposition is more thoughtful and discreet than is common. I need not advise you to distinguish between virtues and amusements, between talents and fancy.

Your country is young, and advancing with more rapid strides than any people ever took before. She will have occasion for great abilities and virtues to conduct her affairs with wisdom and success. Your sex must preserve their virtue and discretion, or their brothers, husbands, and sons will soon lose theirs. The morals of our country are a sacred deposit, and let every youth, or either sex, beware that no part of the guilt of betraying it belongs to him.

Look not for fortune, honours, or amusements, these are all but trash. Look for the virtues of good citizens and good men; with these the others will do little good or no harm; without them they are nothing but vexation and a scourge.

I please myself with the fond hope of conversing with you soon at home. Your brother was at Hambourg on the 4th of April, but I hope is at the Hague by this time.

Your affectionate father, John Adams

THOMAS JEFFERSON

TO

MARTHA JEFFERSON

---

*J*efferson had just begun serving as Secretary of State in the new federal government when he wrote this letter to his eldest daughter, who had just married her cousin, Thomas Mann Randolph. Despite Jefferson's advice to place his son-in-law before even himself, Martha remained her father's "mistress of Monticello" until his death in 1826.

New York April 4. 1790

My dear daughter
I saw in Philadelphia your friends Mrs. Trist and Miss Rittenhouse.

both complained of your not writing. In Baltimore I enquired after Mrs. Buchanan and Miss Holliday. The latter is lately turned methodist, the former was married the evening I was there to a Mr. Turnbull of Petersburg in Virginia. of course you will see her there. I find it difficult to procure a tolerable house here. it seems it is a practice to let all the houses the 1st. of February, & to enter into them the 1st of May. of course I was too late to engage one, at least in the Broadway, where all my business lies. I have taken an indifferent one nearly opposite Mrs. Elsworth's which may give me time to look about me and provide a better before the arrival of my furniture. I am anxious to hear from you, of your health, your occupations, where you are &c. do not neglect your music. it will be a companion which will sweeten many hours of life to you. I assure you mine here is triste enough. having had yourself and dear Poll to live with me so long, to exercise my affections and chear me in the intervals of business, I feel heavily these separations from you. it is a circumstance of consolation to know that you are happier; and to see a prospect of it's continuance in the prudence and even temper both of Mr. Randolph & yourself. your new condition will call for abundance of little sacrifices but they will be greatly overpaid by the measure of affection they will secure to you. the happiness of your life depends now on the continuing to please a single person. to this all other objects must be secondary; even your love to me, were it possible that that could ever be an obstacle. but this it can never be. neither of you can ever have a more faithful friend than my self, not one on whom you can count for more sacrifices. my own is become a secondary object to the happiness of you both. cherish then for me, my dear child, the affection of your husband, and continue to love me as you have done, and to render my life a blessing by the prospect it may hold up to me of seeing you happy. Kiss Maria for me if she is with you, and present me cordially to Mr. Randolph: assuring yourself of the constant and unchangeable love of your's affectionately, Th. Jefferson

*W*riting in response to her father, Martha assured Jefferson that her duties to her husband would be secondary to nothing "except my love for you."

Richmond April 25 1790

I received yours My Dearest Father with more pleasure than is possible for me to express and am happy to hear that you are at last settled at New York as I am in hopes we shall now hear from you often. We are just returned from a visit up the country to Aunt Carr's and Mrs. Flemming's. It has not been possible as yet to carry dear Pol to Eppington for want of horses as Mr. Randolph was unwilling to borrow his father's for so long a time but I expect certainly to be there in ten days at latest. I intend writing to Mr. Trist and Holly by the next post and promise you not to leave Richmond without writing also to my friends in Europe. I hope you have not give over comming to Virginia this fall as I assure you My dear papa my happiness can never be compleat without your company. Mr. Randolph omits nothing that can in the least contribute to it. I have made it my study to please him in every thing and do consider all other objects as secondary to that except my love for you. I do not know where we are to spend the summer. Mr. Randolph has some thoughts of settling at Varina for a little while till he can buy a part of Edgehill. I am much averse to it my self but shall certainly comply if he thinks it necessary. My health is perfectly good as also dear Polly's. I have received a letter from Mrs. Curson who informs me that the Duke of Dorset and Lady Caroline are both going to be married, the former to a Miss Cope. Adieu My Dear Pappa. I am with the tenderest affection yours, M. Randolph

ELIZABETH PARK CUSTIS
TO
GEORGE WASHINGTON

*W*ashington wrote two surprisingly frank letters to his eighteen-year-old grand-daughter, who had initiated this exchange by asking for a "likeness" of her grandfather. Elizabeth and Thomas Law were married "in quite a private wedding," according to her sister Eleanor. Despite Washington's best advice, Elizabeth's marriage to Thomas Law ended in separation in 1804 and divorce.

Hope Park September 7th, 1794

Dear & Honrd Sir.

My Sister's success in her application to you for your Picture gives me courage to make the same request, and as I have no other wish nearer my heart than that of possessing your likeness; I hope you will believe me sincere when I assure you, it is my first wish to have it in my power to contemplate, at all times, the features of one, who I so highly respect as the Father of his Country and look up to with grateful affection as parent to myself and family.

We are, Dear Sir, at present, in distress, which must be my apology for this short letter. Mamma and Patty join me in affection to you with ardent wishes for your health and happiness, I am Honrd Sir, your grateful Grand Daughter Eliza P. Custis

GEORGE WASHINGTON
TO
ELIZABETH PARKE CUSTIS

German Town, September 14, 1794

My dear Betcy:

Shall I, in answer to your letter of the 7th instant say, when you are as near the Pinnacle of happiness as your sister Patcy conceives herself to be; or when your candour shines more conspicuously than it does in that letter, that I will then, comply with the request you have made, for my Picture?

No: I will grant it without either: for if the latter was to be a preliminary, it would be sometime I apprehend before that Picture would be found pendant at your breast; it not being within the bounds of probability that the contemplation of an inanimate thing, whatever might be the reflections arising from the possession of it, can be the only wish of your heart.

Respect may place it among the desirable objects of it, but there are emotions of a softer kind, to wch. The heart of a girl turned of eighteen, is susceptible, that must have generated much warmer ideas, although the fruition of them may, apparently, be more distant than those of your Sister's.

Having (by way of a hint) delivered a sentiment to Patsy which may be useful to her (if it be remembered after the change that is contemplated, is consummated) I will suggest another more applicable to yourself.

Do not then in your contemplation of the marriage state, look for perfect felicity before you consent to wed. Nor conceive, from the fine tales the Poets and lovers of old have told us, of the transports of mutual love, that heaven has taken its abode on earth: Nor do not deceive yourself in supposing that the only mean by which these are to be obtained, is to drink deep of the cup. And revel in an ocean of love. Love is a mighty pretty thing; but like all other delicious things, it is cloying; and when the first transports of the passion begins to subside, which it assuredly will do, and yield, oftentimes too late, to more sober reflections, it serves to evince, that love is too dainty a food to live upon alone, and ought not be considered farther than as a necessary ingredient for that matrimonial happiness, which results from a combination of causes; none of which are of greater importance, than that the object on whom it is placed, should possess good sense, good dispositions, and the means of supporting you in the way you have been brought up. Such qualifications cannot fail to attract (after marriage) your esteem and regard, into wch. Or into disgust, sooner or later, love naturally resolves itself; and who, at the same time, has a claim to the respect, and esteem of the circle he moves in. Without these, whatever may be your first impressions of the man, they will end in disappointment; for be assured, and experience will convince you, that there is not truth more certain, than that all our enjoyments fall short of our expectations; and to none does it apply with more force, than to the gratification of the passions. You may believe me to be always, and sincerely Your Affectionate Go. Washington

ELIZABETH PARKE CUSTIS, GRANDDAUGHTER OF
PRESIDENT GEORGE WASHINGTON, MARRIED THOMAS LAW IN 1796
AND DIVORCED HIM A DECADE LATER.

Philadelphia 10th Feby 1796

My dear Betsey

I have obeyed your injunction in not acknowledging the receipt of your letter of the first instant until I should hear from Mr. Law. This happened yesterday—I therefore proceed to assure you—if Mr. Law is the man of your choice, of wch there can be no doubt, as he has merits to engage your affections, and you have declared that he has not only done so, but that you find, after a careful examination of your heart, you cannot be happy without him—that your alliance with him meets my approbation. Yes, Betsey, and this approbation is accompanied with my fervent wishes that you may be as happy in this important event as your most sanguine imagination has ever presented to your view. Along with these wishes, I bestow on you my choicest blessings.

Nothing contained in your letter—in Mr. Laws—or in any other from our friends intimate when you are to taste the sweets of Matrimony—I therefore call upon you, who have more honesty than disguise, to give me the details. Nay more, that you will relate all your feelings to me on this occasion: or as a Quaker would say "all the workings of the spirit within."

This, I have a right to expect in return for my blessing, so promptly bestowed, after you had concealed the matter from me so long. Being entitled therefore to this confidence, and to a compliance with my requests, I shall look forward to the fulfillment of it.

If after marriage Mr. Laws business should call him to this City, the same room which Mr. Peter & your sister occupied will accomodate you two; and it will be equally at your service.

You know how much I love you—how much I have been gratified by your attentions to those things which you had reason to believe were grateful to my feelings. And having no doubt of your continuing the same conduct, as the effect will be pleasing to me, and unattended with any disadvantage to yourself—I shall remain with the sincerest friendship, & the most affectionate regard always yours. Go. Washington

---

JOHN TYLER
TO
MARY TYLER

---

*A*fter the death of his wife, Letitia, in 1842, Tyler married Julia Gardiner, who was younger than three of his children, including his eldest daughter, Mary.

Despite Tyler's assurance that "this occurance will make no change in aught that relates to you," Mary refused to accept Julia into the family and became somewhat estranged from her father.

Washington June 28. 1844

My Dear Daughter.
Well, what has been talked of for so long a time is consummated and Julia Gardiner, the most lovely of her race, is my own wedded wife. If I can lay my hand on a paper containing a proper account of the ceremonial I will send it. Will not my dear child rejoice in my happiness! She is all that I could wish her to be. the most beautiful woman of the age and at the same time the most accomplished. This occurrence will make no change in aught that relates to you. nor will new associations produce the slightest abatement from my affection for you.

What if we were disposed to visit the farm for a day or two. Could you give us suitable accommodations. I mean a good room to sleep in etc. etc. We shall be at Old Point in a day or two. Can you be there with us, or what arrangements will you make for the summer. I do not think that you should stay in lower Virginia this fall. Write me freely. And will you not also write a suitable letter to Julia. Telling her all about the house and its features and expressive of your pleasure to see her.

> I write hastily. You will write me in full. Yr. Father
>
> J. Tyler

THEODORE ROOSEVELT
TO
ETHEL CAROW ROOSEVELT

---

*R*oosevelt wrote these two ebullient letters to Ethel just days after her April 4, 1913, marriage to Richard Derby. Both letters show a joyous relationship between father and daughter, not readily evident in the correspondence of many other presidents and their offspring. Even Roosevelt jokingly wondered whether her husband might find them a bit wacky.

Sagamore Hill. April 7th 1913

Darling Ethelybyekins,
(I must give you the full title just once) we didn't know whether to laugh or to cry, to be more glad or more sorry, when blessed little Mrs. Dick Derby, and dear Dick, closed the chapter in their and our lives and opened the new one thereby. Well, you were the dearest engaged couple that ever was; and I believe you'll be, with the exception of mother and myself, the happiest married couple. Old Colonel Hallowell, when the Porc brethren met up in the gun room, drank to "the girls of '61["]; and in the same way, and just as mother symbolizes everything to me, so you'll always symbolize everything to Dick.

Well, it was the very nicest, the best arranged and most attractive and most enjoyable wedding I have ever seen; dozens of people have said so, and have written so to mother. We spent a feverish twenty four hours getting the house back into something like normal shape, and now life is back in the usual groove. Archie and I rode, and sawed logs industriously; he started for Andover last night. Yesterday, Sunday, afternoon, mother and I motored in town, very swell with sister, and went to the Henry House Settlement for supper and the play, and then motored out again. stopping to leave the Jake Reis', who were fellow guests at the Penn station. This afternoon mother goes in town to go to the opera this evening; Quentin goes with her, as he leaves for school this evening. I am working with heated intelligence at my "biography"—I fairly loathe it—, now. George, Phil, Mike Landon and Oliver were here at lunch yesterday.

Your loving father

THEODORE ROOSEVELT
TO
ETHEL CAROW ROOSEVELT

Sagamore Hill May 1st 1913

Darling Ethely-bye,
Just after posting my letter, two letters from you came, one to me. we just love them, blessing. Evidently Dick is ever more than all we were sure he was! I really believe you are going to be just as happy as darling mother and I have been.

Well, it's a wonderful thing to be able to have the "first fine careless rapture," and also the companionship of fun and humor, and the liking for the same things.

I have capitulated and enclose the picture letter altho I suppose it will make good loyal Dick wonder, down in the bottom of his heart whether or not he has married an out-patient of bedlam's daughter.

I am glad the ditty box has been started with two treasures.

I understand exactly what you mean about Dick's sometimes reminding you of Kermit. Poor Kerm! He has some hard sledding to do. Mother and I are going down to see him next winter.

I hate to write him about Heller's and my book, for I know how homesick it will make him for Africa. I was surprised, and immensely interested, by your description of how eastern Algiers was.

Mother and I have dear evenings together but I wish I played cards and was more of a companion to her. Love to Dick, Your loving father

---

WOODROW WILSON
TO
JESSIE WOODROW WILSON

$\mathcal{J}$essie was the first of Wilson's two daughters to marry in the White House. She and her husband, Frank Sayre, were on their honeymoon in Europe when her father wrote this letter.

The White House 8 December, 1913

My darling Girlie

I must indulge myself in a short message of love from my own pen (this little machine seems to have taken the place since my hand grew unmanageable!). I cannot put into words what my heart contains about you and dear Frank; but somehow it is a comfort to at least speak to you across the sea. Our thoughts follow you with a yearning which goes to the very roots of our hearts. But they are happy thoughts, because you are happy. We know only what the cable dispatches in the papers have told us about your safe arrival, but they tell us that you are well and show us that it is evident to everybody that you are radiating happiness just as you did before you left, bless your heart! We are content. I know how fine it will be with the Pages. They are of your own taste and will know instinctively what you wish and most enjoy. The wedding has left the most interesting impressions here and the happiest memories on the part of everybody who saw it or heard about [it] from those who did. It is so delightful that the whole country should get just the right impression of it and of you. It helps establish a standard in girls and their sweethearts! Your dear mother is wonderful. She has spoken no word since you left but of happiness and content. I can see in the depths of yearning that she cannot always hide in her eyes what lack her mother's heart feels, but she loves you more than she loves herself and wishes for nothing but your happiness. It is lovely to see her! For the rest of us there is of course the constant pain of the empty place; but we love you, too, with all that is best in us, and want everything to be as it is. For with one accord, and with a common enthusiasm we love Frank, too, and delight to think of him as our son and brother and everything that is dear and sacred.

God bless you both. This is just a message of love which I could not deny myself. We are all well. No one else knows I am writing. Your devoted Father

---

MARGARET WOODROW WILSON
TO
WOODROW WILSON

In these three letters among sisters Margaret and Jesse and their father, the girls seem to have gone overboard in welcoming their stepmother, Edith Bolling Galt. Wilson and Ms. Galt, a widow, were married December 18, 1915, at the bride's house on 20th Street, and the family unity did not skip a beat.

Cornish, New Hampshire [October 5, 1915]

My darling precious Father
I wish that I were going to be with you tomorrow. I know however that you understand perfectly why I did not go down with the Smiths, and that you know that only "business" has kept be [me] away from you so long. I feel that I ought to do all in my power to make it possible for me to give my best in these three recitals.

I am so glad, oh so glad that you are going to announce the glad secret tomorrow for then you will be free to see much more of our sweet Edith. Give her my warmest love and tell her that I can hardly wait to see her again.

Dear Father I am so happy for you and have been ever since I knew what was going to happen, and I am sure you know that I am happy for myself too. It must be evident to you how much I love to be with Edith. Above all however, because I love you so much, I am glad that you are going to have her love and companionship constantly.

I long to see you dearest Father. What terrible times you have been going through! Your patience and poise are mavellous to me—but then every thing about you is wonderful.

The Davids came back today and my work begins again, but after these days alone I shall go at it with more hope and joy than just before they left. I have been in the depths of discouragement, but now I feel brimful of courage and am looking forward to my concerts not only with hope, but with joyful eagerness.

I love you darling Father with all my heart and mind and soul.

Your devoted, Margaret

JESSIE WOODROW WILSON
TO
WOODROW WILSON

Williamstown Massachusetts Oct. 17, 1915

Darling, darling Father
We are so glad that everything has gone off so well, and we are only sorry that we are not nearer to share your joy by seeing it near at hand. The pictures of you, poor as they are, look so happy, it rejoices us.

We have just written to Edith, suggesting that if international complications permit, you run off here and allow us to see you and have the fun of chaperoning you for a little space. You know how quiet you can be here. The country is at its loveliest, a vision of rose and gold, the weather is Indian summer, and the rides in all directions are superb. The Smiths can tell you about the trail, over the alps to Albany is another glorious ride, and you know something about the Pittsfield valley.

Couldn't you come up after voting, right away quick before Germany hears about it and prevents it? We want you both so much and it seems as if we could hardly wait to see you. There is plenty of room for both, and you wouldn't be bothered here, I'm sure.

Francis has a really truly tooth to show you, which came through today on his ninth month birthday, without any attendant ills, not even crossness!

So, you see, we all three want you.

Ever adoringly, Jessie.

MRS. ELLEN AXSON WILSON AND HER DAUGHTERS, JESSIE, MARGARET, AND ELEANOR, ON THE SOUTH PORTICO OF THE WHITE HOUSE IN 1913.

The White House. 25 October, 1915

My darling Jessie,

It was a delight to get your letter. You are constantly in our thoughts, and I would give anything if it were possible to act on your delightful suggestion that Edith and I come up to you before this lovely autumn has passed. Alas! my dear little girl, that is impossible. I not only must stay close at my tasks, but I must, just now particularly, make it evident to the country, that I am doing so, and not galavanting around and seeking my own pleasure. If I followed my heart, Williamstown is the first place I would make for.

I hope that Frank's visit to Montana had a successful outcome. Did it? And is he as well as little Frank seems to be? Now that Francis has begun to get his teeth I hope that he will hurry up and push the job through, bless his heart. How I should like to see him.

While Nell and Mac are in the West Little Ellen is staying with us. She is wonderfully well, and now weighs about thirteen pounds, for she is gaining steadily. She is as good as gold, a singularly serene person, and has now, I am glad to say, an excellent permanent nurse.

Margaret really had a wonderful success in her recitals and has come back quite radiant. Mrs. David has turned out a much better, because much more sympathetic accompanyist than Miss David and all is serene and full of encouragement for the dear little girl.

Edith is greatly distressed by the foolish (and lying) publicity of which she is being made the object, poor girl, but is fine about it, as about everything else. She is very well indeed, and seems (to me, at least) to grow more radiant and lovely every day. I am sure she would send deepest love if she knew that I was writing today.

Margaret and Helen are well, and unite with me in messages of dearest love. I love you very tenderly and very deeply, my darling little girl, and your happiness makes me very happy. I love Frank as if he were my own son, and Francis as if he belonged to me.

Your devoted Father, Woodrow W.

H E L E N   T A F T

T O

W I L L I A M   H O W A R D   T A F T

---

*H*elen and her father reveal the depth and closeness of their relationship in these two letters written when Helen announced her pending engagement to Frederick J. Manning.

Pen-Y-Groes Bryn Mawr Sunday,
Jan. 11 [1920]

Dear Papa.

I meant to have a conversation, or consultation rather with you during the Christmas holidays, on the subject of my private affairs. But I had planned it for the end of the vacation and you went away so often that I missed out. You will be sorry to hear, I am afraid that I spent the vacation persuading Fred to marry me this summer.

He very conscientiously pointed out to me all the objections but had to concede in the end that it would be very difficult to do any thing else and that we would not really be much better off financially another year. So he gave in and agreed that if he were reappointed and if we could find any place to live within our means that it could be done.

I know that the first objection you raise is about my thesis. I did not answer you on that point this Summer I think. But I have thought the matter over very thoroughly and I cannot see that there is very much to be gained in trying to take my PhD. before I marryd. You see I have never intended to stop working when I

GROVER CLEVELAND AND HIS WIFE, FRANCES FOLSOM CLEVELAND, WHO WERE MARRIED ON JUNE 2, 1886, IN THE ONLY PRESIDENTIAL MARRIAGE AT THE WHITE HOUSE, ARE PICTURED WITH THEIR ELDEST DAUGHTER, RUTH. BABY RUTH, AS SHE WAS CALLED IN THE PRESS, DIED AT AGE TWELVE OF DIPHTHERIA IN 1904.

marry. The only question is what kind of work I can find in New Haven or wherever else we are living. It would always be comparatively easy to work on my thesis and that would be what I should do next year unless I hear of some opening of the kind I want. When I chose my thesis originally Professor Abbott said that it could be written without going abroad and while I do not think that I could treat the whole subject as I should like to without going to England I could probably write a pretty good thesis on Canada and wait to publish the whole study until we can go to England. Fred wants to go there for his thesis when we can manage it.

The more important question is what I can do permanently for a career. On the whole I think that writing or editorial work would be the easiest to fit in with having a family and that I should like it quite as well if not better than teaching. The only difficulty is that literature is a hard profession in which to get a start and that was why I said that if there was an opening next year I might take it. Fred is willing to go west if I want to in order that we may both teach but the plan presents a good many difficulties which I needn't go into. But at all events, as to the thesis I don't see why I shouldn't be able to write it after I am married, and if you think that a wedding ring is going to make all work impossible then I don't care much about having a PhD just for the purposes of signing my name. If Fred should die or desert me I really could very easily find something remunerative to do with or without a degree.

The most crucial question is of course the financial one. If Fred is reappointed he will have $1750 next year. (I shouldn't suppose there was any doubt of his reappointment but he makes the reservation because of the projected changes in the Staff history courses) I have about $600 a year (The exact sum depends on Mr. Norton's investments) I reckon that we can live on $2500. We would take the cheapest apartment available and not have a servant. We could cook breakfast and dinner without too much exertion, I think, and go out for lunch. I would want to have a cleaning woman once a week and a laundress. I am quite sure that people still do live like that on $2500 though I haven't gone over budgets yet. But from Ned's mother and Margaret French (who has done her own work ever since she was married I can get a pretty good idea) If I did not have to cook in the middle of the day I reckon that I would be able to do six or seven hours of work pretty easily, on my history. I thought that as you were planning to support me for the next year or two you would not object to giving me $1000 a year for several years. In which case we ought to be able to save up and have a baby if we're lucky.

The most serious financial difficulties are concerned with actually getting married. Fred has had to buy clothes and furniture this year and will have saved very little if any thing by summer. I hope to have at least $500. I think that we can manage it some how but am not counting on an expensive honeymoon. The worst objections are really to one getting married at all for the next nine or ten years. Of course it would be better for F to be unencumbered and to go on with his thesis after next year. Though I doubt wether he could afford to go abroad then. But since we were imprudent enough to fall in love I don't see that there is much for us to do but to get married. I will be 29 next summer and Fred will be

26! I'm not anxious to spend a few years just marking time, as it would be for both of us and for me especially. Moreover, I don't know whether you have observed it or not but we are very much in love and the prospect of a year on different sides of the Atlantic or in a state of being engaged in New Haven is far from pleasing. I know that we have some rather hard years before us but it seems worth it to me and it is all that Fred asks for as long as I am happy.

I am going West next Friday & shall be most frightfully busy for some time to come, which is my reason for writing this now. You don't need to answer it until you get ready. I merely wanted you to know what imprudent schemes have been fostering in my head. We do have to begin to make our plans more or less for next year though of course we can always change them.

I am going to tell Aunt Annie and Uncle Charley when I am in Cincinnati As I think they might otherwise be hurt. I will also write Uncle Horace. So far we have apparently been extraordinarily successful in keeping our affair a secret and I hope that it can be prevented from reaching Bryn Mawr before June.

With loads of love, yours Helen

WILLIAM HOWARD TAFT

TO

HELEN TAFT

New Haven, Connecticut, January 13, 1920

My dear Helen:

I have your letter of January 11th. As you know, I think it would be very much wiser for you to wait another year. As one looks back from my stand-point one year is a small time, and I fear you may regret that you did not improve the opportunity which it gives you to perfect your qualifications for the teaching profession. If you are to be married in July next, I doubt if you [will] ever write your thesis or secure your degree.

But you must carve out your own future, and be responsible for the consequences when they disclose themselves. I yield to your desire and of course will do everything to facilitate your wishes. I have been very proud of the success you have thus far attained and perhaps my feeling in the matter has been colored by my ambition for a career for you to auspiciously begun. Your marriage will probably end that career, if your married life is as happy as I hope it may be. You have a right to welcome married life. It is probably wiser for you to insist on it. Certainly you are and ought to be the arbiter of your own future in this regard. I hope you will find Fred all that you think he is and that he is the one to make you happy, and that you are not stimulated in your enthusiasm for this marriage by the thought that you are approaching thirty and yearn for the happiness of family life. You are a woman of poise and level headed and I can not think this.

The prospect for a comfortable life through Fred's earning or yours is not immediate certainly, and you are facing res auguste for a long time. I am far from saying or thinking that an academic life is not a happy and useful one or that the prospect of having to live with economy should turn you from your purpose. But as I love you, my dear girl, I do not propose to stand aloof and let you encounter hardships just as a lesson of good discipline. On the day of your wedding you can count on receiving from me $1000 for your honeymoon in addition to such presents as your mother shall select, and there after beginning with September 1st I hope to be able to put to your credit on the first day of every month $200 and to continue this indefinitely. This with what you have and what Fred will earn ought to give you an income of something like $4500 a year upon which I would think you could afford a cook and save Fred's digestion, that is, if you can find a cook.

If your mother survives me, I have given every thing I have to her. In that case, I know she will deal generously with you. If I survive her, then by my will half of what I have goes to you, and one fourth to Bob and Charlie each. This ought to bring you at least $5000 a year, unless Edith Morgan's Bolshiviki views obtain and everything is turned "topsy turvy."

I think it will be well to have the wedding at Murray Bay in the latter part of July. My plans, if carried out, will prevent my reaching Murray Bay before the 7th of July. Eleanor does not expect to visit us this summer for reasons you understand. Charles, however, would doubtless come for the wedding, and I hope Bob and Martha and the boys will be there. With the new addition, we shall have a good deal of room. I want to make the wedding all that you would wish it to be.

The question where you shall live in New Haven will not be an easy one to settle. New Haven has not many houses or apartments of reasonable size at reasonable rates. You will have to be looking out for something suitable and I have mentioned the amount I hope to help you with in order that you may plan on that basis. And now, my dear Helen, I hope you will not think this letter cold or unsympathetic. I don't mean it to be. You and I are a good deal alike, more so I think than the boys and I, and when we differ, we differ. When your judgment is vindicated as I warmly hope it may be, I shall be oh only too glad to admit my erroneous judgment. Meantime, my dear, believe me always and ever, Your proud and loving father, Wm. H. Taft

---

RICHARD M. NIXON
TO
JULIE NIXON

---

*N*ixon wrote this encouraging letter to his daughter Julie, who was about to announce her engagement to David Eisenhower, grandson of General and former President Dwight D. Eisenhower. Julie and David were married in New York on December 22, 1968, days before Nixon's presidential inauguration. He wrote a similar letter to his daughter Tricia on the morning of her wedding in 1971.

RICHARD NIXON AND DAUGHTERS, JULIE NIXON EISENHOWER
AND TRICIA NIXON, STAND ON THE EDGE OF THE ROSE GARDEN AT
THE BEGINNING OF THE WHITE HOUSE WEDDING OF
TRICIA AND EDWARD COX ON JUNE 12, 1971.

November 22, 1967

Dear Julie-

I suppose no father believes any boy is good enough for his daughter.

But I believe both David and you are lucky to have found each other.

Fina often says—"Miss Julie always brings life into the home"

In the many years ahead you will have ups and downs but I know you will always "bring life into your home" wherever it is.

Love Daddy

RICHARD M. NIXON
TO
PATRICIA NIXON

The White House Washington June 12, 1971 12:10 a.m.

Dear Tricia—

Well today is the day you begin a long and exciting journey.

I want you to Know how proud I have been of you through the years—some of them—pretty difficult for you I'm sure.

The years ahead will be happy ones because you will make them so. Your strength of Character will see you through whatever comes.

You have made the right choice and I am sure Eddie & you will look back on this time and be able to say—

"The day indeed was splendid." Love Daddy

TRICIA NIXON COX DANCES WITH HER FATHER ON HER WEDDING DAY, JUNE 12, 1971, IN THE EAST ROOM OF THE WHITE HOUSE.

Washington Nov. 27. 03.

It's rare, my ever dear Maria, during a session of Congress, that I can get time to write any thing but letters of business: and this, which is a day of rest to others, is not at all so to me. we are all well here, and hope the post of this evening will bring us information of the health of all at Edgehill, and particularly that Martha and the new bantling are both well, and that her example gives you good spirits. when Congress will rise no mortal can tell: not from the quantity, but the dilatoriness of business. mr Lilly having finished the mill, is now I suppose engaged in the road which we have been so long wanting, & that done, the next job will be the levelling of Pantops. I anxiously long to see under way the works necessary to fix you there, that we may one day be all together. mr Stewart is now here on his way back to his family, whom he will probably join on Thursday or Friday. will you tell your sister that the pair of stockings she sent me by mr Randolph are quite large enough and also have fur enough in them. I inclose some papers for Anne; and must continue in debt to Jefferson a letter for a while longer. take care of yourself my dearest Maria, have good spirits and know that courage is as essential to triumph in your case as in that of the Soldier. keep us all therefore in heart by being so yourself: give my tender affections to your sister, and recieve them for yourself also, with assurance that I live in your love only & that of your sister. Adieu my dear daughter.

Th: Jefferson

23577   Mrs Eppes.

THOMAS JEFFERSON TO MARY JEFFERSON

CHAPTER 5

CHILDBIRTH:
"COURAGE IS AS ESSENTIAL TO TRIUMPH..."

"Courage is as essential to triumph
in your case as in that of the Souldier"
—Thomas Jefferson to Mary (Maria) Jefferson,
November 27, 1803

"You have gone through
this greatest strain in a woman's life"
—William Howard Taft to Ellen Taft,
October 13, 1921

CHILDBIRTH, like marriage and education, is a typical subject of the correspondence between fathers and daughters. Except in the case of Thomas Jefferson, whose wife and later whose daughter Mary died of an illness contracted during childbirth, such presidential letters usually reflect the joyful emotions of the experience.

THOMAS JEFFERSON
TO
MARY (MARIA) JEFFERSON

*J*efferson and his youngest surviving daughter exchanged these emotional letters as the time for the birth of her second child neared and arrived. Following the safe delivery of Maria Jefferson Eppes, on February 15, 1804, Mary succumbed to a raging infection, just as her mother Martha had after her own birth more than twenty years earlier. Jefferson arrived at Monticello in early April just days before the death of his daughter, and recorded in his family register: "Mary Jefferson, born Aug. 1, 1778, 1h. 30 m. A.M. Died April 17, 1804, between 8 and 9 A.M."

Washington Nov. 27. 03.

It is rare, my ever dear Maria, during a session of Congress, that I can get time to write any thing but letters of business: and this, tho' a day of rest to others, is not at all so to me. we are all well here, and hope the post of this evening will bring us information of the health of all at Edgehill and particularly that Martha and the new bantling are both well: and that her example gives you good spirits. when Congress will rise no mortal can tell: not from the quantity but dilatoriness of business. Mr. Lillie having finished the mill, is now I suppose engaged in the road which we have been so long wanting, and that done, the next job will be the levelling of Pantops. I anxiously long to see under way the works necessary to fix you there, that we may one day be all together. Mr. Stewart is now here on his way back to his family, whom he will probably join Thursday or Friday. will you tell your sister that the pair of stockings she sent me by Mr. Randolph are quite large enough and also have fur enough in them. I inclose some paper for Anne; and must continue in debt to Jefferson a letter for a while longer. take care of yourself my dearest Maria, have good spirits and know that courage is as essential to triumph in your case as in that of the Souldier. keep us all therefore in heart by being so yourself:

give my tender affections to your sister, and receive them for your-self also, with assurances that I live in your love only and that of your Sister. Adieu my dear daughter. Th. Jefferson

---

THOMAS JEFFERSON
TO
MARY (MARIA) JEFFERSON

Washington Dec. 26. 03.

I now return you, my dearest Maria, the paper which you lent me for Mr. Page, and which he has returned some days since. I have prevailed on Doctr. Priestly to undertake the work of which this is only the syllabus or plan. he says he can accomplish it in the course of a year. But in truth his health is so much impaired, and his body become so feeble, that there is reason to fear he will not live out even the short term he has asked for it. you may inform Mr. Eppes and Mr. Randolph that no mail arrived the last night from Natchez. I presume the great rains which have fallen have rendered some of the watercourses impassable. on New year's day however we shall hear of the delivery of New Orleans to us. Till then the legislature seem disposed to do noth-ing but meet and adjourn. Mrs. Livingston, formerly the younger Miss Allen, made kind inquiries after you the other day. she said she was at school with you at Mrs. Pine's. Not knowing the time destined for your expected indisposition, I am anxious on your account. You are prepared to meet it with courage I hope. Some female friend of your Mama's (I forget whom) used to say it was no more than a knock of the elbow. The material thing is to have scientific aid in readiness, that if any thing uncommon takes place, it may be redressed on the spot, and not be made serious by delay. it is a case which least of all will wait for Doctors to be sent for. therefore, with this single precaution, nothing is ever to be feared. I was in hopes to have heard from Edgehill last night, but I suppose your post has failed. I shall expect to see the gentlemen here next Sunday night, to take part in the Gala on Monday. give my tenderest love to your sister of whom I have not heard for a fortnight; and my affectionate salutations to the Gentlemen and young ones. continue to love me yourself and be assured of my warmest affections.

MARY (MARIA) JEFFERSON
TO
THOMAS JEFFERSON

Edgehill February 10th [1804]

Your letters My dear Papa have been long unanswered but while low in spirits and health I could not prevail on myself to do it, the hope however of soon seeing you and Mr. Eppes for the time is now approaching makes me feel all of happiness that anticipation can give in my present situation. It is indeed only by looking forward to that much wish'd for moment that I acquire spirits to support me in the tedious interval, but to be with you both again would compensate for any suffering.

In the mean time I have a favor to beg of you that I hope will not be refused. It is one which my sister as well as myself is deeply interested in. We had both thought you had promised us your picture if ever St. Memin went to Washington. If you did but know what a source of pleasure it would be to us while so much separated from you to have so excellent a likeness of you you would not I think refuse us. It is what we have allways most wanted all our lives and the certainty with which he takes his likenesses makes this one request I think not unreasonable. He will be in Washington the middle of this month and I can not help hoping you will grant us this one favor. I am very much afraid you will be disappointed in getting your faeton. Davy Bowles went to Richmond intending to return here before he went on. but it is so long since he left us that as his wife is now staying in Richmond it is most probable he has hired himself there. Your acacias are very beautiful My dear Papa, there are eight of them very flourishing that have changed their foliage entirely. They have remain'd in my room to the warmth of which I believe they are indebted for their present flourishing state as they appear to be more delicate the smaller they are. I wish you could bring us a small piece of your Geranium in the spring if it is large enough to admit of it. Perhaps Mr. Eppes could more conveniently take charge of it than yourself. Adieu dearest Papa. We are all well here and all most anxious for the happy moment that will reunite us again after this long separation. Believe me with the tenderest love yours ever, M Eppes

---

THOMAS JEFFERSON
TO
MARY (MARIA) JEFFERSON

Washington Feb. 26. 04

A thousand joys to you, My dear Maria, on the happy accession to your family. A letter from our dear Martha by last post gave me the happy news that your crisis was happily over and all well. I had supposed that if you were a little later than your calculation, and the rising of Congress as early as we expected, that we might have been with you at the moment when it would have been so encouraging to have had your friends around you. I rejoice indeed that all is so well. Congress talk of rising the 12th of March but they will probably be some days later. You will doubtless see Mr. Eppes and Mr. Randolph immediately on the rising of Congress. I shall hardly be able to get away till some days after them. By that time I hope you will be able to go with us to Monticello and that we shall all be there together for a month and the interval between that and the autumnal visit will not be so long. Will you desire your sister to send for Mr. Lilly and to advise him what orders to give Goliah for providing those vegetables which may come into use for the months of April, August and September. Deliver her also my affectionate love. I will write to her the next week. Kiss all the little ones, and be assured yourself of my tender and unchangeable affection

Th. Jefferson

THOMAS JEFFERSON
TO
MARY (MARIA) JEFFERSON

Washington, Mar. 3d. 1804.

The account of your illness, my dearest Maria, was known to me only this morning. Nothing but the impossibility of Congress proceeding a single step in my absence presents an insuperable bar. Mr. Eppes goes off, and I hope will find you in a convalescent state. Next to the desire that it may be so, is that of being speedily informed, and of being relieved from the terrible anxiety in which I shall be till I hear from you. God bless you, my ever dear daughter, and presserve you safe to the blessing of us all. Th. Jefferson

---

JAMES MONROE
TO
ELIZA MONROE

---

*T*he Monroes, including daughter Maria, who had married Samuel L. Gouverneur in 1820, were taking the waters at Shannondale Spring on the east bank of the Shenandoah River in present day Jefferson County, West Virginia, when Maria's newborn daughter became very ill. Monroe's letter reflects his concern for his granddaughter, as well as for his chronically ill wife, Elizabeth, in this letter to his elder daughter, Eliza. Maria's unnamed infant daughter died just two weeks later on September 4, 1821.

Shennondale Augt. 19 .21

My Dear Daughter
I received today your letter respecting Maria's child, yr. Advice respecting which I communicated to your [mother], & to the parents, who were gratified by your attention to their infant, at a moment of such danger to it, and distress to them. The disease is not as you suppose a complaint of the bowels, nor is she yet teething, tho' under that impression her gums have been lanced two or three times. She had a fever about 3 weeks since, of which on a slight dose of calomel, she in a great measure recovered. It

MARIA, DAUGHTER OF JAMES MONROE, WAS THE FIRST PRESIDENT'S DAUGHTER MARRIED IN THE WHITE HOUSE. PORTRAIT CIRCA 1820.

is now eight days since it return'd on her, & Dr. Craemer, who attends her, who is an able man, says it has assumed the intermittent form. She is very low, her stomach is weak, nothing remaining on it; but her bowels are in a good state. Her fever today is moderate, so that we have much hope of her recovery. The accomodation here, being limited your mother with Maria, her child & nurse will move to Charlestown, 4 miles off, where the physician lives & they will be better accomodated. They go in the morning. Your [mother] is much indisposed, her head being much affected, & her eyes inflame. She will be bled tomorrow. I hope that She will be restored at Charlestown. I am in good health, & Col. Saml has derivd considerable advantage from the water. We hope that you, Mr. Hay & Hortensia, are in good health. Our affectionate regards to you all.

Your affectionate father, James Monroe

JESSIE WOODROW WILSON
TO
WOODROW WILSON

---

*J*essie and her father excitedly discussed the progress of Jessie's son, Francis Woodrow Wilson Sayre, who had been born at the White House on January 17, 1915. She and young Francis had just returned to Williamstown, Massachusetts, where Francis B. Sayre, husband and father, taught at Williams College. Jessie's mother, Ellen Axson Wilson, had been dead less than six months when Francis was born.

Williamstown Massachusetts
March 1st[1915]

My dearest, precious, Father
Here we are safe and sound in Williamstown! How it snowed and how hard the wind blew when we arrived; but that blessed baby

ESTHER CLEVELAND, DAUGHTER OF GROVER AND FRANCES
FOLSOM CLEVELAND, WAS THE ONLY CHILD OF A PRESIDENT TO BE
BORN IN THE WHITE HOUSE ITSELF. ESTHER, WHO WAS TWENTY-ONE
YEARS OLD WHEN THIS PHOTOGRAPH WAS TAKEN IN 1915, SERVED
AS A VOLUNTEER IN ENGLAND DURING WORLD WAR I.

slept without stirring and kept as warm as toast! Our nurse seems
to be a treasure, capable and gentle and a comfort generally, and
our routine is already fairly well established. We are having the
kind of weather I love best. I am beginning to take walks again
and to recover from my first tiredness. It was hard to tell Miss

Harkins 'good bye' this morning. I can't tell you how much it has meant to us to have her here to get things started. Every detail is so well arranged here now for convenience in caring for the baby and it gives one such confidence to know that things are right. She has been lovely in every way.

Oh Father dearest Father, how can I ever find words to express our gratitude for all you have done. I couldn't say a word when I left and now I find it equally hard to write, for it has meant more than you can ever know to me to have a father's tender love and care and thoughtfulness at this time. You seemed to be giving me all mother's love combined with your own, so that I felt here very close and you most wonderfully dear.

Those were blessed hours, dear Father, when you sat and talked with me in your busy hours and I shall cherish them always. They and you and your love are bound up for always in my new happiness with the little son. I wish we were not so far away, or that if I were nearer I could give you a fraction of all the happiness you have given me. How I hope that Frankie will grow up to know and love and be like you.

With dearest love from us both to all but especially to me darling Father, devotedly Jessie

---

WOODROW WILSON
TO
JESSIE WOODROW WILSON

The White House 14 March, 1915

My darling Jessie,
I am ashamed of myself when I think I have been so long acknowledging the dear letter from you that made me so happy, and touched me so deeply. You cannot know, I fear, what it

meant to me to have you say that I had in some sort taken you incomparable mother's place when you were here! Ah! How little I knew how! and how impossible it was to do more than just let you feel as well as I knew how the infinite tenderness I felt and the longing that was at my heart to make up for what can never be made up for either to you, my sweet daughter, nor to me nor to anyone who ever had a chance to know how sweet and loving and infinitely rewarding she was. I cannot yet trust myself to speak much of her, even in writing. My heart has somehow been stricken dumb. I felt so dumb when you were here, dear. I did not know how to say the things that were in my heart about you and the baby and all the crowding thoughts that made my heart ache with its fulness. I had to trust you to see them; and your dear letter makes me hope that you did. I can talk about most things but I always have been helpless about putting into words the things I feel most deeply, the things that mean most to me; and just now my heart is particularly voiceless. But I do love you and yours, my dear, more than words can say, and there is added to my love now the mother tenderness which I know the depths and beauties of in her heart. She was beyond comparison the deepest, truest, noblest lover I ever knew or ever heard those who knew the human heart wish for!

It is delightful to hear how well everything goes with you. God bless you. You will have heard of Mac's operation. He has come out of it finely: and is doing as well as anyone could in the circumstances. Nell is here with us, of course, and as steady and brave as usual. Nothing happens to the rest of us except daily crises in foreign affairs.

Love beyond measure from us all to you all. Your loving Father

*J*essie was recovering from the birth of her daughter, Eleanor, in Philadelphia, Pennsylvania, when she wrote this wistful letter to her father, who was about to embark on his presidential reelection campaign.

May 10, 1916

Dearest Father,

I realize with dismay how long I have been home with no word of my love and gratitude to you. I had to let Frank do the writing for me, for these first two weeks have been very tiring ones, and very busy. Our new routine is, however, happily established. We have an excellent nurse who gets things done so quickly and efficiently and yet is so sweet with the children that she bids fair to prove a treasure.

Eleanor has not done well since we came home, has not gained at all since the Monday after our arrival, but we feel that she is over the upset now and that all will be well. She looks well, still, and is a joy to have in the house.

I am gaining strength steadily. Spring is at last here and we are all out of doors a great deal. It is so heavenly that I wish you and dear Edith could be here to share the entrancing beauty of spring on these hills with us. Dearest Father, we love you so, you can't know how wonderful it was to see you in Philadelphia and to see my darling in your arms. I shall always remember it. Dear Father, I am wordless when I try to express all our love for you and our appreciation of your generosity towards us. It makes me cry when I try to write.

I can only say again how much I love you both, Devotedly your own daughter Jessie

WOODROW WILSON'S DAUGHTERS, JESSIE (STANDING) AND ELEANOR, CIRCA 1912.

WILLIAM HOWARD TAFT
TO
HELEN HERRON TAFT

*T*aft was overjoyed at the October 5 birth of Helen, the first of two daughters born to Helen Taft and Frederick Manning. When Helen's second daughter, Caroline, was born in 1925, then–Chief Justice Taft went to church upon hearing of his daughter's lying in, reporting in a January 18, 1925, letter to her: "Then while I was at Church the good news came." Taft also asserted his preference for "another little girl. Your mother would have been glad to have a boy but I don't have that feeling. She will grow up and give you delight."

Supreme Court of the United States October 13, 1921.

My Dear Helen:

Your letter, written by Fred, came yesterday, and we were delighted to get the report of progress. I presume you see all you say you see in your baby, but I assume that others are perhaps deprived of the vision that you and Fred have in this matter. It is delightful, however, to hear that you have gone through this greatest strain in a woman's life, and find yourself now so rapidly on the way to complete activity. It delights your mother and me to have another grandchild in the family, and the feeling is only a bit qualified by the thought that we are not to have you and Fred and the baby at Murray Bay next summer, if you carry out your present plans. It is possible you may conclude to change them and postpone your going. Fred hasn't as yet the right to a sabbatical year, and it may seem wiser to wait until that right accrues. However, you and he know your own business, and I haven't sufficient knowledge of all the circumstances to make my advice useful. I know that this coming of the little stranger will add to you expenses, so that from now on I shall expect to send you $250. a month instead of $200. I hope the expenses attending the birth and your stay at the hospital have not been excessive.

Your mother has been doing great work in getting us settled in the house. We feel very well satisfied with the house. There are a good many thing that need to be done to it, but it is in such excellent condition on the whole that we can postpone doing things so as to take them gradually, rather than to do them all at once. The house needs painting, the electric light fixtures need attention, and possibly the plumbing needs furbishing up, but I was most agreeably surprised to find how little really needs to be done to make the house most habitable and most comfortable. We have a great deal of extra furniture, but just what we wish to part with and what we wish to retain, it needs considerable deliberation to determine. I am awaiting the furnishing of my two rooms in the house which I use as judicial chambers, and which under the practice the Marshal of the Court pays the expense of furnishing. It is the getting of little things done that take such time. The Marshal has had the order for my bookcases placed for nearly a month, and I doubt if I get them done before the first of November. However, I have temporary cases which serve my purpose partially. The house needs painting on the outside, and the shrubs and trees and vines need pruning. It is now a fine looking place, but can be made much more presentable. We have ample room for guests, and should you and Fred wish to bring the baby down at Christmas, you can be sure of a very warm welcome and of plenty of space.

I am doing very steady work now, and find a great deal of work to employ me. I have tried the experiment of beginning at 6 o'clock in the morning, rising at a quarter after five, working until eight, breakfast for half an hour, then working until a quarter after ten, and then walking to the Supreme Court. The Capitol is about three miles from our house, and it takes me just about an hour to walk. When I get there, I am in a state of perspiration, my underwear is wet, and it gives me time in the bath room we have there to change my clothes, rub down, and leaves me an interval of half an hour perhaps to take up matters there and look up authorities. Court begins at 12 o'clock, and continues until two. We have half an hour for luncheon when Court lunches together. At half past two we return to Court for two hours, and adjourn at half past four. Then Tom meets me with the Dodge and I come home. I work from five until seven until dinner, and then from half past seven until ten when I go to bed. This gives me seven hours' sleep. Up to this time I have found no difficulty with this program, but I may find a change necessary. The members of the Court are very congenial. Brandeis and I are on excellent terms. We haven't had conferences, with the clashes of opinion which are sure to come, but I hope I can get used to them, and as I have been through a similar experience.

Your mother is going to have some social duties in receiving on Mondays, and I suppose we shall have to entertain in a small way, and I presume that when the dinners begin, I shall have to introduce a rule not to go out more than once a week, because this work is incessant, and does not permit dissipation.

I hope you are going to find that your quarters are sufficiently large to take care of that youngster, whose lungs will doubtless need development, and have it. I hope Fred proves to be a good entertainer of the baby. I never was with our babies, but perhaps he will be.

With dearest love from both of us to you and Fred, believe me, my dear Helen,
Your affectionate father, Wm H Taft

[P.S.] You should train Fred by making him walk at night with the baby, I did that with you. Hence my career.

ANNA ROOSEVELT
TO
FRANKLIN D. ROOSEVELT

---

*R*oosevelt's daughter was recovering from the birth of her son, John, when she wrote this letter to her father.

Swedish Hospital, Seattle, Washington
April 6th [1939]

Dearest Pa,

(My first attempt at letter writing since March 30th!)

Your letter from Warm Spring meant a great deal to both John and me. I felt cheated that I hadn't been able to talk to you on the phone—and the letter made up for it, and made you seem much closer to us than the three thousand physical miles between us.

We're so happy about little Johnny! You should see big John learning how to handle him and feed him his bottle. I thought Mother would die laughing at John's concentration, facial expressions and efforts to "catch" the baby's head as it rolled from side to side!

Ma was such a comfort before the event, during & after. After, she spent supper time and every evening with Sis and Rus so that their noses would not feel out of joint. They, too, have been in every day for a visit. Sis is already making plans for the feeding she intends to give the baby.

We're all excited at the prospect of seeing you in July. Ma seems to hope you'll make the trip in June, but the date doesn't matter just so long as you come. (Slightly peculiar English!)

We have heard nothing as yet from Curt about the children's summer visit to him, and we're holding our fingers crossed and hoping he won't ask for them until after your visit.

I hope you and Missy and Harry got at least a little rest at Warm Springs. We're having beautiful weather here and as a result I'm beginning to long for the feel of a horse under me once more.

We all five send you much love. Your youngest (for the moment) precocious grandson has a most excellent pair of lungs and vocal chords with which to welcome you in July!

So very much love to you from Anna

LYNDON B. JOHNSON
TO
LYNDA BIRD JOHNSON

*J*ohnson wrote this endearing letter to his elder daughter when she was expecting her second child, Catherine Lewis Robb.

April 24, 1970

My dear daughter Lynda:

Enclosed is a dear letter one of your nice friends wrote to me while I was in the hospital. I was so proud to read what she thinks about you.

Should another little girl-child come to join our family next month, don't think for one minute there will be any disappointment down this way because I know she will be "sugar and spice and everything nice"—smart as a whip besides—all just like her mother.

On the other hand, if you think Lyn needs a boy cousin for companionship and decide in his favor, this grandfather is easy to please and only hopes for a little girl as lovely as you or a young boy as fine as Chuck.

My love to all of you.
Your father, lbj

GEORGE H. W. BUSH
TO
DOROTHY BUSH

*B*ush, then serving as President Ronald Reagan's vice president, wrote this letter of August 8, 1984, to his daughter, just after the birth of her son, Sam.

8–31–84

Dear Doro,

Monday was a special day in my life—a very special day. Sam is beautiful. He has 2 great parents who will give him love all his life.

Seeing that little guy made many thoughts run through my head. Thank God he's strong & well. Thank God he's born into a family of love and kindness and caring. Then I must confess I thought—I am 60—it doesn't feel old but it is pretty old: and here's Sam, 1 day old, just starting out in life, with much joy and happiness ahead of him and a mother who has given her own Dad nothing but happiness & love; and a father who will be at his side teaching him about decency—honor and the importance of family.

Sleep on fat little Sam—a lot of fun awaits you and when you hurt your beautiful wonderful Mom will hug you. Devotedly, Dad

---

DOROTHY BUSH
TO
GEORGE H. W. BUSH

---

*D*orothy wrote this thankful letter to her father immediately after receiving a gift for her newborn daughter, Ellie.

[undated, 1986]

Dear Dad

I can't begin to thank you for your gift for Ellie. It will be such a help as you can imagine. I know that amount of money is not exactly chicken feed to you and Mom so I appreciate it So very much. You and Mom have always been such a Support in every way and when I get down for any reason, I just think of you. Dad, you have always made us proud and you will be an inspiration to Sam and Ellie I am glad they will know you for themselves.

Ellie is a beauty—big round cheeks. You will love her.

Thanks Dad. I love you, Doro

1826

Williamstown June 26

My Darling Little Girl:

This morning Mr. Rockwell brought your letter and Miss May's. I cannot tell you how glad we all are to hear from you and learn that you are doing so well. Did you really write your letter all alone. It was so well written that I could scarcely think you did it yourself. Papa says you did, and I hope he is right. The boys are having a grand time. Prof. Perry has two boys just their ages

CHAPTER 6

ENCOURAGEMENT:
"YOUR LATE SUCCESS"

"Congratulations on your late success"
—Abigail Adams to John Adams,
May 10, 1783

*"I write you about the
little flock of which you are the leader."*
—James Garfield to Mary (Mollie) Garfield,
June 26, 1876

ENCOURAGING words were offered in some form in most letters between presidents and their daughters. These letters, from the exchange between Abigail Adams and John Adams to the ebullient letter from George H. W. Bush to Dorothy Bush, seemed designed to uplift the spirit rather than convey any important information or elicit any particular action.

ABIGAIL ADAMS
TO
JOHN ADAMS

*A*dams, one of America's peace negotiators in Paris, had concluded the treaty ending the American Revolution when young Abigail wrote this letter assuring him of her love and support even if he continued his service abroad. At that time, she did not know that she was to be invited to join her father the next year as a parental device to separate her from Royall Tyler, the young man to whom she was engaged to be married. In his reply, Adams hints at her future invitation to Europe.

Braintree May 10 1783

No opportunity of writing has presented since I was so happy as to receive two excellent letters from my Dear Pappa, neither of them of a date later than actober. Not a vessell has sailed for Europe these many months. All the return that it is in my power to make, is to indeavor to assure you Sir that I feel a greater degree of gratitude for all your favours, than it is possible for me to express. It is the foundation of virtue, and I hope is fully impressed on my heart.

I assure you my Dear Sir that I have suffered, not a little mortification, whenever I reflected that I have requested a favour of you that your heart and judgment did not readily assent to grant. Twas not that your refusal pained me, but the consciousness that there was an impropriety in my soliciting whatever you should consider incompattiable to comply with. It has rendered me so througherly dissatisfied with my own opinion and judgment, that I shall for the future take care to avoid the possibility of erring in a similar manner. and shall feel doubly gratified by the receipt of aney favour unsollicited.

Whatever Books my Dear Sir you think proper to recommend to me, I shall receive with particular pleasure, those of your choice, cannot fail, to gratify your Daughter. I have not that taste for history which I wish and which might be greatly advantagous, but I hope it is yet to be acquired.

Permit me my Dear pappa to join the general voice in addressing my congratulations on your late success in your publick station. None I believe refuse to acknowledge and express the gratified that is due to those who have been immediately instrumental in accomplishing this great event, altho many persons do not appear gratified with it. It does not so intirely coincide with their own interest, as they wish, and this principle of self-interest is too often the governing power of the mind. It is upon the same motive that I am so intirely gratified, but it—as it leads me to look forward with pleasure to your return. I hope the period is not far distant. Yet I still have an ardent desire to cross the atlantick, it is quite as powerfull as ever. Was you to continue abroad I should not feel contented with the distant prospect I have had of it for these few years, past.

I wrote you last December by Mr. Robbins a young gentleman who was for some time an instructor to my Brothers. He has been detained all Winter in Virginia and I suppose my letter will never reach you.

It seems almost an age since we have received any direct accounts from my Brother John. I feel at times as it we were growing into Life strangers to each other. It is a painfull reflection to my mind. I hope he has not lost in any degree his affection for his friends, or the remembrance of them. His advantages are great, and I flatter myself that his improvements in every thing necessary, and usefull, will be in proportion.

I hope my Dear Sir that you will receive this; before you leave Europe. It will remind you of a Daughter who derives her happiness from the anticipation of y[our] return, who is ever solicitous of your remembra[nce] and whose greatest pleassure is in subscribing yours Dutif[ully] and affectionately,

AAdams

JOHN ADAMS
TO
ABIGAIL ADAMS

Paris, August 13th, 1783

My Dear Daughter:

I have received your affectionate letter of the 10th of May, with great pleasure, and another from your mother of the 28th and 29th of April, which by mistake I omitted to mention in my letter to her to-day. Your education and your welfare, my dear child, are very near my heart; and nothing in this life would contribute so much to my happiness, next to the company of your mother, as yours. I have reason to say this by the experience I have had of the society of your brother, whom I brought with me from the Hague. He is grown to be a man and the world says they should take him for my younger brother, if they did not know him to be my son. I have great satisfaction in his behaviour, as well as in the improvements he has made in his travels, and the reputation he has left behind him wherever he has been. He is very studious and delights in nothing but books, which alarms me for his health; because, like me, he is naturally inclined to be fat. His knowledge and his judgement are so far beyond his years, as to be admired by all who have conversed with him. I lament, however, that he could not have his education at Harvard College, where his brothers shall have theirs, if Providence shall afford me the means of supporting the expense of it. If my superiors shall permit me to come home, I hope it will be soon; if they mean I should stay abroad, I am not able to say what I shall do, until I know in what Capacity. One thing is certain, that I will not live long without my family, and another is equally so, that I can never consent to see my wife and children croaking with me like frogs in the Fens of Holland, and burning and shivering alternately with fevers, as Mr. Thaler, Charles, Stephen, and myself have done: your brother John alone had the happiness to escape, but I was afraid to trust him long amidst those pestilential steams.

You have reason to wish for a taste for history, which is as entertaining and instructive to the female as to the male sex. My advice to you would be to read the history of your own country, which although it may not afford so splendid objects as some others, before the commencement of the late war, yet since that period, it is the most interesting chapter in the history of the world, and before that period is intensely affecting to every native American. You will find among your own ancestors, by your mother's side at least characters which deserve your attention. It is by the female world, that the greatest and best characters among men are formed. I have long been of this opinion to such a degree, that when I hear of an extraordinary man, good or bad, I naturally, or habitually inquire who was his mother? There can be nothing in life more honourable for a woman than to contribute by her virtues, her advice, her example, or her address, to the formation of an husband, a brother, or a son, to be useful to the world.

Heaven has blessed you, my daughter, with an understanding and a consideration, that is not found every day among young women, and with a mother who is an ornament to her sex. You will take care that you preserve in a course of conduct, worthy of the example that is every day before you. With the most fervent wishes for your happiness, I am your affectionate father,

John Adams

THOMAS JEFFERSON
TO
MARY (MARIA) JEFFERSON

The emotion of Jefferson's poignant attempt to encourage his daughter to join him and her sister in France is more than matched by the plaintive reply sent by the seven-year-old Mary. Despite her protest Mary was brought to Paris, where she lived for several years until the Jeffersons' return to America in late 1789.

Paris Sep. 20. 1785

My dear Polly

I have not recieved a letter from you since I came to France. If you knew how much I love you and what pleasure the reciept of your letters gave me at Philadelphia, you would have written to me, or at least have told your aunt what to write, and her goodness would have induced her to take the trouble of writing it. I wish so much to see you that I have desired your uncle and aunt to send you to me. I know, my dear Polly, how sorry you will be and ought to be, to leave them and your cousins but your [sister and m]yself cannot live without you, and after a while we will carry you back again to see your friends in Virginia. In the meantime you shall be taught by her to play on the harpsichord, to draw, to dance, to read and talk French and such other things as will make you more worthy of the love of your friends. But above all things, by our care and love of you, we will teach you to love us more than you will do if you stay so far from us. I have had no opportunity since Colo. LeMaire went to send you any thing: but when you come here you shall have as many dolls and playthings as you want for yourself, or to send to your cousins whenever you shall have opportunities. I hope you are a very good girl, that you love your uncle and aunt very much, and are very thankful to them for all their goodness to you; that you never suffer yourself to be angry with any body, that you give your playthings to those who want them, that you do whatever any body desires of you that is right, that you never tell stories, never beg for any thing, mind your book and your work when your aunt tells you, never play but when she permits you, nor go where she forbids you. Remember too as a constant charge not to go out without your bonnet because it will make you very ugly and then we should not love you so much. If you will always practice these lessons we shall continue to love you as we do now, and it is impossible to love you more. We shall hope to have you with us next summer, to find you a very good girl, and to ... of our affection to you.

Adieu my dear child! Yours affectionately Th. Jefferson

MARY (MARIA) JEFFERSON
TO
THOMAS JEFFERSON

[May 22, 1786]

Dear Papa

I long to see you, and hope that you and sister Patsy are well; give my love to her and tell her that I long to see her, and hope that you and she will come very soon to see us. I hope you will send me a doll. I am very sorry that you have sent for me. I don't want to go to France. I had rather stay with Aunt Eppes. Aunt Carr, Aunt Nancy and Cousin Polly Carr are here. Your most happy and dutiful daughter,

Polly Jefferson

JAMES GARFIELD
TO
MARY GARFIELD

*M*ary was only nine years old when her father urged her to take up her role as eldest child in the family home in Ohio. Her brothers Irvin, Abram, and Edward were respectively six, four, and two.

Williamstown June 26 1876

Mollie Darling

Papa was sure that you wrote the letter yourself. How nice it will be when you write as nicely as any woman! And when Papa and Mamma can show your letters to their friends, as specimens of nice hand writing!

I came from Ohio, the same day that Mamma left home, and I met her & the boys at Albany New York and came on here with

FRANK LESLIE'S
ILLUSTRATED
NEWSPAPER

No. 1,317.—Vol. LII.   NEW YORK, JULY 23, 1881.   [Price 10 Cents.

THE ATTEMPTED ASSASSINATION OF THE PRESIDENT.—A MORNING GREETING BY THE PRESIDENT'S WIFE AND DAUGHTER.
FROM A SKETCH BY A STAFF ARTIST.—SEE PAGE 346.

MARY (MOLLIE) GARFIELD AND HER MOTHER, LUCRETIA,
VISIT HER FATHER, JAMES GARFIELD, DURING HIS LINGERING
DEATH FROM AN ASSASSIN'S BULLET IN 1881.

them. I don't yet know what day we shall leave, but we shall see you all, before the End of this week.

Kiss old Benton and old Dobe and Baby Brewster for me and then Kiss yourself for me, and tell all my four precious children how much papa loves them, and then please try to remember what Each one of them says so that you can tell me when I get home. Just think of it! You are our eldest child now at home; indeed you are the head of our family and so I write you about the little flock of which you are the leader. Give our love to Miss Mays & all the girls at home.

Ever Your affectionate Papa J.A.Garfield

THEODORE ROOSEVELT
TO
ETHEL CAROW ROOSEVELT

---

*R*oosevelt encourages his youngest daughter and her husband, Dr. Richard Derby, to press on with their voluntary ambulance service in France late in 1914, just six months after the birth of their son, Richard Derby Jr., who was left to the care of nurses and his maternal grandparents. After the United States entered the war, Roosevelt tried to secure an active military commission for himself, but was denied the opportunity.

Osyter Bay, November 4, 1914

Darling Ethel,

Of course we think of you and Dick all the time. I know you are having a hard time, of wearing anxiety and sorrow and effort; but I am very proud of you both and very glad that you have been able to go over to do your part—and a portion of this nation's part—in helping those who suffer in this terrible cataclysm. I am utterly sick of the spiritless "neutrality" of the Administration; and I have at last said so, in emphatic language, in an article that appears next Sunday; I shall send it to you.

Richard is the dearest, merriest little fellow that ever was. He is always smiling, and is such a cuddly baby. He adores his grandmother's amber beads, puts them in this mouth, and then the string hangs out of each corner of his mouth like the moustache of a Chinese mandarin. His grandmother calls him Littlejohn Bottlejohn; and he sits up in his chair and hugs his bottle with both hands. His grandmother read aloud to me the enclosed piece from the Atlantic Monthly about merry souls that "waggle," like nice bow wows; and we send it to you because Littlejohn Bottlejohn is always so cheerful and friendly. My drawings are only good for grownups who can be caricatured! I can't draw the blessed baby. He is a great comfort; and we most earnest hope that in another month or so you will be starting back to him.

November has opened with beautiful weather. Mother and I have had two lovely rows, and a good walk. Somehow this always seems to me one of the loveliest seasons of the year; I like the wintry sunsets, and the tang in the air, and the wood fires in the North Room and Library.

As of course I expected the Progressives went down to utter and hopeless defeat; I don't think they can much longer be kept as a party. They are way ahead of the country as a whole in morality, and the country will need too long a time to catch up with them. It will be, from the selfish standpoint, a great relief to me personally when and if they do disband. But it is rather pathetic for the remnant who stood fast. Well, they really have shoved a good many reforms quite a distance forward.

We are somewhat concerned about Kermit and Belle, in view of the harrying of English ships by the Germans; we can only hope that the too-newly-weds managed to show efficiency enough to get on the very earliest ship that went.

Good bye, darling; I wish I could stroke your neck and hair. Give my dearest love to Dick. Your loving father

HARRY S. TRUMAN
TO
MARGARET TRUMAN

*S*ixteen-year-old Margaret had become a "full-fledged driver" when Truman wrote her this letter discussing her driving and studies.

Washington, D.C. August 28, '40 2:30 P.M

Dear Daughter:

Mother tells me you are a full-fledged driver now, and that you go to church, to town, and all around without a helper. I'm glad of that. Maybe you can be my chauffeur in the campaign.

She also tells me you are going to study Spanish. That is a very useful language these days. Maybe I could get you an interpreter's position at Panama, Guatemala, or Santiago, Chile, someday. Anyway, I hope you'll be good at it & your music. Would have liked to be with you on the ride. Did Chief behave himself? He be rather tall to play Prince of Wales. Wish I could see the Ramparts Watch.

Mr. Stark is a ham, whether it is governor, candidate, or judge.

I thought I'd be starting home tomorrow night, but I won't be able to make it. We'll probably finish this bill today, the big appropriations tomorrow, and then take up the transportation bill Saturday. That means no home for me this weekend. I'll have to miss the meeting in St. Louis, and the legion convention in Sedalia too.

I suppose you have started to school almost by now. Are you a Junior this year?

Senator Burke is giving a party at the Army & Navy Club tomorrow to celebrate my victory. Five senators and five representatives. Nice of him, isn't it? Wish you & Mamma were here. I miss you terribly.

Kiss Mamma. Love to you. Dad
XXXXXXXXXXXXXXXXXXXX
OOOOOOOOOOOOOOOOOOOOOOO

*J*ust months before his death, the former president wrote this letter praising the efforts of his daughter and her husband. Lynda and Charles Robb went on to become powerful figures in Virginia and national Democratic political circles.

September 27, 1972

Dear Lynda and Chuck:

Thank you for your nice letters. I always enjoy hearing about the many wonderful things that both of you are busily doing.

Chuck, I believe you made a very level-headed and well thought out choice in accepting Judge Butzner's offer. Since you always have done so many things in the past with incomparable perfection, I am confident that you will excel in this position also—nonetheless, you have my best wishes and highest hopes.

Lynda, I know my girl must have set the house afire at those meetings of the Women's Conference—you make a good and effective spokesman for any cause, and you have picked one that has always sorely needed every dedicated and talented lady it could get. I'm glad, and I'm sure the Women's Conference is too.

Give those two little sweeties of yours a big hug for me–I love all of you very much.

Affectionately, lbj

[P.S. autograph note] We can & will arrange the loan on the Worthington acreage when you are ready to close.

HARRY S. TRUMAN, BESS TRUMAN, AND THEIR DAUGHTER,
MARGARET, IN THE WHITE HOUSE SHORTLY AFTER
TRUMAN BECAME PRESIDENT.

JULIE NIXON
TO
RICHARD M. NIXON

*T*he younger Nixon daughter was a veteran of America's political forums when she wrote this note of encouragement to her father, who then faced a lengthy impeachment trial in the Senate as a result of the Watergate investigations. Nixon resigned just three days later on August 9, and Julie remained his most vocal family defender.

August 6 [1974]

Dear Daddy
I love you. Whatever you do I will support. I am very proud of you.
   Please wait a week or even ten days before you make this decision. Go through the fire just a little bit longer. You are so strong!
I love you Julie

[P.S.] Millions support you.

*P*resident Bush had only been in the White House three months when he wrote this letter to Dorothy, who was just beginning work as a planner of business conferences for the Maine tourist bureau.

Camp David Sunday 3–12–89

Dear Doro,

I loved the clipping about your new job—good ink.

Advice from ole Dad—do not worry about the shots they fire at you in the press or letters to Ed. I have learned that lesson the hard way. It is surprising how different I feel now about all this. A year ago it was 'up tight time', but now I say 'let them do their thing' (Don would say Thang) and I'll do mine.

You'll do just fine up there.

The weather here at CD is still on the brisk side with the snow covering all but the new horse shoe pit; but soon March will give way to April and this place will be heaven.

Only one problem. Millie, fat and fidgety keeps me from sleeping. She is gigantic and looks up with mournful eyes. In a week plus we should have about 6–8 new puppies at the White House.

Love to all, Devotedly Dad

P.S. Here we are with the Flying Pidgeons given us in China.

Nashville, Tennessee.
Saturday, 12, O'clock, April 15th

My dear, dear Father

The sad, sad news
has just reached us, announcing the
death of President Lincoln. Are you
safe, and do you feel secure? Our city
is filled with excitement. It presented a gala appearance this morning but our joy was suddenly turned
into grief. The Stars and Stripes have
all been taken down, and now
nothing but the booming of cannon
is heard, and returning soldiers to
camp. I never felt so sad in all my
life, and poor Mother she is almost
deranged, fearing that you will be
assassinated. Our distracted and torn
up country. How I long to be with
you this sad day, that we might weep
together as a Nation's calamity

2634 [Rec: 1865 Ap 22 A Patterson to A J 2]

CHAPTER 7

HEALTH AND CONSOLATION: "THE SAD, SAD NEWS"

*"The Sad, Sad news has just reached us,
announcing the death of President Lincoln . . .
I never felt so Sad, in all my life"*
—Martha Johnson to Andrew Johnson,
April 15, 1865

*"The sore throat which you recollect
I had all the time we were at Long Branch last
summer has proven to be a very serious matter."*
—Ulysses S. Grant to Ellen Grant,
February 16, 1885

GOOD HEALTH, bad health, and death were major topics of presidents and their daughters. Although the public sees presidents primarily as public figures, a full range of personal emotions can be seen in this selection of letters.

JOHN ADAMS
TO
ABIGAIL ADAMS

*A*dams took the occasion of the death of ten-year-old Abigail's grandmother, Elizabeth Quincy Smith (1721–1775), to console and encourage her.

October 20th, 1775

My Dear Daughter

I condole with you, most sincerely for the loss of your most worthy grandmamma. I know you must be afflicted at this severe stroke. She was an excellent instructress to you, and a bright example of every amiable virtue. Her piety and benevolence; her charity; her prudence, patience, and wisdom, would have been, if it had pleased God to spare her life, an admirable model for you to copy. But she is no more: however, I hope you will remember a great deal of her advice and be careful to pursue it.

Now you have lost so valuable an ancestor, I hope you will be more attentive than ever to the instructions and examples of your mamma and your aunts. They I know will give you every assistance in forming your heart to goodness and your mind to useful knowledge, as well as to those other accomplishments which are peculiarly necessary and ornamental in your sex. My love to your brothers and all the rest of the family. Your father, John Adams

GEORGE WASHINGTON
TO
ELIZABETH PARKE CUSTIS

*E*lizabeth had just married Thomas Law, when Washington wrote this letter of condolence on the death of Martha Washington's niece, Frances Bassett Washington Lear.

Philadelphia, March 30, 1796

My dear Betsey:

Melancholy as the event is, on which you wrote the 25th instant; and unwelcome as you knew the information must be, yet it was the part of prudence to communicate it as early as you did: and the precaution you took of writing to me, was well judged; and wd. have been necessary, had we not been previously prepared for the shock, by letters from Mr. Lear; giving an account of her situation, which left no hope, in me of a different result.

Mrs. Lear was good and amiable, and your Society will feel the loss of her. But the Dispensations of Providence are as inscrutable, as they are wise and uncontroulable. It is the duty therefore of Religion and Philosophy, to submit to its decrees, with as little repining as the sensibility of our natures, will permit.

My compliments to Mr. Law. In a joint letter, written a few days ago to him, by your Grandmamma and myself, we offered you both our congratulations on your union, and I repeat them again, with sincerity, being Your Affectionate. Go Washington

*W*hile at one of his plantations, Oak Hill in Loudoun County, Virginia, Monroe wrote this to Eliza a month after the death of her young niece. Eliza's daughter, Hortensia, recovered fully from the illness mentioned in this letter.

Oak hill Octr. 8th. 1821

We were very much distressd my dear Eliza to hear by your last letter, that Hortensia was so seriously indisposed, but hope for the best. J. Coburn left this on Saturday with Mr. G. & your sister, for Washington on their way to N. York. We expect him back on Wednesday, and as soon as possible after his return, I will send him on horseback to attend you here. One day only will be necessary for him to rest. We hope to hear from you again, & by every post, of the state of Hortensia's health. We returnd from Albemarle on Wednesday last. All were in good health here, and on the whole route, under this mountain, except of Mr. Madisons, where the family of Mr. Richd & Mrs. Cutts & some of her children, had a malignant fever. Your mother is tolerably well; I am so also. Our most affectionate regards to the child & best wishes & anxious hope for her recovery. Remember us to Mr. Hay, Generl Ringgold, Lady, & family. Your affectionate father & friend. James Monroe

[P.S.] I address this to you, not knowing whether Mr. Hay or Genl. Ringgold are there.

JAMES MONROE
TO
MARIA MONROE

*M*onroe covers the health of virtually every member of the family in this letter to Maria. Eliza's daughter Hortensia had married Nicolas Lloyd Rogers of Baltimore in 1829. Her husband, George Hay, did not survive his illness and died on September 21, 1830, followed two days later by Monroe's wife, Elizabeth Kortright Monroe.

Oak Hill June 6th 1830

My dear Maria

Your mother has recieved a letter from you, which informs us, that you have been lately indisposed, and threatend with a chill, from which, altho' thin, you have recovered. We are delighted to hear that you have recovered., & that the children, & Mr. Gouverneur are in good health. Your mother has likewise been for a few days, indisposed, but is now perfectly restord. Her complaint was bilious, but she took some calomel, which has had the best affect. My own health has improved much, since you were with us, tho' I am still, compared to my former state, weak. I ride on horseback every day, when the weather permits, which has a good effect.

Your sister has sufferd much of late, by the duties she has been called on to perform, to her daughter & her husband. She left us, more than a month since, with him, for the city, to avail himself of the aid of phisicians there, who were acquainted with his constitution. From him, she was called to attend Hortensia in her confinement, and who has added to the family a daughter. She has been forc'd for the last week, to return to her husband, who is reduced to a very low state. His complaint was thought to be Rheumatic in the first instance, & afterwards bilious, and the process deemed necessary, in those cases, with the force of the disease itself, has reduced him so low, that altho' all medicine is stopped, he cannot now return home, nor is it certain when he will be able to do it. Your sister is with, & nurses him at the office. His recovery is uncertain. The phisicians Drs. Hisnett & Warfield, advise that he go to the Warm Springs in this state, should be able, & as soon as he is able. We hope that your sister will be able to bring him here, in which case, we may relieve her, from a portion of the heavy and distressing duty she has to perform. Of whatever change may take place, you and Mr. Gouverneur shall be advised, either respecting him, or any of the family.

It would be delightful to us to see you, Mr. Gouverneur, & the children, but you must not think of it at this moment. The period is delicate & difficult, and nothing must be risked, but in cases of imminent danger, & great emergency. Your visit to see me, when I was threatend, with such danger, in the winter, was most gratifying to us all, but I am happily relieved from that danger, & no emergency now exists, & your mother is well. Take care of your children who are dear to us, as well as to you and Samuel. Our affectionate regards to you all, & to the whole connection to whom we are much attached. Your affectionate father, James Monroe

---

JOHN TYLER
TO
MARY TYLER

---

*T*he chronic bad health of Letitia Christian Tyler was the subject of this letter from her husband to their eldest daughter. The plan to install a bath tub for its curative values is of particular note. In 1839 Letitia suffered a paralytic stroke, and she died in 1842 during her husband's presidency.

Washington June 15. 1832

My dear daughter:

I suppose that by this time you have settled down in solitude after your late extensive frolicking. So comes the calm after the storm. These alterations in life constitute its real zest. Who could

SHERWOOD FOREST, THE VIRGINIA HOME OF JOHN TYLER
AND HIS DAUGHTERS, MARY AND LETITIA.

be content to be always engagd in dissipation. The highest enjoyments of life pale upon the apetite when indulgd in for too long a time. The opposite of this will likewise only do for a season. Solitude brings with it real pleasures if its hours be properly improvd–as reflection—meditation and study. It is calculated also to heighten the pleasures of society when we return to it. The person who is a stranger to sickness is equally a stranger to the highest enjoyment of health. So that I have brought my self to believe that the variableness in the things of the world are designd by the Creator for the happiness of his creatures. In truth what exists but for some wise purpose: All our crosses and the numerous vexations which assail us are designd to improve our moral condition. But I am running into a lecture, when I design merely to write a short letter. I was concernd to learn from your mother that she had suffered from a severe headache the day after you had company. This proceeds from ones anxiety on her part aided by a predisposition to dissease. Tell her that Doctor Gaither says that a free use of the pills I gave her would serve to keep off those attacks, and that she would derive great benefit by using the bath. I have no doubt of this. When I was at home I had designd to have fixd up the room now used as a dairy for the bathing tub. Nothing more is necessary than to move it into that room and with an augur to bore a hole through the floor so as to let off the water from the tub when it was proper. Once or twice a week, a tub or two of salt water might be put into it or a barrell might be filld and then you would have a salt bath exclusively. It might be made warm enough with a tea-kettle or two of boiling water. The warm bath has in all ages been esteemed the greatest luxury and you might all enjoy it at little or no trouble. Burwell could take the tumbler and bring up a Barrell of salt water whenever it was wanting. Gaither says that nothing contributes so much to health. Persons flock annually to old point to enjoy the advantages of sea-bathing, and altho' we live on the Salt water no one has ever used it. I promise you all one thing that if you use the bath once you will never consent to be without it. The proper time is either early in the morning, at 12 o'clock or at night—in other words on an empty stomach. Once or twice a week would be often enough.

So much for the bath which I am anxious for you all to try.

Mrs. Minge & Mr. Bolling and his wife reachd here yesterday. He brought me a letter of introduction and I have to play the gallant. I perceive that they have been pleas'd at my having mentiond Sandy point in my speech on the tariff. I shall call on them to day. Every body male and female coming from Virginia bring letters of introduction to me or become acquainted after reaching here. This gives me a good opinion of my popularity at home.

Washington Irvine is now here. He stands at the head of our literati. His productions are numerous and well spoken of in Europe. His face is a pretty good one altho' it does not blaze with the fire of genius. It is deeply markd with the traces of hard study and altho' sometimes lighted up with a smile, is for the most part serious and contemplative. There is a late work of his now offerd for sale in the book stores which I will bring on when I come, if Congress ever will adjourn. We cannot get away sooner than the 1 July and possibly not until the 15th. Harvest will in the mean time be over. Tell John to take good care of the harvest whiskey.

With my love to all, Yr. father J. Tyler

[P.S.] Mr. Waggaman is very low—in fact I do not expect him to recover. Mary leaves this to day for Chs. City.

MARTHA JOHNSON
TO
ANDREW JOHNSON

*M*artha tries to convey the reaction in Nashville, Tennessee, when it first heard of Abraham Lincoln's assassination. Shock, anger, grief for Lincoln and the nation, and fear for her father's life are all evident in this brief, poignant letter. Johnson was to rely on the support and advice of his daughter during his presidency and his postpresidential political career.

Nashville Tennessee
Saturday 12 O'Clock April 15th [1865]

My dear, dear Father
The Sad, Sad news has just reached us, announcing the death of President Lincoln. Are you Safe, and, do you feel Secure? Our City is wild with excitement. It presented a gala appearance this morning but our joy was Suddenly "turned into grief." The stars and stripes have all been taken down, and now nothing but the booming of cannon is heard, and, returning Soldiers to camp. I never felt so Sad, in all my life, and from Mother she is almost deraanged fearing that you will be assassinated. Our distracted and torn up country, How I long to be with you this sad day, that we might weep together at a Nations calamity and be ever mindful of Him who watches over and preserves us from all harm. The City now presents a gloomy aspect, almost every thing is draped in mourning, and the house we occupy is also draped, much I should say to Mrs. Browns chagrin. She walked in here the other day, and inspected things, without observing the common ceremonies of entering a house. and then asked to see no one. I had a better opinion of her ladyship but then she is a rebel, and nothing better could be expected.

I presume she thinks we are an arrogant sort of people, half civilized and refugees from upper E. Tennessee. I have written more than I intended. I will enclose her note, written to Mother, asking "for her rooms, in her own house". I made no reply to her note.

We heard from Sister of Knoxville had a pleasant trip, but uncertain as to the time, when she would leave there for home. Frank was unwilling to return, and will go home with her. Rob had promised to go with her, but was in his usual condition, and could not go, he is here, but not sensible of the awful calamity, which has befallen a nation. Rob is all packed to go to East Tennessee. How much we would prize a few lines from you.

Judge Milligan and family go to Knoxville in a few days.

All are tolerably well at this time, and we were made happy to hear through Mr. Long, that you were so well. We are hoping to hear from you by telegram to day. I will write again in a few days,

Your ever affectionate daughter, Martha J. Patterson

ANDREW JOHNSON
TO
MARTHA JOHNSON

---

*J*ohnson, who had received little if any formal education, wrote this letter sharing his concerns about his wife's chronic illness with his daughter. Despite her chronic battle with consumption, which reduced her to a semi-invalid, Eliza McCardle Johnson spent her life educating her husband, parenting five children, helping in the family business, and urging her husband on in his political career. When she died in 1876, she had survived her husband by six months.

Greeneville Tenn June 13th 1871

My dear daughter,
Your mother does not seem very will to day continues in bed, yet complaing of nothing unusual with less cough than common. Mary is a way and none of the family have been over to see her to day and makes her some what lonesom. If convenient it would

be well enough to come down to morrow perhaps it would have some influence on her mind and spirits.

The House seems abandon by all and I am as salitary as though I were in the wilds of Afrika. If you can't come drop a not that you will be dawn soon &c.

Your devoted father Andrew Johnson

ULYSSES S. GRANT
TO
ELLEN GRANT

---

*G*rant breaks the news to Ellen that his chronic sore throat is more than merely troublesome. Ultimately, he would die from throat cancer in less than a year despite his optimism that the "ulcers" would yield to the treatment prescribed by his doctors. Before his death, he completed his memoirs, which provided his widow a comfortable support.

February 16th 1885

Dear Nellie:

Your letter of the 2d of February, to your mother, came two or three days ago. Algy arrived a few days before and came up and stayed with us until after dinner. all the family are well except me. The sore throat which you recollect I had all the time we were at Long Branch last summer has proven to be a very serious matter. I paid no attention to it until it have been five months. I found then the doctor considered it a very serious matter. Even now I have to see him twice a day. It has troubled me so much to swallow that I have fallen off nearly thirty pounds. It has only been within the last two days that the doctor has been willing to say that the ulcers in my throat are begining to yeald to treatment. It will be a long time yet before I can possibly recover.

It would be very hard for me to be confined to the house so long a time if it was not that I have become interested in the work which

I have undertaken. It will take several months yet to complete the history of my campaigns. The indications now are that the book will be in two volumes of about four hundred and fifty pages each. I give a condensed biography of my life up to the breaking out of the rebellion. If you ever take the time to read it you will find out what cut of a boy and man I was before you Knew me. I do not Know whether my book will be interesting to other people or not, but all the publishers want to get it, and I have had larger offers than have ever been made for a book before. Fred helps me greatly in my work. He does all the copying and looks up references for me.

We have all been as happy as could be expected considering our great losses and my personal suffering. Philosophers prefer to believe that what is is for the best. I hope it may prove so with our family.

All join me in sending love and Kisses to you and all the children.

Your affectionate, Papa

BENJAMIN HARRISON

TO

MARY HARRISON

Caroline L. Scott Harrison died on October 25, 1892, just two weeks before the presidential election in which her husband was defeated for reelection by Grover Cleveland. When Harrison married his deceased wife's niece, Mary Scott Lord Dimmick, in 1896, his daughter Mary was one of several family members who had difficulty accepting the marriage.

Monday Morning [May 16, 1892]

Dear Mamie

You will want fuller information about your Mother than a telegram can give. She has not shown the improvement we had hoped. There seems to be no reason why she don't come right up except her nerves. She is a little "hypo'd" & it is hard to get her to brace up & take an interest in anything. We will try to day to give her a fishing or crabbing expedition & hope when she gets a bite she will cry out for a landing net. We are most comfortably fixed. The boat is as quiet as a sick room. Every man moves about on tip toe—the cook is very good & everybody as attentive as possible. It is warm & clear but with a delightful breze on the bay. Your mother has no trouble except that she don't give over her groans & moans. She will I am sure gain to day for nobody could resist the healthful & pleasant conditions about her. Lynn was off yesterday with a sick headache but is out again this morning. Mame & Josie gone up to the sea, Sunday morning crossing the Bay, but have apparently been the better for it. Yesterday at lunch we had baby soft shell crabs. Not much bigger than a silver dollar. Mame ate seven I think.

The Col Comd Ft. Monroe is now coming off to call & I must close now. I wish you & the dear children were with us. Kiss them many times for Grandpa and Grandma.

Your affectionate Father, Benj. Harrison

BENJAMIN HARRISON

TO

MARY HARRISON

Loon Lake July 8 1892

Dear Mame

We sent you a telegram yesterday announcing our safe arrival & I am glad to give you a good account of your mother this morning. The ride over from the Station (four miles) on a buckboard was pretty hard on her & she complain a good deal & felt very much exhausted when we got her into bed. But she rallied at once & before the day was over she showed very marked improvement especially in her nerves. She took an interest in Evything—had an improved appetite & slept eight hours last night. The Doctor feels very much encouraged. She has just called to me from her bed room to know if I had telegraphed to you. Our little cottage is new & Evything as sweet & clean as possible. Mrs. Chasse is very attentive and wants to do Evything for us. The place is very quiet—save for some blasting on Dr. Webb's RR which is building a few miles from here. There are

SHORTLY AFTER BENJAMIN HARRISON'S INAUGURATION IN 1889, THIS PHOTOGRAPH OF BABES OF THE WHITE HOUSE WAS TAKEN BY FRANCES B. JOHNSTON. FROM LEFT, MARY SCOTT HARRISON MᶜKEE, DAUGHTER OF THE PRESIDENT, MARY LODGE MCKEE, MARTHENA HARRISON, MRS. RUSSELL HARRISON, DAUGHTER-IN-LAW OF THE PRESIDENT, AND BENJAMIN HARRISON MCKEE.

quite a number of people at the Hotel but Mrs. Chase says she has only "Sensible people" & it seems so.

I will return to Washington Sunday Evg. or Monday—to be there by Tuesday at least. Mrs. Halford was sick again when I left.

I sent to Chicago the other day for some rubber Stamps to make "Brownies" for Ben. I suppose he will have them by this time. Tell him to print some & send them to Grandpa. Love & Kisses. Russell wired yesterday that they were all nicely settled at Cape May. Your Ma asked at once after getting here if the house was large enough for the Children.

Your affectionate Father, Benj Harrison

JESSIE WOODROW WILSON
TO
WOODROW WILSON

---

*J*essie wrote this touching letter to her father on the eve of the first major holiday after the death of her mother, Ellen Louise Axson Wilson, of Bright's disease on August 6, 1914. The reference to her mother is a brief, but a meaningful acknowledgment that she would be "with us in spirit."

November 20th, 1914

Dearest sweetest Father,

The Springfield Republican, a paper you recommend, says today that you are coming here for Thanksgiving. Of course we don't believe any paper, but it gives me an excuse for asking you again. Oh if you only could, it would be such a blessing on us and on our home! And if you could get here for Wednesday evening, our first wedding anniversary, our joy would be complete, as complete as possible with one so necessary for our happiness not with us in person. We know she is with us in spirit and you would be, too, father darling, even if you stay in Washington but to have you under our roof and at our board would make us so wonderfully thankful that we must beg you to come. But, darling father, you know we wouldn't ask you to do one little thing that means extra fatigue or strain, and so we will understand perfectly whatever you decide to do. We only want you to know how we want you.

The Garfields are more than anxious to stow away all extra people so you and Cousin Helen, Margaret and Uncle Stock and the Doctor all will be welcome and find room in plenty.

If you can't come Wednesday, too, we will be more than grateful for Thanksgiving Day and after.

With a whole overflowing heartful of love, from your adoring daughter, Jessie

[P.S.] I am sure people would let you be quiet here. They have been thoughtful to me in many ways.

THEODORE ROOSEVELT
TO
ETHEL CAROW

In this poignant letter to his daughter, the former president celebrates the success of her brother and commiserates in the death of a friend's son. Little did they know that Quentin's "day of honor and triumph" would be so short: in slightly more than a week (on July 20) they would learn of Quentin's death in aerial combat over France.

Oyster Bay, July 12, 1918

Darling Ethel,

Your letter was delightful; but it renewed all my homesickeness for you and for Pittypat and Tippytoe. The company with whom you associate seem a thought elderly; but Ann and Linda will help out; and some of the old ladies sound as if they were nice.

Of course we are immensely excited over the press reports of Quentin's feat. We got the news just as I was going in to act a pall-bearer for poor Puroy Mitchell. Whatever now befalls Quentin he has now had his crowded hour, and his day of honor and triumph. Mitchell had neither; he died before he was able to get to the front and to render service and to feel the thrill generous souls ought to feel when they have won the honorable renown of doing their duty with exceptional courage and efficiency. How pleased and proud Flora must be.

Eleanor's cable about Archie would indicate, if one didn't know Archie, that when he recovers from this operation (I presume his arm was broken again) he would come home, as he has a prospect of six or eight months before he can get back to active service; but what Archie will no I have no idea—and most certainly I shall not write to advise him!

Mother has just come in from a ride with me. She is really enjoying Oriole.

I am always prompt for breakfast now; I have no darling, lovely baddy baby girl to keep me. The little sweetheart sister! I delighted in the picture of Richard taking care of her while you were shopping for the household. Of course we miss the children more than we can express. Today when I mounted Truxton I began to laugh, as I remembered, one time when I was mounting him, Richards coming full speed round the corner of the piazza on his tricycle, with the train of cars hitched to the rear axle; the racket made even Truxton's dull nerves give way, and he crouched trembling like some huge fawn.

Cousin Christine and Cousin Laura both genuinely sympathize with me over Edie's absence! And well they may! And over Richard's. And over their mother's! You can imagine how we have enjoyed you all.

Your loving father

WILLIAM HOWARD TAFT
TO
HELEN HERRON TAFT

*T*aft's health was a major concern for his daughter. Grossly overweight for most of his life despite his daily walking regimen, he continued to serve as Chief Justice of the Supreme Court until his death in 1930 from arteriosclerotic heart disease and high blood pressure. This exchange of correspondence about Taft's health, politics, family, and Helen's education reflects the close familial relationship between father and daughter.

Supreme Court of the United States
April 27, 1924

My dear Helen:

I assume that you are working night and day to get that thesis of yours into shape for the first of May, and I don't want to delay you by having an obligation to read too long a letter. For two or three days I have been suffering from a rapid heart—what they used to call a "palpitation". While I haven't given up going to Court, I have stayed in bed until it was time to go to Court and have come back to bed after court. This was a compromise I made with the Doctor, because I did not want to give it publicity and have people make a fuss over my staying away. This is a week end so that I am in bed for Sunday. The Doctor does not give any good explanation of what brings these attacks. I don't suppose he knows, except that the heart is out of whack in some way. It isn't the most desirable part of one's body to be out of whack.

We have one more week of hearings. I don't expect to have between next Monday, the 5th of May, and the 9th of June so much work that I can not get through it without undue exertion, unless I am permanently or really disabled.

I haven't heard from your mother since she left Paris. She must have met Maria on the morning of the 15th, and therefore we soon ought to begin to hear from her from Seville and learn something of the hobnobbing of herself and Ambassador Moore with the King and Queen of Spain, as well as her experiences in getting to Seville.

I do not ask to know how you are getting on with your thesis. I am content to wait news of that until after you have got it done.

Politics is boiling. The death of Murphy in New York has added to the chaos of the Democratic situation, and perhaps increased the chances of McAdoo. While I do not minimize McAdoo's strength with the labor people and his strength with the so-called radicals, I am inclined to think that he would be the weakest candidate for us. If Coolidge will only use the veto in two or three conspicuous instances, it will so separate him from the moth-eaten crown of Republicans in the Senate and the House and put him so far above the Democrats of the same kind in Congress that the Republican party will be born again. He certainly has manifested remarkable vote getting capacity, and I think that that is due to the complete disgust of the rank and file of the regular

WILLIAM HOWARD TAFT IS PICTURED WITH HIS WIFE AND THEIR THREE CHILDREN, HELEN, CHARLES, AND ROBERT, IN THEIR WASHINGTON, D.C., HOME.

Republican party at the lack of leadership and a desire on their part to rally behind a conservative and consistent Republican. The strength of Coolidge is with the business men. He has it now and a few vetoes will give him a sound platform. But I must stop in my talk about politics, and send my love to you and Fred and the baby, with every good wish for your thesis.

Your loving father, Wm. H. Taft

HELEN HERRON TAFT
TO
WILLIAM HOWARD TAFT

May 31 [1924]

Dear Papa,

I have just had letters from you and Mama and Fred in the same mail so I feel well in touch with my family. I was much amused at Mama because she was very indignant that the Doctor said you were too fat. She almost cabled you that you weren't to diet any more but she said she knew it wouldn't do any good because you were so set on doing what the doctor told you. I know that she will be overjoyed to hear that her belief is vindicated.

I am taking my exams on Tuesday and Wednesday and then my troubles are over at least for the present. The exam will be very hard I have no doubt. I don't feel as if I know enough to write for six hours no matter what they ask me.

I enclose the bill from my typist. It seems a good deal but I suppose it is really very reasonable for she had a very hard time deciphering some of the manuscript I gave her. It can't be printed for two years at least so this and the bill from the binder are all there are to be paid at present.

I am just taking little H. out for a walk so I must stop. Little H. refuses to send her love as she doesn't seem to have any confidence in my power to convey it. Affectionately Helen

ANNA ROOSEVELT
TO
FRANKLIN D. ROOSEVELT

*A*lthough he had suffered the aftereffects of polio, high blood pressure and arteriosclerosis presented the greatest challenges to Roosevelt's life. He was just sixty-three when he died on April 12, 1945, of a cerebral hemorrhage. Anna's and the president's exchange about his diet demonstrates her ability to cajole and humor her often temperamental father.

7100 Fifty-Fifth Avenue South, Seattle, Washington
Wednesday [June 1941]

Dearest Pa,

If you do have a moment to relax, the attached diet suggestion from the Olympic Hotel Chef may amuse you—especially such suggestions about "repose" for your "estomac!" I've thanked the gentleman. He's the one who always sends us elaborate & indigestable though delicious dishes when Mother is here—& makes Katie furious!

We've been really worried about you—but Ma writes you are fine again, thank goodness.

Am sure Mother has given you all the news from here, so this is just to send you loads & loads of love from us all always.

Devotedly, Anna

P.S. Thanks no end for my June 1st check which is most welcome now we've acquired a new house!

FRANKLIN D. ROOSEVELT
TO
ANNA ROOSEVELT

June 25, 1941

Dearest Sis:

I am dictating this because at last I expect to get away (tomorrow) and get four or five days at Hyde Park. I am much better but still fairly weak—and poor Missy is still laid up although she is better.

Seriously, that diet from the Olympic Hotel chef makes sense and I would like it—on condition that the chef cooked it. Strictly between ourselves, I wish you could get Mother to hire him or for that matter any other chef for a large hotel known as the White House. Do Not tell anybody I suggested it!

Thank John for his note. I do wish you would both come East. I have less reason than for some time to insist that Seattle is about to be bombed by the Japs so I have to give the excuse that you are both needed for the defense of the East Coast.

> Much love to all five of you.
>
> As ever,

LYNDON B. JOHNSON
TO
LYNDA BIRD JOHNSON

---

*J*ohnson was majority leader of the U.S. Senate when he wrote this letter to his elder daughter. The letter extols the virtues and bemoans the death of her paternal grandmother, Rebekah Baines Johnson (1881–1958), who had just been lost to cancer. Although Johnson claimed an exceptionally close relationship to his mother, members of his staff later claimed to have written his weekly letter to her, including Mother's Day greetings. As he frequently did, Johnson here encouraged his daughter in her efforts to lose weight.

September 17, 1958

Dear Lynda:

When I read your sweet letter first thing this morning, I decided right then and there that you are the girl for me. Beginning immediately you can just warn any boys that might be hanging around that I am a very jealous man and that I'll be coming to town pretty soon and I better not catch any of them pinching you! From now on you are going to have to take care of your daddy so just get yourself ready.

These last few days have been sad and lonely and I know you have felt that way too. But one thing we can take comfort in is the knowledge that so many people are standing by us in our time of distress. I have learned that a great many people loved Mother as you and I did.

She lived a beautiful life and left many beautiful monuments to her memory. I hope that you grow up to be as good a woman as she was. She was a truly great woman and a wonderful person. She was wise, gentle, kind and understanding. She knew and understood so much about life. She could tell you who reigned in France during the 18th century, who wrote what book and little known facts of interest. But she was more than erudite. She would run her house, tend to her husband and children, and always be sitting in the first pew at church on Sunday. All of us would do well to study her life and learn from it.

I couldn't be happier to know that you are losing some weight. But as for your face looking like two tomatoes, I don't know. At any rate, I hope you don't feel too bad and it will all be over soon.

Your mother sends her love and I send a hug and a kiss. We will be seeing you before long.

Love,

LUCY (LUCI) BAINES JOHNSON
TO
LYNDON B. JOHNSON

---

*J*ohnson had suffered a heart attack on April 8, 1972, while in Charlottesville, Virginia. The exchange of letters with his younger daughter during the aftermath of the attack illustrates her deep concern for her father and his great desire to have his family around him. Johnson died of a heart attack on January 22, 1973.

2706 Macken St., Austin, Texas Sunday April 9, 1972

Dearest Daddy:

You are sorely missed and deeply loved. I do not believe that there is a soul in Austin whom you know who hasn't reached me to express their love and concern—this includes:

1 Everybody I met at church from the priests to Frank Ikano's daughter-in-law.

2 every clerk at the grocery store

3 100 of Houston area's phycologists, educators and optometrists—where you serving as my inspiration (because in my heart I dedicated my speech to you) helped me to make one of the best talks of my life (not all of my speeches have had quite the zip I like lately)

4 Every neighbor I have—all of them have offered to keep the children if and when you feel I might be able to help—I'm packed and ready and oh so anxious to be near you.

5 nearly every member of the Junior League. We are going to the library tomorrow as part of our Know your Community and I've arranged for a tour and coffee & sweetrolls (Harry & John Gronouski are speaking

6 dozens of my friends, your friends from Patsy Steves to Carolyn Bengston

7 And Patsy wants to offer you & or mother her house located 3 minutes from Brook if you should go there when you return to Texas.

I LOVE YOU

I am including in this note a memo (on a separate sheet) concerning my rentals since you expressed an interest last week in them. I thought when you are better you might like to have them on file or at least know that I have some idea of what I am doing.

Please know that you are loved and that we are all ready and so willing so wanting to do anything to make the days to come a bit easier.

Lyn is very concerned he tells me "Mamma I pray in my mind for Boppa all the time—I know Baby Jesus is going to help him—he's just got to. I love him so." Out of the mouths of Babes.

Lyn said in a few words what we all feel and he sends the enclosed art work dedicated to you by his own decision and desire.

We love you, Your Luci

LYNDON B. JOHNSON
TO
LUCY (LUCI) BAINES JOHNSON

April 27, 1972

Dear Luci:

Most of all I needed your love, and after that—pajamas.

Thank you so much for them and bringing your little family to see me. As much as I appreciate Brooke General Hospital, I could not have stood it without all those visits. Come to the ranch whenever you can, and meanwhile love and hugs and kisses for everyone.

Your Daddy, lbj

RONALD REAGAN
TO
PATRICIA REAGAN

*R*obert F. Kennedy was shot in Los Angeles on June 5, 1968, just hours before then-Governor of California Reagan wrote this reassuring letter to his fifteen-year-old daughter, Patti, who was hoping to leave the Orme School in Arizona.

June 5, 1968

Dear Patti:

As you know, and as Mommie has told you, I've been in and out and up and down the state, so I'm a little late in answering your letter.

We still have some time about your questions as to schools, so let me see what I can find out about everything around here with regard to that senior year.

I know you are concerned, as all of us are, about what happened here. It is a great tragedy, just as it was a great tragedy for his brother. I've been here in the office all day, and feeling almost sick most of the time. Even though I disagree with him on political matters and even though I disapprove of him and his approach to these problems, I still feel very deeply the tragedy of this young man taken from his family in this way. I don't mean to make this sound so final, but the latest word we've been getting is one that the condition is very grave. Of course you'll know the answer by the time you read this as to how great the tragedy is or whether things are going to turn for the better.

In all of this sometimes one can learn why a certain course has been followed. There are many times when I have wondered why I'm doing what I'm doing. Now is one of those moments when I'm grateful that I can be in a position to perhaps change things to see that we do start a return to sanity and law and order and turn away from this whole creed of violence that seems to be so prevalent in our land.

Isn't it strange, a few months ago our friend in Washington told me that she foresaw a tragedy for him before the election. She didn't know whether it would be in the nature of illness or accident, but that there would be a tragedy befall him.

I must run now. Love, Dad

Answd
10/26/06

Simsbury October 22nd 1906 —

Dearest Father:

Thanks so
much for sending me
Lord Minto's letter. It
doesn't sound particularly
encouraging — though I see
no reason why next year
we shouldn't be away
in the autumn as at
that time he said the
weather wouldn't be so
disagreeable. but there is
plenty of time to decide
and I want to talk it
over with you and see

ALICE ROOSEVELT TO THEODORE ROOSEVELT

CHAPTER 8

POLITICS:
"THE GREATEST VICTORY
OF YOUR LIFE"

"I feel it is the greatest victory of your life,"
—Martha Johnson to Andrew Johnson,
January 29, 1875

*"I fear that the party, who have hitherto
embarrassed the President by their cabals. . .
will continue their utmost endeavors to render
it as uncomfortable a situation as possible."*
—Abigail Adams to John Adams,
January 20, 1797

"this last group resent your November victory,"
—Anna Roosevelt to Franklin Roosevelt,
January 10, 1937

POLITICS dominates the lives of presidential families, severely testing the fabric of their emotional ties. How the family operates and cooperates under the ever-watchful eye of the media and political arena is often a clear measure of the strengths and weaknesses of its relationships.

Many presidents, such as John Adams, Andrew Johnson, William H. Taft, and Harry S. Truman, had detailed, introspective dialogues on politics with their daughters. In turn, some daughters provided their fathers with politically astute behind-the-scenes advice—sometimes exalting, sometimes encouraging, sometimes cautionary, always supportive. Such letters reflect an equality of insiders in political events. For instance, John Adams took to heart his daughter Abigail's warning in 1797 that "I fear that the party, who have hitherto embarrassed the President by their cabals . . . will continue their utmost endeavors to render it as uncomfortable a situation as possible."

Other presidents wrote about external, real-time events, such as elections, public appearances, and speeches. Most of the presidential exchanges fall into this category. The letters of the Roosevelts, John Tyler, Woodrow Wilson, and Lyndon B. Johnson clearly illustrate this broader band of interest. For example, Franklin Roosevelt's daughter, Anna, made public appearances on behalf of her father.

A few presidents, to judge from their surviving or publicly available letters, confined familial communications to the topics of health, education, children, marriage, and personal behavior. This was particularly prevalent among the nation's early presidents: George Washington, Thomas Jefferson, James Monroe, Ulysses S. Grant, and Rutherford B. Hayes. Although politics occasionally entered their letters, particularly in times of great crisis or elation, it was not a major focus of their correspondence.

JOHN ADAMS
TO
ABIGAIL ADAMS

---

*A*bigail had just returned to the United States from London, where in 1786 she had married William Stephens Smith, Secretary of Legation while John Adams was serving as the United States' first minister to Great Britain. Adams confided to his daughter his resolve not to accept any minor political office, while urging her to convince her husband to become a lawyer. Adams was elected vice president in the new federal government, but his son-in-law never did settle on a profitable profession.

Braintree, July 16, 1788

My Dear Child:
Your mamma's hand has been wholly unable to hold a pen, without exquisite pain, from the time of our arrival; and I am afraid your brothers have not done their duty in writing to you. Indeed, I scarcely know what apology to make for myself. Would you believe this is the first day that I have taken a pen into my hand since I came ashore?

I am happy to hear from all quarters a good character of all your brothers. The oldest has given decided proofs of great talents, and there is not a youth of his age whose reputation is higher for abilities, or whose character is fairer in point of morals or conduct. The youngest is as fine a youth as either of the three, if a spice of fun in his composition should not lead him astray. Charles wins the heart, as usual, and is the most of a gentleman of them all.

You, my dear daughter, are in new scenes, which require new duties. Mr. Smith's mother has a right to all the dutiful filial respect, affection, and attention, that you can show her; and his brothers and sisters you ought to consider as your own. When I say this, I say no more than what I know must long ago have occurred to a lady of your reflection, discretion, and sensibility.

I wish to be informed, as fully as may be with propriety, of Mr. Smith's views. My desire would be to hear of him at the bar, which, in my opinion, is the most independent place on earth. A seeker of public employments is, in my idea, one of the most unhappy of all men. This may be pride; but if it is, I cannot condemn it. I had rather dig my subsistence out of the earth with my own hands, than be dependent on any favour, public or private; and this has been the invariable maxim of my whole life. Mr. Smith's merit and services entitle him to expect employment under the public; and I know him to be a man of too much spirit as well as honour, to solicit with the smallest degree of meanness for any thing. But I would not be dependent; I would have a resource. There can be none better than the bar. I hope my anxiety for his and your welfare, has not betrayed me into any improper expressions, or unbecoming curiosity.

You may be anxious, too to know what is to become of me. At my age, this ought not to be a question; but it is. I will tell you, my dear child, in strict confidence, that it appears to me that your father does not stand very high in the esteem, admiration, or respect of his country, or any part of it. In the course of a long absence his character has been lost, and he has got quite out of circulation. The public judgment, the public heart, and the public voice, seem to have decreed to others every public office that he can accept of with consistency, or honour, or reputation; and no other alternative is left for him, but private life at home, or to go again abroad. The latter is the worst of the two; but you may depend upon it, you will hear of him on a trading voyage to the East Indies, or to Surrinam, or Essequibo, before you will hear of his descending as a public man beneath himself.

Write me as often as you can, and believe me, Your ever affectionate father, John Adams

---

ABIGAIL ADAMS
TO
JOHN ADAMS

---

*I*n her response to Adams's July 16, 1788, letter, Abigail correctly predicted that her father would be elected vice president. Moreover, she openly discussed plans to move the national capital. This event eventually occurred in 1790 after Alexander Hamilton, James Madison, and Thomas Jefferson made a famous dinner deal that led to the federal assumption of state debts and changed the capital from New York to Philadelphia and then to Washington, D.C. Abigail also correctly foresaw the struggles that her husband, William S. Smith, would have in establishing himself professionally or commercially in New York. The Smiths' path to prosperity was eased by President Washington's appointment of Smith as U.S. Marshal for the District of New York in 1789 and by President Adams's appointment of Smith as Surveyor for the Port of New York in 1800.

Jamaica, Long Island, July 27th, 1788

Last Thursday I had the pleasure of receiving my dear papa's kind letter of July 16th. I was very impatient to hear of your welfare. My mamma's letter received a few days before, was the first particular account I had heard of the situation of the health of my dear parents since your arrival. My brothers have been very inattentive to me; I fear they have forgot the duties they owe to an elder and only sister.

It gives me great pleasure, my dear sir, to hear from you that they sustain good and amiable characters. Young men who pass through college without any imputation of misconduct, have laid a very good foundation, and are less liable to fall into errors afterwards. The habit of well doing is not easily overcome, and when it is the result of principle and judgment, the impression is so strong upon the mind as to influence their conduct through life. May you, my dear sir, never have occasion to regret the conduct of your children; but that you may have cause to rejoice in the character which they may support through life, is my most ardent wish.

I thank you, sir, for your solicitude respecting my friend and his future pursuits. As yet, I believe, he has formed no determination respecting his future career. At the bar there are so many persons already established by a course of practice, who are known in the State by common report, that there is but little encouragement for one who by long absence has been lost in public view. There is a strong propensity (perhaps it is a natural consequence) in the people of this country, to misplace the absent by those who are present. A few combining accidental circumstances may bring a man into notice; he will, without any extraordinary exertions on his own part, rise in the opinion of the people; the enthusiasm catches like wildfire, and he is in the popular voice more than mortal.

I think I can, in our own State, recollect a few instances of this kind, and I believe it is the case throughout the continent, both in public life and in particular professions.

For myself, I confess my attachment to the profession of the law. I think the study of it most conducive to the expansion of the mind of any of the learned professions; and I think we see throughout the continent, the men of the most eminence educated to it.

With respect to yourself, my dear sir, I do not quite agree with you in opinion. It is true that a very long absence may have erased from the minds of many your services; but it will not take a long time to renew the remembrances of them, and you will, my dear sir, soon find them not obliterated. You have, in a late pretended friend, a real rival. The attention lately shown you was the highest proof of policy, grounded upon fear, that could have been given; it was intended to blind the popular eye (perhaps it may for a time) but every person of any discernment saw through the veil.

It is my opinion that you will either be elected to the second place upon the continent, or first in your own State. The general voice has assigned the presidentship to General Washington, and it has been the opinion of many persons whom I have heard

JOHN ADAMS, SECOND PRESIDENT OF THE UNITED STATES AND FATHER OF ABIGAIL ADAMS, STANDS NEXT TO A GLOBE IN THIS LITHOGRAPH AFTER A 1783 PAINTING BY JOHN SINGLETON COPLEY.

mention the subject, that the vice-presidentship would be at your option. I confess I wish it, and that you may accept it. But of the propriety of this, you must judge best.

This State has adopted the Constitution by a majority of three only. It has given great joy to many, that at any events they are admitted to the Union. There have been great exertions made by the opposers of it, to prejudice the minds of the populace against its adoption, by such arguments as would have most weight with them—the addition of taxes, the rise of provisions, and some of the most improbable, though affecting to the lower class of people, that could be invented. The motives of some persons in power in the State, in opposing it, have been attributed to selfish views; whether just or unjust, I know not. It is now a great question in debate, whether Congress shall remove from New-York, and great exertions are making by some of the southern members, to get them to return to Philadelphia. Upon this question, I presume that selfish views actuate all who are violent upon either side, for I do not see that any material advantage can arise to the country from the local situation of Congress, except such as contribute to the convenience of their residence.

Believe me your affectionate daughter, A. Smith.

ABIGAIL ADAMS
TO
JOHN ADAMS

*A*bigail congratulated her father on his election as the second president of the United States. He received seventy-one electoral votes; Thomas Jefferson, his chief rival for the presidency and leader of the Jeffersonian Republicans, received sixty-eight. Under the federal constitution, Jefferson, who received the second highest vote for president, became the vice president. Abigail correctly warned her father that the opposition would dog his administration. Indeed, he was defeated in his bid for a second term in 1800.

East Chester, January 20, 1797

My Dear Papa:

I had the pleasure of a few days since to receive your favour of the 11th inst. and was happy to hear of your health: the season has with us, been extremely severe, and my faculties have been, I believe, congealed by the cold. I have scarcely had any intercourse with any of my friends; and this must be my apology, for having omitted to offer you my congratulations upon your election to the Presidency of the United States, a station in which no one can more sincerely wish you happiness, peace, and tranquility, than your daughter; but I fear that the party, who have hitherto embarrassed the President by their cabals, and who have exerted themselves to divide the election, will continue their utmost endeavours to render it as uncomfortable a situation as possible.

You will suffer much inconvenience from the absence of my mother, in the interior arrangement of your affairs.

Believe me, my dear, Sir, at all time, and in all situations, Affectionately your daughter,

A. Smith

MARY (MARIA) JEFFERSON
TO
THOMAS JEFFERSON

---

*M*ary expressed her concern about the presidential election to her father, the acknowledged leader of the Republican Party, who had defeated the incumbent president, John Adams, but then became embroiled in a seventy-three-vote tie with his own vice-presidential running mate Aaron Burr of New York. The election was ultimately decided in the House of Representatives, when the Federalists, fearing military action on behalf of Jefferson and believing they had received assurances that as president he would not remove them from office, switched enough votes to elect Jefferson the third president of the United States.

Bermuda Hundred Dec. 28. 1800

I feel very anxious to hear from you My Dear Papa. It is a long time since you left us, and it appears still longer from not having heard from you, opportunitys from Eppington to Petersburg so seldom occur that I could not write to you while there, here I hope we shall receive your letters more regularly. By directing them to City Point which Mr. Eppes thinks will be best, we can get them the same day they arrive there and in the expectation of hearing from you a little oftener I shall feel much happier. We have had the finest spell of weather ever known allmost for the season here, fires were uncomfortable till within a day or two past, and it still continues very mild and pleasant. It happen'd fortunately for us, as the house was not in a very comfortable state and every thing was to be moved from Mount Blanco here. We have not finish'ed yet moving and the carpenters are still at work in the house but we have two rooms that are comfortable and I prefer it infinitely to living in a rented place. We are still in anxious suspence about the election. If the event should be as it is expected I shall endeavor to be satisfied in the happiness I know it will give to so many tho I must confess mine would have been greater Could I be forever with you and see you happy. I could enjoy no greater felicity but it is very late and I must bid you adieu My dear Papa. May every blessing attend you. Your affectionate daughter M Eppes

---

THOMAS JEFFERSON
TO
MARY (MARIA) JEFFERSON

---

*J*efferson assured his youngest daughter that he would ultimately be elected president by the House of Representatives, because Burr would not succumb to the blandishments of the Federalists. Like John Adams, Jefferson correctly credited Maria with understanding the intricacies of national politics. Ever the doting (or some might say controlling) father,

he reminded his daughter that he expected her to come to Monticello when he arrived in April. Jefferson's two daughters were usually very diligent in serving as hostesses for their father during his stays there.

Washington Jan. 4 1800 [1801]

Your letter, my dear Maria, of Dec. 28. is just now recieved, and shall be instantly answered, as shall all others recieved from yourself or Mr. Eppes. this will keep our accounts even, and shew by the comparative promptness of reply which is most anxious to hear from the other. I wrote to Mr. Eppes Dec. 23 but directed it to Petersburg. hereafter it shall be to City point. I went yesterday to Mount Vernon, where Mrs. Washington & Mrs. Lewis enquired very kindly after you. Mrs. Lewis looks thin, & thinks herself not healthy; but it seems to be more in opinion than any thing else. she has a child of very uncertain health.

The election is understood to stand 73.73.65.64. the Federalists were confident at first they could debauch Colo. B. from his good faith by offering him their vote to be President, and have seriously proposed it to him. his conduct has been honorable & decisive, and greatly embarrasses them. time seems to familiarise them more & more to acquiescence, and to render it daily more probable they will yield to the known will of the people, and that some one state will join the eight already decided as to their vote. the victory of the republicans in N. Jersey, lately obtained, by carrying their whole congressional members on an election by general ticket, has had weight on their spirits. should I be destined to remain here, I shall count on meeting you & Mr. Eppes at Monticello the first week in April, where I shall not have above three weeks to stay. we shall there be able to consider how far it will be practicable to prevent this new destination from shortening the time of our being together. for be assured that no considerations in this world would compensate to me a separation from yourself & your sister. But the distance is so moderate that I should hope a journey to this place would be scarcely more inconvenient than one to Monticello. but of this we will talk when we meet there, which will be to me a joyful moment. remember me affectionately to Mr. Eppes; and accept yourself the effusions of my tenderest love. Adieu my dearest Maria

---

THOMAS JEFFERSON
TO
MARY (MARIA) JEFFERSON

---

*I*n the midst of the presidential election battle, Jefferson wrote to Mary about the difficulties of the electoral process and the scheming that had enveloped both parties as they tried to cope with the first major constitutional crisis of the federal government. When, on February 17, the House of Representatives finally elected him president at the 36th ballot, the House established the principled precedent of the peaceful transfer of power from one political party to another no matter how contentious or close the election.

Washington Feb. 15. 1801.

Your letter, my dear Maria, of the 2d inst. came to hand on the 8th. I should have answered it instantly according to our arrangement, but that I thought, by waiting till the 11th I might possibly be able to communicate something on the subject of the election. however, after 4 days of balloting, they are exactly where they were on the first. there is a strong expectation in some that they will coalesce tomorrow; but I know no foundation for it. whatever event happens, I think I shall be at Monticello earlier than I formerly mentioned to you. I think it more likely I may be able to leave this place by the middle of March. I hope I shall find you at Monticello. the scene passing here makes me pant to be away from it; to fly from the circle of cabal, intrigue & hatred, to one where all is love and peace. tho' I never doubted of your affections, my dear, yet the expressions of them in your letter give me ineffable pleasure. no, never imagine that there can be a difference with me between yourself & your sister. You have both such dispositions as engross my whole love, & each so entirely that there can be not greater degree of it than each possesses. Whatever absences I may be led into for a while, I look for happiness to the moment when we can all be settled together, no more to separate. I feel no impulse from personal ambition to the office now proposed to me, but on account of yourself and your sister, and those dear to you. I feel a sincere wish indeed to see our government brought back to it's republican principles, to see that kind of government firmly fixed, to which my whole life has been devoted. I hope we shall now see it so established, as that when I retire, it may be under full security that we are to continue free & happy. as soon as the fate of the election is over, I will drop a line to Mr. Eppes. I hope one of you will always write the moment you receive a letter from me. Continue to love me my dear as you have ever done, and ever have been & will be your's affectionately, Tho. Jefferson

JOHN ADAMS
TO
ABIGAIL ADAMS

*R*etired from personal involvement in politics, Adams settled back on the family farm in Quincy, Massachusetts, where he continued to keep a close eye on national politics. In this letter to his daughter, he expounded upon the influx of French refugees from the slave uprising in Santo Domingo, which established the first government in the Americas led by blacks and former slaves.

Quincy, September 26th, 1802

My Dear Daughter:

I received last night your favour of the 17th, and thank you for the pamphlet you sent me; I had read those before. Most of the pamphlets are sent me by one and another, as well as the newspapers.

To read so much malignant dulness is an odious task, but it cannot well be avoided. I have the history, too, of my administration. Good God! Is this a public man sitting in judgment on nations; and have the American people so little judgment, taste, and sense as to endure it?

The history of the Clintonian Faction, as it is called, I shall be glad to see. The society he asserts to exist, and which you say has not been denied, I fear is of more consequence than you seem to be aware of.

But to dismiss this society for the present. There is another set of beings who seem to have unlimited influence over the American people. They are a detachment, I fear, from a very black regiment in Europe, which was more than once described to me by Stockdale of Piccadilly, whom you must have seen at my house in Grosvenor Square. "Mr. Adams," said the bookseller, "the men of learning in this town are stark mad. I know one hundred gentlemen in London of great learning and ingenuity, excellent writers upon any subject, any one of whom I can hire at any time for one guinea a day, to write upon any theme, for or against any cause, in praise, or in defamation of any character." A number of the most profligate of these have come to this country very hungry, and are getting their bread by destroying all distinction between right and wrong, truth and falsehood, virtue and vice.

You speak of "moderate people on both sides," if you know of any such, I congratulate you on your felicity. All I know of that description are of no more consequence than if there were none. Commerce will decline, and the revenue fail. What expedient the government will have recourse to, I presume not to conjecture. I mourn over the accumulated disgraces we are bringing on ourselves, but I can do nothing.

The prisoners from St. Domingo will be dangerous settlers in the southern states. The French care very little whether turning them loose is insult or injury, provided we will cordially receive, or tamely connive at them.

My health is good, and my spirits would be high, if the prospect before us did not present clouds portending bad weather.

My love to Col. Smith and the children. The young gentlemen, I hope, think of Greece and Italy. I am your affectionate father, John Adams

---

JOHN TYLER
TO
MARY TYLER

---

*T*yler was nearing the end of his term in presidential office, when he wrote this emotional letter to his daughter, who had married William N. Waller, urging her to ask her husband to reconsider his support for the Whig presidential candidacy of Henry Clay, who opposed Tyler's plans to make Texas a state. Even though Tyler was a leader of the Whig Party, he believed that the Democratic Party candidate, James K. Polk, would be more likely to carry out his expansionist plans.

I am still abused by all the papers in his (Clay's) advocacy, and he urged on that conspiracy in 1841 which was designed to ruin me personally and politically. His opposition to Texas, his attempt to revolutionize the government—through the abolition of the veto power—in short, his total want of principle of every sort renders him the most obnoxious man in the Union. Mr. Polk is, to say the least, a gentleman in principle and conduct. If he comes into power, his administration will be a continuance of my own, since he will be found the advocate of most of my measures. Mr. Clay leads the Federal cohorts; Mr. Polk the Democratic. My friends will be treated with regard and attention, and a rally on their part will secure the election. They have rallied en masse in Pennsylvania, New Jersey, Maryland, Massachusetts, Connecticut, New York, etc. etc. I hope Mr. Waller will seriously ponder before he commits himself to Clay.

ANDREW JOHNSON
TO
MARTHA JOHNSON

---

*J*ohnson succeeded to the presidency on the assassination of Lincoln, only to barely escape conviction on impeachment charges. The Republican Party had abruptly discarded him as a presidential candidate in 1868 in favor of U. S. Grant. When Johnson and his daughter exchanged these letters, he was in a successful race to win a seat in the U.S. Senate. Martha's letters reveal her intimate knowledge of politics; her husband, David Trotter Patterson, was a former U.S. Senator from Tennessee. President Johnson, who had no formal education, exposed his poor spelling and grammar in written correspondence.

Greeneville Tenn Dec 29th 1874

My dear dughter
I returned from Memphis this morng and found you letter here
and was very much rejoice to heir that your mother was no worse.
is there no way that the night sweats can be broken or abated. I
hope she will recover from them soon and restored to her usual
health if restored alltogether. I hope Mary will settle upon somthg
in reference to scheduling her Children, for it is time had done so.
However she will have her own way and if they succeed she will
have no one to find fult with. I hope they will all do well in the end.

In regard to the Senators at questions I think all look very well
now and will Came out right in next month which will soon be
here. The while in Memphis was disagreeably warm followed last
night and to day by rain and now looks as it might snow.

Tell Andrew he must write to me and give all the local news
about Greeneville and how the printing press is baring on. I do
not think I shall return before the Senatorial election draws off:
but very soon thereafter. There is no news to write more than
what you see in the papers of the day.

I am quite will and all of you are will and doing will.

Give the best wishes of my heart to all.
Your devoted father, Andrew Johnson

MARTHA JOHNSON
TO
ANDREW JOHNSON

Home Tennessee Sunday Jan 24th [1875]

My dear Father
A week of anxiety and suspense just passed, and the contest not
ended. How earnestly I have prayed, that it would be as we wished.
Each day has seemed a week of itself, Andrew goes to town, and

then goes down to the Depot before day, when the mail passes to learn if any despatches have been received at Bristol but no result.

Today has been one of the most disagreeable of days good for plotting treason.

A letter from R.A. Crawford at Nashville stating he was there in your interest, which of course, none of us believed a word of, unless he thinks the Radical ship is sinking, and he wants a berth on the Democratic Vessel which he knows will sail soon.

Be of good cheer dear father, and it should be otherwise then desired, it will all be for the best.

Mother has been very unwell I think from excitement, however she is better today, She sends much love to you, and hopes for the best.

Affectionately Your Daughter Martha

MARTHA JOHNSON

TO

ANDREW JOHNSON

Home Tennessee Jan. 29th 1875

My dear Father,
Your cup of joy already full, and ours too great to express. It would be better to wait until the multitude had dispersed, before writing you I feel it is the greatest victory of your life, and your friends, their power is legion.

I see among the Congratulatory telegrams Mrs. Hawkins' name. How well I recollect her during the Impeachment Trial.

A telegram I enclose taken off at Jonesboro and sent to this office.

Mother has been very feeble and since the result has seemed very much better indeed. Rose early this morning and took her breakfast.

Hoping to see you very soon, and hear the time you will be there. No news. Quite warm, heavy rains.

Affectionately Your Daughter Martha

ULYSSES S. GRANT
TO
ELLEN GRANT

*G*rant was nearly nominated for president at the 1880 Republican Convention in Chicago, June 2–8, but was defeated by James Garfield on the 36th ballot, 399 to 306. Grant's two letters to his daughter provide valuable information on this little-known aspect of his political career.

Galena Ill. June 27th 1880

Dear Daughter:
I received your nice long letter a day or two ago. We were all delighted to hear that you are all well and enjoying your self. If

little Algie is such a bother to his pa send him over to us and we will bring him up "And away he will go." I am very sorry you are not all here now to go with us. On the 1st of July we start for the Rocky Mountains to be gone during the hot weather. Fred is out on the Rio Grande, and Ida & Julia, Will Smith and probably Buck will be with us. That country is now so intersected with rail-road that all the fine scenery can be visited without any difficulty. It exceeds Switzerland in grandeur and immensity. Buck & Fred have been with us a little this Summer, but not together, and last Jesse. Jesse just left here a few days ago. He was just on his return from Arizona and Northern Mexico, where he had been for about three months looking after Mines. Jesse has quite a large interest in mines and one of them has developed very rich. You know I presume that he is in business in New York City! He is doing quite well too.

I felt no disappointment at the result of the Chicago Convention. In fact I felt much relieved. The most unscrupulous means had been resorted to by the friends of the other candidates—no doubt by their advice—and even then a good majority of the delegates chosen were for me. But means were resorted to to displace them and give a small majority for all the other Candidates Combined. Had I been nominated there would have been the most violent campaign ever Known in our Country made against me. This I have avoided.

Next Summer we will be at Long Branch and then we will expect you. It may be that we will get a house in Washington for the winter. If we should could not you, Algie & the Children Come over, as soon as the fact is ascertained that we do?

All send much love to you, Algie & the Children.

Yours Affectionately U. S. Grant

[P.S.] Give my respects to Mr. Sartoris, Sr. and say that I am sorry he is not with us to take this summer trip. U.S.G.

ULYSSES S. GRANT
TO
ELLEN GRANT

New York City Nov. 4th 1880

My Dear Daughter:

The presidential election is now over and I have time to write, and attend my own business for the first time for a month. The country, in my judgement has escaped a great Calamity in the success of the republican party. A month ago the result attained was not expected. You know Buck is married! Every one speaks most highly of the young lady. She is quite pretty with all. Fred & Ida have been with us since our arrival in New York, now nearly four weeks. They return to Chicago however this evening. It now looks as if we would make our permanent home in this City. If we do I shall be engaged in some occupation giving me a good income. I will also expect to secure a place for Fred and have him resign and come here to live. We will then be all together except you. But we will have a home and expect you and Algy to spend much of your time here.

Possibly you might come here to live. Algy would not have to become a Citizen if his interests were averse to it. Buck & Jesse are both doing well in their business, and are entirely independent. We are boarding at the Fifth Av. hotel for the present, and will continue to do so until I Know I am fixed to be entirely independent. I will then purchase or lease a house. The latter is cheapest, but the former is more pleasant. I do not Know whether any one has described Jesse's wife. She is quite small with beautiful large eyes, a very small face but prominent nose, light auburn hair, and by some thought quite pretty. I do not think her as pretty as either Ida or Buck's wife. But she is very pleasant and not a bit spoiled. The same may be said of all your sisters-in-law.

We are all just as well as we can be and looking forward to the time when we can have you, Algy and the children with us again. With love and Kisses to you all. In my next letter I want to send you a draft to get your Chrismas things with.

Yours Affectionately U. S. Grant

ELLEN (NELLIE) GRANT POSES AT THE WHITE HOUSE AFTER HER 1874 WEDDING TO ALGERNON SARTORIS.

ALICE LEE ROOSEVELT
TO
THEODORE ROOSEVELT

*I*n the middle of his second term as president, Roosevelt and his eldest daughter exchanged these enthusiastic letters about the Congressional campaign of her husband, who went on to serve as Speaker of the House of Representatives for six years. She and Nicholas became one of the nation's leading political couples and, after his death in 1931, Alice remained a fixture of the captial's social/political scene until her death in 1980. One of the office buildings occupied by members of the House is named for Nicholas Longworth.

Sunday October 22nd 1906

Dearest Father:

Thanks so much for sending me Lord [?] letter. It doesnt sound particularly encouraging—though I see no reason why next year we shouldn't be away in the Autumn as Oct that time he said the weather wouldnt be so disagreable. But there is plenty of time to decide and I want to talk it over with you and see what you think about it. Nick has been very busy campaigning for the past few weeks. He seems to feel perfectly sure of being elected. And there has been practically no fight put up on the other side so far. The labor people have kept absolutely quiet. The Roosevelt Club has endorsed him and the Enquirer came out in an editorial for him the first time it has openly supported any Republican candidate, and that should mean a great many democratic votes. It certainly all looks as if it were going our way, but I never can feel perfectly at ease until election is over. We have been around the state to several places where Nick has spoken and then we both shake hands with most of the population. The last town we stayed in was Marietta—where they were celebrating their hundred and eighteenth anniversary which is a grand old age for out here. It is quite like a New England town with nice old houses and broad streets and big trees. Mr. Fairbanks was there and spoke. It [I] think he feels that the White House would set him off very well. On the way to the meeting he would rise in his open car and bow right and left to the populace who appeared here not in the least enthusiastic about him. Marietta is in Beeman Dawes district and we stayed with him at his farm almost three miles out of town. He is the third of his family to be in Congress—his great grandfather Manassa Cutler his father and now himself. He had such a really nice quiet wife, but looking so thin and poor and ...with a large family of children and having to do most of the work herself. But they were such thoroughly nice people. Quite different from another of our hostesses who when she saw Nick smoking a cigar pitched a spitoon towards him with her dainty foot to make him feel entirely at home! Beveridge was here for the opening meeting of the campaign and stayed with us. He has...utterly conceited Man I have yet seen lives. I wish I could see you and tell you some of the impossible things he said. There are meetings here nearly all day from sun up, and Nick...away twice again. Poor dear he has the worst frightful cold and he has to speak every night this week. How is it all coming out in New York. Hearst surely has no chance there has he? Best love my dearest dearest Father. I do wish I were going to see you soon, because I feel a pretty sad cat at times though these last weeks have been great fun really.

Your very dearest Alice

THEODORE ROOSEVELT

TO

ALICE LEE ROOSEVELT

Washington, November 7, 1906

Dear Alice:
First let me thank you heartily for the really beautiful glasses. They make a very nice birthday gift and were just what I wanted.

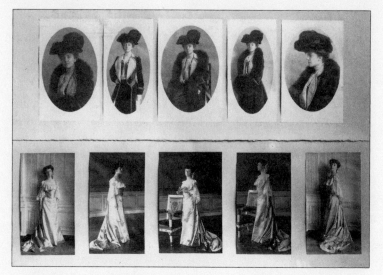

ALICE LEE ROOSEVELT, ELDEST DAUGHTER OF THEODORE
ROOSEVELT AND ONLY CHILD OF ALICE LEE ROOSEVELT, IS SHOWN
IN A MONTAGE OF TEN PHOTOGRAPHS TAKEN BY FRANCES
JOHNSTON OVER A TWENTY-YEAR PERIOD, 1890 TO 1910.

Next let me congratulate you and Nick with all my heart upon the successful way in which both of you have run your campaign. I tell you I felt mighty pleased with my daughter and her husband—especially comparing them with certain other American girls and their spouses, as for example, the Duke and Duchess of Marlboro, of fragrant presence!

Well, we have certainly smitten Ammon hip and thigh. I had no idea that we were going to do so well in the Congressional campaign. If the Republican, Goodling, is elected in Idaho there won't be anything to regret of any consequence. Next to beating Hearst in New York, I was most anxious to see Goodling elected in Idaho; that is, of course, aside from the Congressional campaign. It is very gratifying to have ridden iron-shod over Gompers and the labor agitators, and at the same time to have won the striking victory while the big financiers either stood sullenly aloof or gave furtive aid to the enemy.

With love to Nick, Ever yours, TR

P.S. Yes, we have elected Goodling Governor in Idaho; it is a big
victory for civilization, to have beaten those Western Federation
of Miners scoundrels.

THEODORE ROOSEVELT
TO
ALICE LEE ROOSEVELT

---

*D*uring the 1904 election, Roosevelt, who had become president upon the assassination of William McKinley, had announced he would only serve one full term. He was attempting to secure the Republican Party nomination for his Secretary of War, William Howard Taft, who became president in 1909. Because Taft was an Ohio politician, Roosevelt knew that his daughter, who was married to Ohio Congressman Nicholas Longworth, would understand and appreciate his comments on the complexities of the local politics.

Washington, November 10, 1907

Darling Alice:
I was much concerned to learn that you were not well; and very
glad when Mother heard thru Mrs. Longworth that you were better. I hate to think of you so far away from us when you are sick.

A Harvard man named Keys, who I think was a '77 football play-
er and an A.D. man, but whom I would not know if I saw him, sent
me a foolish and impertinent telegram about Cincinnati political
conditions three or four days before the election, which really made
me feel as if he was an outpatient of bedlam. I shall have to find out
from Nick if he is a Roosevelt Club man, and what the Roosevelt
Club has been doing. I wish to Heaven that Taft had never gotten
me into the organization. You are quite right about the Taft movement being hurt by what has happened, especially in Cleveland. I
still think that he is the most likely man for the nomination, and it
may be that the movement for him will spring up with fresh vigor

after he gets home; but I do not think much of Vorys, and in spite of the most explicit talk with him on my part and on Jim Garfield's, in which I explained that while I would prefer to have Taft succeed me rather than anyone else, yet that I certainly could not undertake to dictate his nomination, and that our final action must be determined by disinterested effort to find out who would be the best and most valuable candidate—in spite of this talk he keeps trying to give the impression that I am in honor bound to come out and declare myself for Taft and intend to do so. If I had done anything of the kind hitherto, New York would have been a unit for Hughes; and the worst thing the Taft managers could do would be to make Correlyou get out of a race which he has a perfect right to enter.

Excepting for Cleveland the results of the elections were exceedingly good.

I had a most interesting trip down the Mississippi, and enjoyed my hunt.

Give my love to Nick, Your loving father, TR

[P.S.] If, as I think likely, we now have six or eight months depression, then poor Taft will suffer because he is my close friend and representative, for if times are at all hard many men will, to use the vernacular of our own provincial city, try how they can "vote furdest away from" me.

WOODROW WILSON
TO
JESSIE WOODROW WILSON

𝒲ilson wrote this chatty letter just months after the United States had entered the war against Germany. In the midst of its family news, he comments adversely on a demonstration by the suffragettes at the White House that occurred during a meeting with the

Russian foreign delegation. Jessie was an early advocate of women's suffrage, while the president only came to support the movement in 1916. The suffragette movement successfully used women's vital roles in the war effort and Wilson's idealistic war aims to argue for the Nineteenth Amendment to the Constitution granting women the right to vote.

22 June 1917

My darling Daughter:

Thank you with all my heart for your letter from Siasconset. It eased my heart not a little, and along with it came a letter from Frank in New York which spoke of the arrangements he has been making for the summer, which look as if they were satisfactory as far as one can judge from this distance. At any rate, I am quite willing to trust his choice.

It is delightful to think of you and the little ones successfully transplanted to that quiet place. My heart longs to come up and be with you all, but apparently that is something I must not allow myself to hope for even.

Do let us know, my dear girlie, from time to time how you are all faring, because our hearts will wait anxiously for news. We are all well, over head and ears in work of course but keeping our heads above water by hard swimming. Edith and I have resumed horseback riding and I am sure it is going to do both of us a great deal of good.

I dare say you heard of the fracas raised by the representatives of the Woman's Party here at the gates of the White House. They certainly seem bent upon making their cause as obnoxious as possible.

It was indeed a delight to see you and Frank, and the only trouble of it was that it was too short. Nell was quite broken-hearted that she was not here to see you. Mac is overworking himself as usual and the dear girl is very anxious, but I am depending on Mac's extraordinary powers of recovery. He seems tough in spite of his high-strung nerves.

All unite in sending you and the little ones and Frank messages full to overflowing with love,

Lovingly yours,

ELEANOR RANDOLPH WILSON
TO
WOODROW WILSON

*W*ilson was convalescing from a severe stroke when Eleanor wrote this optimistic letter about the acceptance of the Treaty of Versailles and of American participation in the League of Nations. Wilson had championed the international organization as a means of maintaining peace in the world after World War I, but his incapacitating illness plus strong opposition led by the isolationist Senator Henry Cabot Lodge doomed the acceptance of the treaty in the U.S. Senate. The United States never joined the League of Nations.

Nov. 3rd 1920

Darling, darling Father
I want just to send a line to tell you that I know that this is not a repudiation of the League. Everywhere we went people told us that it was the common belief that Harding would have to give us the League, in spite of what he said—and that the election would be settled on all sorts of entirely different issues. People are stupid, beyond words, but they want the League—the majority—I know it darling Father. And those that don't want it feel that way only because they have been lied to so constantly and so long.

Nothing can destroy what you have done—nothing in the whole wide world.

I love you so much—and I want so much to see you—can I go down soon darling?

With all my love to you both.
Your adoring daughter Nell

WOODROW WILSON
TO
JESSIE WOODROW WILSON

*W*ilson had left the presidency when he wrote this letter to his daughter, but he obviously retained his animosity toward U.S. senator Henry Cabot Lodge.

Washington DC 9th November 1922

My dearest Jessie,

Unhappily it turns out that the defeat of Lodge forecast in your telegraphic message of Tuesday was not verified by the event. But I hope that his reduced majority gave him a jolt which may make even him comprehend the new temper of the voters.

We now have the serious duty of making the best use of our victories.

I am getting along about as usual, and we are looking forward with much satisfaction to seeing you at Thanksgiving.

Edith joins me in warmest love to you all and I am,
With a heart full of love, Your Devoted Father

WILLIAM HOWARD TAFT
TO
HELEN TAFT

*T*aft was Chief Justice of the U.S. Supreme Court and his daughter was writing her doctoral dissertation at Yale University when he wrote this letter about the 1924 presidential campaign, in which he correctly predicted Calvin Coolidge's nomination and the divisions in the Democratic Party that would lead to Coolidge's victory over John W. Davis on November 4, 1924.

My dear Helen:

I sincerely hope that you are getting along successfully with your thesis. I don't expect to hear from you in any lengthy correspondence while this burden is on you. I hope that you have settled down now to a satisfaction with your plan. There is real pleasure, after your plan is adopted, in filling it out and carrying out your general purpose. There is also a great advantage in finishing up what you have on hand. If you let it go for another year, you may want to change the plan and you will fool along, so that it will take you another full year, whereas that ought to be behind you. The project of the book may well take you a long time, but it is wise to get the thesis out of the way.

Since your mother left I had a visit from Mrs. Irving Chase. She telegraphed me from Florida to know whether she could stay over night at the house or else to engage a room for her at the New Willard. I was very glad to have her come and stay, and she left me the next afternoon at 2 o'clock. She lives several months at Palm Beach where she has a house, and where she has made some fortunate speculations. She has the little girls with her part of the time, but Irving, her husband, takes another kind of outing. He goes down into the Carribbean Sea and entertains a party of a dozen people as the host in Jamaica. Mrs. Chase left on Friday and Lucy and Harry Lippitt came on Saturday, and they are with me now. Lucy had to come here to have the oculist look at her eyes, and Harry came here just to take a glance at Washington. Yesterday I furnished Tom to them and they went sightseeing around Washington seeing the things they had not seen when they were here six or eight years. They saw a lot of things they did not know about.

We lunch with the Irvin Laughlins to-day in order that Irvin and Lucy may have a talk. Irvin leaves for Greece to be Minister there, at the end of the month, and of course Lucy's children are interested in the Laughlin business so that they ought to have a talk.

The weather is beautiful. Your mother's cherry blossoms are now blushing out in full luxuriance and one loves to be in Washington at this time.

Coolidge seems to be gathering in the delegates, and in spite of the abuses of Johnson, he goes on toward certain victory in the convention. The Democrats are gathering the hosts but they are in a bad way for a candidate. What between the wets and the drys and between the Klu Klux Klan and the Catholics, the selection of a candidate for them is a matter of very great doubt. McAdoo seems to be still holding a good deal of strength, and while I can not think they will nominate him, he certainly hasn't given up.

All the Democrats seem to think that this dirty police court work is going to prejudice the Republican party and Coolidge,

WILLIAM HOWARD TAFT AND HIS DAUGHTER HELEN, ABOUT THE TIME OF HIS ELECTION TO THE PRESIDENCY IN 1908.

and they may be right about it, but there are evidences that Coolidge continues to be a vote getter, and that people separate him from the environment which made some abuses possible. The new Attorney General and the new Secretary of the Navy are really very excellent appointments. They are both able men and they have a most honorable record. Johnson, the foul-mouthed, is getting what he has long deserved, and as he is being quenched, he continues to emit the same cries with which he was to command the populace, but the populace doesn't now respond.

We are on our last lap in the Supreme Court. We have finished one week of the four weeks of hearings that still remain. I walked to the Capitol every day this week, and on the whole I think I am in fairly good condition, though I speak with due caution.

I had a cable from Ambassador Moore in Madrid last night announcing that they had taken your mother in as a guest of the Embassy, and were very glad to have her—that she had arrived in good health. If she carries out her plan, she leaves Madrid today for a day journey to Cardova and Seville and looks for Maria not tomorrow but next day. It will be a great comfort to have her under Maria's guidance.

Give my love to Fred and the baby, and believe me, as always,
Your loving father, Wm H. Taft

ANNA ROOSEVELT

TO

FRANKLIN D. ROOSEVELT

---

*A*nna had married Clarence John Boettiger and moved to Seattle because her husband had been appointed editor of the Seattle Post Intelligencer. From this vantage point, she often provided political observations to President Roosevelt and often represented him at public events despite public criticism of the William Randolph Hearst–Roosevelt connection.

Benjamin Franklin Hotel.
Seattle Washington Jan. 10th [1937]

Dearest Pa,

I do love my embroidered white jacket from Trinidad and it is a
perfect fit besides. Ever so many thanks!

Ever so many thanks, too, for the picture. It is already framed
and ready to be hung as soon as we get into our house.

The jobs prove more interesting and absorbing, day by day,
and we are loving it. All will be complete when the kids join us
on the 27th—except for the ever present fact that we miss being
able to see you, Ma, Granny and the boys every now and then.

The people as a whole—better known as the peo-pul—out
here are grand. Even the society, with a capital "S" have been very
cordial to us. But, Oh, how this last group resent your November victory, and the local politicians you carried in with you!
They are, of course, extremely wealthy and control most of the
business interests. The few liberals among the business group
keep their views to themselves. It seems to me that this state is
badly in need of a liberal leader someone who is not branded as
"just a politician." It would be grand to get some new blood out
here among the wealthy. Men who would understand and rec-
ognized the labor crowd, and beat the present die-hards at their
own game, and, incidentally temporize some of the "Red" inflence
among the labor crowd, which is the cause of much of the violence, beatings etc.

Our circulation has gone up 3500 over what it was when the
paper was closed last August. Our advertising is doing corre-
spondingly well except in a few cases where the advertisers have
frankly said that they are afraid of us as a New Deal paper!

I have taken advantage of having no house keeping to do, and
have been very busy with some reorganization of our women's
departments, helping with some promotion work, and attending innumerable womens' club's shindigs.

We are really excited at the prospect of meeting Katie and
Ivan and the dogs, bright and early next Thursday morning. We
move into our newly rented domain on Friday. I sent Ma a cou-

ple of pictures of the house and hope she showed them to you. It is low and rambling, with plenty of room and is made of those big, oversized cedar shingles they call "shakes" red here. Our lawn runs down to the Sound and we have a gorgeous view of the Olympic range.

We listened to your message to Congress. It was simply grand and came over beautifully.

Every time I read of one of the journal receptions at the W.H. I think of you and wonder if Mrs. Hehn slipped a couple of hundred extras in to you or if you caught them on the list first!

Loads of love, Sis

ANNA ROOSEVELT

TO

FRANKLIN D. ROOSEVELT

---

*A*nna asked for advice on several political issues in this letter to her father, who was beginning his second term in the White House. Her main concern was an invitation to the dedication of the Golden Gate Bridge.

4315 Semple Street,
Seattle, Washington March 16th. [1937]

Dearest Pa:

Ever so many thanks for the green cigarette case with the little white sloop. It is very much appreciated.

A letter from Ma has just brought me your wire to her saying 'think Anna and John will be invited Golden Gate dedication but have nothing definite'. This, unfortunately does not answer my dilemma! I am enclosing a typical clipping which is just one of many which have been published here. Mr. Brown, who is the gent who called on you in Washington, did come to see me, and told me that you had said to him that you wanted me to represent you at the dedication. I told him that I had not heard from you on the subject, and while I would not think of trying to 'represent' you, as I thought that that was too great an undertaking! I told him in addition that I had been sent a clipping from a paper operated by the longshoreman leader, Mr. Bridges, in which (an editorial) they 'lowed that it would be fine to have you there but that it was just too much to have to put up with a member of your family in the shape of yours truly, and suggested that it would be much better to have you represented by someone official like Jim Farley! John and I realize full well that it will be a grand sight, and we would love to go if you think we should, but don't feel that you must tell us to go because of the publicity as we are as busy as one armed paper hangers, with the itch too, right here in Seattle, and we can still refuse the invitation giving this as an excuse. Will you please, however, let us know your thoughts about it at the earliest moment as I do think that for politeness sake we should let them know as soon as possible

This is the first letter I have written either on the typewriter or longhand in three weeks as I have had a seige of neuritis; but it is about gone now. I blame it all on the huge amount of handshaking I have to do since we came out here! You would honestly get a laugh at the multitudinous invitations both John and I get a week to speak at gatherings of all sorts—shake hands afterwards. You have many many ardent friends out here, and it is surprising to find how far away they feel themselves to be from Washington, D.C. and yet how close they feel to you as a personality. The women, too, think that Ma can do no wrong, and follow her doings avidly from day to day.

I do so hope that you are getting a real rest. The strain of the last weeks have been great, even though you probably would not admit it.

Ever so many thanks for my March the first allowance check. I am putting these checks now into a savings account for the children. They, by the way, are fine. Sis, of course, adjusted herself almost immediately to her new surroundings. Buz has taken a bit longer, particularly in school. But now they are both very happy

and settled. They go to public school—a very good one, new building and fine teachers—and I think that at first Buz found the other boys to be a bit rougher than he was accustomed to.

Things are progressing slowly but surely with the paper. We had the best financial week we have had so far this last week, and both advertising and circulation are growing steadily.

Give our love to Bets and Missy, and loads to you from the four of us. Anna

*A*nna had wanted support for a highway from Washington State to connect with the nearly completed Alaskan Military Highway, but in this letter her father cited practical reasons for the project to be shelved until after World War II. Despite the pressures of the war, the president had found time for fishing, one of his favorite means of recreation.

The White House, Aug. 10, 1943

Dearest Anna:

I have just returned to Washington after a grand six days of fishing in the northern waters of Ontario off Georgian Bay. We got a lot of black bass, several wall-eyed pike and pickerel. I am rested and browned and all ready for the next bout which you will read about by the time you get this.

Mother showed me yours about the connecting highway. It is substantially the same I think as the plan proposed by Slim Williams when he drove his dog team down to the White House seven or eight years ago, and it is undoubtedly the road that eventually will have to be built, together with landing fields along it.

The trouble is that I feel certain nothing can be done about it until after the war. The other route is through but by no means finished and we have not got the manpower.

I think the only thing that Seattle can do about it is to get it listed as one of the major post-war projects—and in the last analysis Congress will decide this—plus the Canadian Government. I am glad people are discussing the through route to Siberia. I feel certain that Siberia is going to be one of the greatest developments to new territory in all history.

I had hoped, as you know, to see you this month but now it does not seem probable that I shall go to the Coast.

Lots of love to the children. I hope the paper survives and does not become too W.R. ish!

Affectionately.

HARRY S. TRUMAN
TO
MARGARET TRUMAN

---

*T*ruman was his plain outspoken self when he wrote this letter to Margaret on the eve of the July 11–15, 1960, Democratic Party Convention in Los Angeles, California. The seventy-six-year-old former president's political sense failed him when he predicted the defeat of John Kennedy by an anti-Catholic coalition.

July 9, 1960

Dear Margie:

Your note of the 4th cost my vest and shirt two buttons' space. Of course your dad's as proud as Punch of your two boys. If someone had been thoughtful enough to hand Kiffie up to me for the other arm we'd have had no difficulty—and no pictures!

I couldn't lean over to pick him up with the other boy holding me down or up.

Looks like I'm in a hell of a fix as regards the Dem. Convention. Old man Joe Kennedy has spent over 4 million dollars to buy the nomination for his son!

Then the anti-pope and the Lutherans, Baptists and Methodists, with the Presbyterians and the Campbellites will beat him. Love from, Dad

HARRY S. TRUMAN WITH HIS DAUGHTER, MARGARET,
WHO IS CASTING HER BALLOT IN A PRIMARY.

LYNDON B. JOHNSON
TO
LYNDA BIRD JOHNSON

---

*J*ohnson had not been president for several years when he wrote this letter to his daughter. However, the content reflects the continued activity undertaken by all retired politicians—attending funerals, club luncheons, and appreciation dinners.

November 19, 1971

Dear Lynda:
We had a strenuous, but enjoyable trip to Rochester, Washington, and New York, and every minute that we loved the most were those you spent with us.

Be sure to tell Lucinda and Cathy that I saw all of Santa Claus' toys in New York, and that I picked out a lot of things I know they will like to have for Christmas.

Yesterday a letter and a newspaper supplement story arrived from one of our Desha relatives in Tennessee. I am having it sent to you and will save it as a surprise until you read the kind of business in which he has been engaged.

Today I am flying to Oklahoma to attend the funeral of Howard Edmondson who was formerly the Governor and then the United States Senator. He was only 46 years old—so much too young to die, but he certainly made the most of all his abilities and opportunities during the little time that he had.

Tonight I go to Greenville, Texas for a much happier occasion—an appreciation dinner for Congressman Ray Roberts given by the Democratic Women's organization of Hunt County.

And tomorrow your mother and I will fly down to Houston to the noon luncheon of the Mayo Alumni Association. I am the guest speaker. Then we fly to Dallas for a dinner the Lawrence Hardings are having for Mary Lasker.

Next week I think I will start on vacation.

Please do send me the names of your friends who would like bookplates. I would love doing this for you.

Tell those darling little girls we look forward to have them come to the ranch for another visit, and they can scurry through the house like little mice all they want to—I enjoy and admire watching inquisitive minds. But I absolutely forbid anybody moving any of my things out of the drawers and off of the tables where I put them.

Thank you for the clipping. That was an expensive journey I made from the Waldorf to Saks!

Your mother is involved this morning with local "beautification." I know she joins me in sending all the love we have to you and your little family, and I will give her your letter to read later.

Your father and best friend, Lbj

RONALD REAGAN
TO
PATRICIA REAGAN

*R*eagan was in his first presidential term when he wrote these two letters to his daughter, Patti, about a "personal private visit" she had arranged for her father with Helen Caldicott, founder of Physicians for Social Responsibility and an outspoken opponent of nuclear weapons. Patti had also become an antinuclear activist, in contrast to her father's stand. UPI later reported that Caldicott spoke about her visit with Reagan and said that Reagan claimed the United States could win a nuclear war against the Soviet Union.

[c. December 1982]

Dear Patti:

We've had to go to the Kennedy Center. As you know I've been in South America and only got in late last night when I discovered our meeting has been moved to 5:15 tomorrow afternoon. Had you been notified of this? If not can you let Dr. Caldicott know?

We'll meet downstairs in the library instead of the office—no interruptions there.

Patti I think we should keep this a personal private visit. I won't be saying anything to the press about it and I don't think you or the doctor should either. That way they can't get into any stories about family disagreements etc.

We'll see you later. Love, Dad

RONALD REAGAN
TO
PATRICIA REAGAN

May 23, 1983

Dear Patti:

The enclosed appeared in today's Washington Post. It has caused quite a stir in the press. Of course no such conversation took place nor have I had any conversation with her since we met in December. And as you know her words about my believing we could win a nuclear war were never part of that visit in December (I don't believe such a thing). So her speech is a complete falsehood both as to having a conversation with me at all and as to the subject of the supposed conversation.

Patti it isn't easy to learn we've misplaced our faith and trust in someone. I know. I've had that experience—once with someone I thought was my closest friend. But when it happens we must be prepared to accept it and not shut our eyes to the truth.

There was a time in ancient days when a messenger bringing bad news was put to death. I hope you won't call for my execution. I'm afraid the doctor is so carried away by her cause she subscribes to the belief that the end justifies the means. Such a belief if widespread would mean the end of civilization.

Love, Dad

Strassburg i. E. den August 1902
Bahnhofplatz.

(Wm. H. Taft)

Dear Pappa:

We just have raced all this week and haven't had time to do anything else. We have been to Dresden, Weimar, Eisenach, Nuremberg, Rotenberg and Strassburg all this week.

The Andersons have just left, and we leave at four for Baden Baden where we expect to stay about two weeks.

The Andersons have gone to Paris and from there I think they are going to Tours.

We stayed almost a week at Dresden part of the time the Andersons were there but the last part they went to Berlin. We saw the Picture gallery the Green Vault, the Johanneum and took an all day trip a mountain called the Bastei from which we got a beautiful view of The Elbe. We went part way in a train and they took a large wagon but Rob, Maria & I and I walked most of the way as it was up hill. In going back we went to several different places

CHAPTER 9

OVERSEAS VENTURES: "SOME VERY DECIDED STEP"

> *"I fear that we shall have to take some very decided step,"*
> —Woodrow Wilson to Jessie Wilson,
> August 21, 1915

> *"The prospect of war alarms me much;"*
> —Abigail Adams to John Adams,
> April 29, 1794

> *"I am curious to hear of your Philippine experiences."*
> —Theodore Roosevelt to Alice Lee Roosevelt,
> September 2, 1905

JOHN ADAMS
TO
ABIGAIL ADAMS

---

*A*s vice president, Adams wrote this insightful letter to his daughter, during the height of the foreign policy crises sparked by the undiplomatic actions of the French minister to the United States, Edmond Charles Genet. President Washington was struggling to hold a neutral course for the U.S. when Genet publicly threatened to involve his nation in the internal politics of the United States to secure American support against Great Britain.

Philadelphia, December 14, 1793

My Dear Daughter:
I thank you for your kind letter of the tenth of this month.

Mr. G[enet]. may well be shocked at the Message. It is a thunderbolt. I cannot but feel something like an apology for him, as he was led into some of his enterprises by the imprudence of our fellow-citizens. The extravagant court paid to him by a party, was enough to turn a weak head. The enthusiasm and delirium of that party has involved us, and will involve us, in more serious difficulties than a quarrel with a Minister. There is too much reason to fear that the intemperance of that party has brought upon us an Algerine war, and may compromise us with all the maritime powers of Europe.

It is a very difficult thing for a man to go into a foreign country, and among a strange people, and there act a prompt and sudden part upon a public political theatre, as I have severely felt in France, Holland, and England; and if he does not keep his considering cap always on his head, some party or some individual will be very likely to seduce him into snares and difficulties. This has been remarkably mr. G's unhappy case. Opposition to the laws, and endeavors to set the people against the government, are too gross faults to be attempted with impunity in any country.

The scandalous libel on the President, in a New-York paper, is a proof to me, that foreign politics have had too much secret influence in America; indeed, I have known enough of it for fifteen years to dread it; but this desperate effort of corrupt factions, is more than I expected to see so soon.

Present my love to my two dear boys. You have a great charge upon you, my dear child, in the education of these promising children. As they have not had the regular advantages of public schools, your task in teaching them literature must be the more severe. A thirst for knowledge early excited, will be one of the best preservatives against that dissipation and those irregularities which produce the ruin of so many young men; at the same time that it will prompt them to acquire those accomplishments which are the only solid and useful ones, whether they are destined to any of the liberal professions, to the gallant career of soldiers, or to the useful employments of merchandise and agriculture.

Your mamma complains that she has not received a letter from you in a long time. Remember me to Colonel Smith. Your affectionate, J. Adams

---

ABIGAIL ADAMS
TO
JOHN ADAMS

---

*P*resident Washington dispatched U.S. Chief Justice John Jay to London to negotiate a treaty with Great Britain in an attempt to prevent war over a wide range of issues including impressment, the return of captured slaves, the continued occupation of British forts in America's West, and the seizures of American ships. Abigail was right to worry about the results of Jay's mission, as Jay's treaty subsequently badly divided the nation and provided the springboard for Thomas Jefferson's presidential candidacy in 1796.

New York, April 29th, 1794

My Dear Father:
Your letter of the 21st of March, has lain by me some time.

The prospect of a war alarms me much; many persons express their apprehensions respecting the safety of this town in particular—supposing that in case of a war, it would be of great consequence for the British to have possession of it, and presuming they will attempt to invade it; but I hope they will find other objects to engage their attention, and that we shall be permitted to enjoy peace, however little we may merit its continuance.

Our fortifications do not proceed with much rapidity. I cannot but lament that the Baron Steuben has been wholly unnoticed; he would have considered it as complimentary, if he had been appointed to superintend the buildings, and I believe would be allowed by the best judges, to be as capable of the business as those who are honoured with the attentions of the President.

I hope Congress will not continue in session until the approach of the hot weather, or, if they are obliged to, that they will adjourn out of that uncomfortable city. I shall be distressed from an apprehension of the return of the fever.

Do you, my dear sir, flatter yourself with the idea, that the mission of Mr. Jay will secure to us the blessings of peace? He is to carry the olive branch in one hand, and the sword of defence in the other. I wish the former may soothe, and the latter strike them with terror; but I fear that we are too incapable of exciting their apprehensions on the subject of self-interest; and until they find us necessary to their prosperity, they will not pay us much respect. I not only wish the cause prosperity, but I wish Mr. Jay, individually, success. I confess I do not feel very sanguine upon the subject.

From the debates in the British Parliament, we find that the opposition make honourable mention of our government, and of the President's measures; but the opposition does not gain much strength or many numbers, and there are so many persons interested in the support of their government, that the minister is generally sure of carrying his points.

Will you be so good as to let me know when you think it probable that you shall return?

Yours, affectionately, A. Smith

ULYSSES S. GRANT
TO
ELLEN GRANT

ℱ̲ormer President Grant was on the final leg of his two-year odyssey around the world when he wrote this letter about his "very delightful" visit to Japan. He and Mrs. Grant were overwhelmed by the open and lavish receptions they received during this trip; however, his appreciation for the Japanese was not widely shared in Europe and America. Shortly after his return, the Grants spent the winter months in Cuba and Mexico before settling for a time in New York City.

Tokio, Japan August 10th, 79

Dear Daughter:

We are now nearly through our visit to this interesting country, and ready to start home. We sail on the 27th of this month for San Francisco. We expect to meet Buck & Ida there, and possibly Jesse. Our visit here has been very delightful. The Country is beautiful abounding in green mountains, beautiful & highly cultivated vallies, clear mountain streams & picturesque Waterfalls. The people are docile & intelligent as well as industrious and frugal. Education is now becoming universal both among the Mails & females. The Country is advancing beyond all precedent. How the government & the people retain their temper and Kind treatment to the foreigners under the insults heaped upon them and overbearing and bullying policy of the foreigners and their diplomatic representatives I cannot understand. The Course of the average Minister, Consul & Merchant in this Country & behavior towards the native is much like the Course of the former slave owner towards the freedmen when the latter attempts to think for himself in matters of choice of Candidates. The present policy towards these two countries cannot continue much longer without a terrible Calamity and one that will fall heavy upon life and property. I hope there will be a speedy change. We should change the most of our representatives in these two Countries. Not our Minister here however.

Your Ma will send from here by express a double gown—silk—which she has got for you. It should arrive soon after this. We will stop a few weeks in the Pacific Coast and visit Oregon & Washington Territory. On the Way east we will stop a few days at Virginia City, Nevada, a few days at Salt Lake, and go from Chienne to Denver where I will leave your Ma & Ida while I and the boys go to Leadville, the New Eldorado. When we leave there we will go directly to our house in Galena. What we will do for the winter is not yet determined. But if your Ma is willing we will go to Havanna & Mexxico. Your Ma & Fred join me in love to you Algie & the children, Remember me also to Mr. & Mrs. Sartoris.

Yours Affectionately, U. S. Grant

ELLEN GRANT WITH HER MOTHER, JULIA, HER GRANDFATHER, FREDERICK DENT, AND HER BROTHER, JESSE.

*T*aft was serving as governor-general of the Philippines, and his eleven-year-old daughter was on a "grand tour" around the world with her brothers and mother, when these letters were exchanged.

Salzburg July 28 [1902]

Dear Papa:

Nothing very much has happened since I saw you last so I have not very much to say.

We got to Venice safely and I thought it is beautiful.

I think St. Marks is really prettier than St. Peters though of coarse it is not half so large.

The first evening we were there we went to St. Marks Square but it is really spoiled by the falling of the campanile at least so Mama says. When we were going into the Church an old guide came up and offered us his services for half a franc saying that the Church would be closed the next fifty days (which was all a lie). So Mama took him and after dragging us around the Church full speed he dragged us into a mosaic shop all the time saying he was taking us to the School of the Church and Mama had to give him a franc to get away.

The next morning we went to the Palace of the Doges which I think one of the handsome buildings in Europe, but I got very tired walking all around there was so much in it. That afternoon we took a trip up the Grand Canal to look at the palaces some of which are very handsome.

The next morning we went to two or three churches. One of these was Santa Maria Formossa which contains the picture of Santa Barbara which I think is the prettiest picture in Venice.

That afternoon we went to the Lido and had a lovely bath. Mama did not go in and when it was time for us to come out she came down to the [Lido] to call us and not being able to [reach] us she became very frightened and went to call a girl and if I hadn't come in just then I don't know what she wouldn't have done.

But its way past bedtime and so I must stop with much love from your loving Helen.

Malaoañan Palace. Sept. 24, 1902

My dear Helen:

I write to thank you for sending me your two nice letters. I think your spelling in one or two instances was original, that is different from the way most of us spell, but I was able to understand what you meant, even if you did not follow Mr. Noah Webster in his dictionary. I hope that you and Robert and the Baby have had a good time on your trip around the world and that you have not troubled your Mother or made her regret that you did not come with me.

The deer was taken away from the grounds when we left and is now in the Zoological garden, but Mr. Carpenter says that he is going to get it and bring it back. The palace has been painted and decorated since we left, but I am not quite sure how your Mother will like it. Major General and Mrs. Chaffee and Mrs. Wright are going to leave next Tuesday on the Transport McClellan going by way of Suez to New York, and I found it necessary therefore to give them a reception on Monday the 29th. I shall have about twelve hundred persons, perhaps more than that. The food for the company has been turned over to the cook to furnish. He is going to get Chinese boys and thinks that he can do it all himself. I have had bought for Malaoañan extra plates and knives and forks and spoons and cups and saucers. I employed a decorator to string lanterns around and he is working on the floors which were in a bad condition owing to the refitting of the house. I am going to have an orchestra of thirty-five musicians and if there is room enough we will have a dance. I am hoping and praying that it will not rain, but this is the rainy season and I fear my prayer may not be answered. Tell Charlie that Josè and Capito are still here and waiting to see him. The gardener wants to know about him and Dominga is just waiting to come back and be his nurse. Dorothy Baldwin is waiting anxiously to see you. I occasionally meet a number of boys and girls riding on the Luneta. I do not think you will find a very great change from when you were here before and that you will easily slide into the old life. I hope that you will have a pleasant passage on the Rosetta Maru which is the largest boat that runs between Hongkong and Manila. She does not run to Australia, but makes the Hongkong trip in forty-eight hours. It may necessitate your waiting in Hongkong two or three days, but I think you can rest there and it is a great deal better to come over in a big steamer than in a small one at this season.

Tell your Mother that Mrs. Worcester expects to give her a reception three or four days after she arrives here. The Times has notices of coming events and has kept in that column the fact that Mrs. Taft is expected to arrive in Manila the first week in October. I understand there are other entertainments awaiting her in the shape of dinners and receptions. I have had so much of this going out at nights that I do not know whether I can go through it all again. Still less certain am I that your Mother ought to. Things are quiet here and are going along fairly well. The amount of work is not at all less than what it was and for four or five months it will be a constant pressure. Judge Smith has left us because he wished to go to a house of his own; so that Mr. Carpenter and I are all alone and we feel very much the need of a family. I hope that Mr. Gifford Pinchot will find you all. He is a very pleasant gentleman, a Yale man, and I am sure will do everything that is needed to make you all comfortable. He is on his way to Manila to look at the forests, for he is the Chief forester of the United States. Tell your Mother that she might very well buy some more wicker chairs to make things look homelike. But I must stop now.

I send love to Mama, Robert and Charlie. If I am not mistaken, you ought to be here so that we shall have dinner together two weeks from tonight, possible you may be here the night before. I sincerely hope so.

Good-night dear, Your loving father,

[P.S.] Your mother might very well invest in some rough bath towelling.

THEODORE ROOSEVELT
TO
ALICE LEE ROOSEVELT

---

*A*mong Roosevelt's noted achievements was his negotiation of peace between Russia and Japan during the Russo-Japanese War. In this remarkable letter to his eldest daughter, the president details his strategy and tactics in securing a negotiated end to the war in the Treaty of Portsmouth, for which Roosevelt received the Nobel Peace Prize in 1906.

Oyster Bay, September 2, 1905

Dear Alice:

I hope you will enjoy your Chinese trip. I am curious to hear of your Philippine experiences.

Well, I have had a pretty vigorous summer myself and by no means a restful one, but I do not care in the least, for it seems now that we have actually been able to get peace between Japan and Russia. I have had all kinds of experiences with the envoys and with their Governments, and to the two latter I finally had to write time after time as a very polite but also very insistent

Dutch Uncle. I am amused to see the way in which the Japanese kept silent. Whenever I wrote a letter to the Czar the Russians were sure to divulge it, almost always in a twisted form, but the outside world never had so much as a hint of any letter I sent to the Japanese. The Russians became very angry with me during the course of the proceedings because they thought I was only writing to them. But they made the amends in good shape when it was over, and the Czar sent me the following cable of congratulation, which I thought rather nice of him:

"Accept my congratulations and warmest thanks for having brought the peace negotiations to a successful conclusion, owing to your personal energetic effort. My country will gratefull recognize the great part you have played in the Portsmouth peace conference."

It has been a wearing summer, because I have had not Secretary of State and have had to do all the foreign business myself, and as Taft has been absent I have also had to handle everything connected with Panama myself. For the last three months the chief business I have had has been in connection with the peace business, Panama, Venezuela, and Santo Domingo, and about all of these matters I have had to proceed without any advice or help.

It is enough to give anyone a sense of sardonic amusement to see the way in which the people generally, not only in my own country but elsewhere, guage the work purely by the fact that it succeeded. If I had not brought about peace I should have been laughed at and condemned. Now I am overpraised. I am credited with being extremely longheaded etc. As a matter of fact I took the position I finally did not of my own volition but because events so shaped themselves that I would have felt as if I was flinching from a plain duty if I had acted otherwise. I advised the Russians informally to make peace on several occasions last winter, and to this they paid no heed. I had also consulted with the Japanese, telling them what I had told the Russians. It was undoubtedly due to the Japanese belief that I would act squarely that they themselves came forward after their great naval victory and asked me to bring about the conference, but not to let it be known that they had made the suggestion—so of course this is not to be spoken about. Accordingly I undertook the work and of course got the assent of both Governments before I took any public action. Then neither Government would consent to meet where the other wished and the Japanese would not consent to meet at the Hague, which was the place I desired. The result was that they had to meet in this country, and this necessarily threw me into a position of prominence which I had not sought and indeed which I had sought to avoid—though I feel now that unless they had met here they would never have made peace. They met, and after a while came to a deadlock, and I had to intervene again by getting into direct touch with the Governments themselves. It was touch and go, but things have apparently come out right. I say "apparently," because I shall not feel entirely easy until the terms of peace are actually signed. The Japanese people have been much less wise than the Japanese Government, for I am convinced that the best thing for Japan was to give up trying to get any indemnity. The Russians would not have given it; and if the war had gone on the Japanese would simply have spent—that is wasted and worse than wasted—hundreds of millions of dollars additional without getting back what they had already paid out.

At present we are having a house party for Ted and Ethel. Ted and Ethel count themselves as the two first guests, and then, by the way of a total change, Steve and Cornelia Landon, and finally Jack Thayer and Martha Bacon. Today is rainy and I look forward with gloomy foreboding to a play in the barn with the smallest folks this afternoon. Mother and I have had lovely rides and rows together. I chop a good deal and sometimes play tennis. I am still rather better than James Roosevelt and Jack.

Give my regards to all who are with you and thank the Griscoms especially for their hospitality. Your loving father. TR

*A*lice was on her honeymoon with her husband, Nicholas Longworth, when she received this missive from her father. Roosevelt's discussion of the diplomatic and political implications of the couple's honeymoon trip shows that, for presidential family members, politics are never out of mind.

Washington, June 24, 1906

Darling Alice:

I have just cabled Nick that if he and you go to Austria and stop at Vienna, I want you to stop, however briefly, at Budapest. With this end in view, write to Count Apponyi or wire him through our Ambassador, Francis. The Count has written me urging that he be given the chance of seing you both, and that you stop in Budapest so that you shall not seem to ignore Hungary and pay heed only to Austria. If you go to Austria and Hungary I should avoid stopping either at Vienna or Budapest, or else I should stop at both; and if you do go let you and Nick listen smilingly to anything that anyone, from an Austrian archduke to a Hungarian count, says about the politics of the dual empire, but, as I need hardly add, make no comment thereon yourselves. Of course you many not be going to Austria at all, in which case all this is needless. I hope you will go to Paris; and indeed I take it for granted that you will.

Also, I feel that after you have been back a little while it would be a good thing for you to go to Cincinnati for a short time. Tell Nick I think his people will like to feel that you have a genuine interest in the city and come out there to make yourself one of Nick's people. I have been watching very carefully to see if there are any symptoms of this European trip having hurt Nick at home. So far I have failed to find any; but of course his opponents will do all they can to make it injure him, and though so far you and he have carried yourselves so that no excuse has been offered for criticism, still I think it would be just as well for you to make a visit to Cincinnati while Nick's canvass was on.

Apparently you have both had a great time. I took sardonic pleasure in the fearful heartburnings caused the American colony in London, and especially among the American women who had married people of title, by the inability of the Reids to have everybody to everything. Nothing was more delightful than the fact that some of the people who were not asked to the dinner, but who were asked to the reception, hotly refused to attend the latter. The Americans of either sex who live in London and Paris, and those who marry titled people abroad, are, taking them by and large, a mighty poor lot of shoats, and the less you and Nick see of them the better I am pleased. Of course there are exceptions, who are as nice as possible.

I have been having a series of rough-and-tumble fights in the closing days of Congress, but it looks as if we were coming out pretty well. All the children are at Oyster Bay, where Ethel is bossing the entire family, to their profit and her pleasure. Mother and I have had lovely times here. We breakfast and lunch on the portico and dine on the west terrace, unless the weather is bad, and we have lovely rides together. Your loving father TR

WOODROW WILSON
TO
JESSIE WOODROW WILSON

---

*W*ilson struggled to maintain U.S. neutrality in the face of the ever-increasing toll of the German submarine campaign. In this letter to his daughter, the president poignantly juxtaposes the difficulties of keeping the United States out of the war with its impact on a planned family get-together and his concern for his grandson's teething difficulties.

The White House. 21 August. 1915

My precious Jessie,

Another week has gone by, and, alas! has brought a new evidence of the critical difficulties that are in our way in keeping this country out of the war. The case of the Arabic seems to me in a way worse than that of the Lusitania because none of the excuses they alleged in her case seem to have been present in this. I fear that we shall have to take some very decided step, probably the severance of diplomatic relations with Germany. I am awaiting the full facts before making up my mind, of course.

One of the things that distresses me about the matter is, that it will be likely keep me in Washington. I had planned to be in Cornish next Saturday. I had set my heart on it. And now it is doubtful when, if at all, I can get away. I know that you will understand, but that does not make it any less of a real and great disappointment.

The enclosed is an extract of a letter from Edith, and is so sweet an indication of her feeling that I thought she would not mind my sending it just as she wrote it, for you and Margaret to read. Will you not send it to Nellie the next time you send her a letter? I know now that Edith never says a word of this kind that she does not mean down to the bottom of her heart.

I think of you all constantly, my darling little daughter. I hope that, if Frank is really teething the poor little chap will be relieved presently by the teeth coming through. Are there any further or clearer indications? Frank, Sr. will be back, when?
Please tell dear Margaret how I loved her letter to me. It brought me some very happy thoughts.

Give my dearest love to Sister Annie, little Annie, Josephine, and to my precious Margaret. You are all very much in my heart.

I am well, chiefly, I think, because I am so generously loved.

Your loving,

JESSIE WOODROW WILSON
TO
WOODROW WILSON

$\mathcal{W}$ilson was in the midst of his fight to secure approval of the League of Nations when Jessie wrote this letter praising him for staying "the right course." He suffered his worst political defeat when the League of Nations was rejected by the U.S. Senate and he also suffered a major stroke during his fight for the League.

May 4th [1919]

Dearest, dearest Father,
Have you time in the immense pressure of events over there to read just a wee note of love and adoring reverence from your little daughter over here? Oh I can't tell you how my heart beats

with exulting pride and joy at every word you say and at everything you do. And I know you will win out. I don't see how anyone can stand out against the right course when it is so simply and clearly put. It must be an intense strain but I know that you don't allow yourself to think of that or even to feel it. You are sustained, I know, by thousands and hundreds of thousands of loving confident yearning prayers both here and over there.

Our little family is flourishing here. Woodrow is not as fat as he should be. When you caught cold he followed suit and is only beginning to gain now. But he is good as gold and no trouble at all.

The children are adorable with him and so careful of him and helpful, eager to run errands and to help in other ways with him.

We leave here in about a month now for Martha's Vineyard, a whole afternoon nearer mainland than S'conset is, because Frank has to teach here all summer. We are very near Margaret and Lewis Perry, and right on the water's edge with beautiful bathing right there are our steps. It looks most promising and we are eager to begin.

Perhaps we shall see the Mayflower at the Vineyard Haven dock some fine day this summer. Wouldn't that be jolly. And we might arrange for the Christening there, but all that's unimportant and premature just now.

Frank joins me in dearest love to Edith and your darling darling self, my dear dear Father.

Ever your own little girl Jessie

The United States was beginning its withdrawal from the active internationalism of Woodrow Wilson when U.S. Supreme Court Chief Justice Taft wrote this highly informative letter to his daughter, who was completing her doctorate in American History at Yale University.

Supreme Court of the United States.
October 28, 1923

My dear Helen:

Another week has rolled around, and I hope you have made progress on your book. I have been able to write four opinions, and while I haven't a baby on hand, I am sitting for a picture, which is something of an interruption. I shall be glad to show you the picture and get your judgment on it when you come with the baby. I am sure that the baby has not any artistic judgment, but possibly you have, though you did not inherit it from me.

We have been a good deal with Lloyd George this week and have enjoyed his visit very much. He is a most interesting character. I am not sure that he is not the most interesting character in the World to-day from the standpoint of politics, although for the time being he is quite out of the running in Great Britain. Still the present government is getting into shoals and quicksands and they have a way of turning over in Great Britain just as they have here. Politics here in Washington is full of guessing, full of wonder at what the Congress is going to do and how far the Radicals and Progressives are going to be able to make themselves affirmatively felt. They hold the balance of power, but that in an important possession to defeat legislation rather than to put it through. What Brockhart would call the corrupt hordes of capital are much more content with legislation that is on the statute book than La Follette and his followers, and it seems to me as if they were going to find it a very much more difficult thing to get legislation off the statute book than it is to prevent its going on.

Coolidge seems to be making headway by keeping his mouth shut, only saying things when he has them to say. Hughes' communications on the subject of reparations, especially the last one, have produced a great impression in the country and in Europe. Lloyd George was especially delighted with them. How far they may be effective with France, and how far the movement may solve what has seemed up to now insoluble, are questions of course for the future. We shall hear in the Congress a great deal of protest from Hiram Johnson and others of the Senate who were the irreconcilables, but I rather think the country is strongly with Hughes in his present position.

The dinners are gradually beginning, and I am going to have a struggle to confine them to one a week. I like to go Monday night. Indeed that is about the only night in the week when I can go and not lose time, but your mother says that Monday is a bad night for dinners, because the markets are not so good Monday morning. But when a woman writes us and says she would like to give us a dinner between certain dates, I don't see why I can not select Monday, and why she can not keep her things over Saturday night. It may require a little more refrigerating, but if we are content with the result, I don't see why she should object.

We had a letter from Lucy asking for your address, from which I infer that she expects to come down perhaps and see one of the games and visit the boys, so you may expect here.

George Seymour wrote he had had you and Fred at a dinner with John Burton Adams, and enjoyed it much. I hope you saw all George's interesting things and are now competent to tell whether a piece of furniture was made in the 16th, 17th or 18th century. But I must stop and go to church.

Your loving father, Wm H. Taft

[P.S.] Lucy writes that Annie Rorther who, wrote you, had broken her hip, is very sick with kidney trouble.

HARRY S. TRUMAN
TO
MARGARET TRUMAN

*T*ruman was just months into his presidency when he went to Potsdam for critical post-European war talks with Churchill and Stalin. In the midst of the conference, Prime Minister Churchill was replaced in British elections by Clement Atlee. Truman conveys a colorful account of this in a letter to his twenty-one-year-old daughter.

Berlin July 29, 1945

Dear Margie:

It was sure nice to talk to you and Mamma night before last, or yesterday morning here.

I had been sitting around all day waiting for the British to come. The pouch came in about 10 A.M., and there were letters in it! One from you, two from Mother, and one from Aunt Mary. So I had a field day. I know you and Janice must have had a nice time, but considering the heat wave and everything you can probably get more sleep without a guest. Glad you went to see Aunt Mary and your grandmother. I suppose your Cousin Harry is at home by this time.

I have been able to help out a lot of soldiers since coming over here. The bread they were giving them was terrible. I sent Mr. Canfil to make an inspection and you should have seen it straighten out.

The British finally arrived at 9:30 p.m. yesterday. Mr. Atlee is not so keen as old fat Winston, and Mr. Bevin looks rather rotund to be a Foreign Minister. Seems Bevin is sort of the John L. Lewis type. Eden was a perfect striped pants boy. I wasn't fond of Eden—he is a much overrated man; and he didn't play fair with his boss.

I did like old Churchill. He was as windy as old Langer, but he knew his English language, and after he'd talked half an hour, there'd be at least one gem of a sentence and two thoughts maybe, which could have been expressed in four minutes. But if we ever got him on record, which was seldom, he stayed put. Anyway, he is a likeable person, and these two are sourpusses.

Atlee is an Oxford graduate and talks with that deep-throated swallowing enunciation, same as Eden does. But I understand him reasonably well. Bevin is a tough guy. He doesn't know, of course, that your dad has been dealing with that sort all his life, from building trades to coal miners. So he won't be new.

Marshal Stalin and Molotov are coming to see me this morning. I am hoping we can get things in shape so we can quit about Tuesday. If we do, I may be home a week from Today—and how I'll like it. The next thing I'll want are a couple of truants back in the White House.

Kiss your mamma for me and lots & lots of 'em for you.
Dad
OOOOOOOOOOOOOOOOOOO
XXXXXXXXXXXXX

HARRY S. TRUMAN
TO
MARGARET TRUMAN

---

*T*ruman wrote this letter to Margaret explaining his public denunciation of the Soviet Union and Communism. As usual, he added some parental instructions about the need to "learn self-discipline."

Key West, Florida. March 13, 1947

Dear Margie:

We had a very pleasant flight from Washington. Your old dad slept for 750 or 800 miles—three hours—and we were making 250 to 300 miles an hour. No one not even me (your mother would say I) knew how very tired and worn to a frazzle the chief executive had become. This terrible decision I had to make had been over my head for about six weeks. Although I knew at Potsdam that there is no difference in totalitarian or police states, call them what you will, Nazi, Fascist, Communist or Argentine Republics. You know there never was but one idealistic example of communism. That is described in the Acts of the Apostles.

The attempt of Lenin, Trotsky, Stalin et al. to fool the world and the American crackpots' association, represented by Joe Davies, Henry Wallace, Claude Pepper and the actors and artists in immoral Greenwich Village, is just like Hitler's and Mussolini's so called socialist states.

Your pop had to tell the world just that in polite language.

Now in addition to that terrible—and it is terrible—decision, your good old 94–year-old grandmother of the 1860 generation was unlucky and broke her leg—you—the "apple of my eye"—my sweet baby always had bad luck with your first appearance. Well daughter the dice roll—sometimes they are for you—sometimes they are not. But I earnestly believe they were for you this time. I

HARRY S. TRUMAN AND HIS DAUGHTER, MARGARET, DEPART ON A TRIP.

am just as sure as I can be that Sunday night at 8:00 p.m. another great soprano will go on the air. So don't worry about anything—just go on and sing as you sang that "Home Sweet Home" record for your dad—and nothing can stop you—even the handicap of being the Daughter of President Truman!

Then you come back to the White House and let me arrange a nice warm rest for you and your lovely mamma and we'll go on from there.

You must learn self-discipline—that is you must eat what you should, drink what you should,—and above all sleep at night and always give people the benefit of good intentions until they are proven bad. Don't put your comfort and welfare above those around you. In other words be a good commonsense Missouri woman—daughter of your mother—in my opinion the greatest woman on earth—I want you to be second.

More love than you can realize now. Dad

MARGARET TRUMAN

TO

HARRY S. TRUMAN

---

*M*argaret was on a trip to Europe when she wrote this excited letter about her experiences in Sweden and Norway.

Helsinki & Oslo [August 23, 1951]

Dear Daddy

Now I am making a valiant effort to keep my temper under control and I have simmered down somewhat! I believe your Ambassador in Stockholm is about as stupid and pompous an ass as I have ever seen. Having a man with so little mental poise in a position of trust like that is frightening. I am speaking of course of that silly incident involving the S.[ecret] S.[ervice]

boys. I didn't get exercised over it until Butterworth tried to throw them to the wolves to save his own skin. He didn't bother to ask me about it, but began apologizing to the Foreign Office and anyone else who would listen. He lost his head completely because and now comes the real heart of the matter the incident as reported by the press did not occur. No photog was threatened, in fact he was told that nobody would stop him from taking a picture at the Town Hall, but that I was inside and it might be difficult. That is all that was said. The thing mushroomed because without asking anyone the facts Butterworth got scared. He had the chance to embarrass the United States and the man running for reelection as Prime Minister. It's funny because the PM is not particularly pro-American and the two things don't go together! The press man at the Embassy was also totally inadequate. Fortunately the S.S. boys kept their heads or it would have been much worse. B. wanted them to apologize, which would have been ridiculous. The crux of it is that as reported nothing of the kind happened. I can't stress that enough. Now wait 'till I get home, and I am quite serious, I want to talk with you and Mr. Acheson together. I hate to bother you with this but I have never seen firsthand before a man in high position try to put the blame on the little man who couldn't fight back, namely the S.S. boys. I get sick and tired of them and they make mistakes, but I will not sit calmly by and listen to a complete lie about a situation which was the fault of the chief of the mission.

Stockholm was a beautiful city, but that Town Hall wasn't worth the trouble it caused. We had a wonderful boat ride to Helsinki and a huge crowd cheered us off the boat. There were some Americans on the boat. Helsinki is a bright, clean-looking city. The Legation is quite nice and the Cabots are very hospitable. Everything has gone fine here thanks to the a capable Ambassador & a fine Press Attaché. Now I have been carrying this in my case for two days so I'd calm down even more before sending it. Goodness knows you have enough important troubles without having any from me. However, I still believe Butterworth and his

attachés to be to blame for the whole thing by their pusillani-
mous attitude. I changed some of this letter and I'm sorry it's so
messy, but I haven't the strength to copy it.

Give it to 'em on sept. 1st and show everybody who's still on
top and in control of the situation. I see you and Mother are going
to Europe without me next year. I have news for you, you just try
to take that whole trip without me! Please, I'd like to come.

See you next weekend. Lots of love Margie

JULIE NIXON
TO
RICHARD M. NIXON

---

*J*ulie sent her father this supportive note on foreign affairs after he had delivered a national television address following an American led "incursion" into
Cambodia. Nixon was trying to once again to explain American actions, intentions,
and goals in Vietnam.

[April 30, 1970]

Dear Daddy,
I was very proud of you tonight. You explained the situation in
Vietnam perfectly—I am sure the American people will realize
why you made your decision. I especially want to tell you how
effective—and heartfelt—your final message to the people of
South and North Vietnam, the Soviet Union, and the United
States was. I feel that the strongest message which resulted from
your speech was: We cannot abandon 17 million people to a living death, and we cannot jeopardize the chances for future world
peace by an unqualified pullout of Vietnam.

I know you are right and, again, I am so proud.

Love, Julie

My dear Papa,

I was very sorry
to have you go away but of course
you had to. Papa the old white
hen has hatched some of the
little chickens but I saw an
egg which had some of the
shell broken off and I guess
she will come off all right.
Miss Mays is not feeling
well a bit she was laying
down almost all day. Irwin
went to Hiram today with
Grandpa and Grandma.
Hal took the grey horses to
be shod in Painsville this

CHAPTER 10

AT HOME: "THOSE COMFORTS WHICH LONG HABIT HAS RENDERED NECESSARY..."

"The men are going to begin the barn tomorrow,"
—Mary (Mollie) Garfield to James Garfield,
May 28, 1877

*"The way you take care of the
children and keep down the expenses and cook
bread and are just your own blessed busy cunning self"*
—Theodore Roosevelt to Ethel C. Roosevelt,
June 21, 1904

WHEN PRESIDENTS and their spouses were in the nation's capital, their children—particularly daughters—were often expected to maintain the family home and business. The limits of travel in the nineteenth century often contributed to such familial arrangements.

*J*efferson's eldest daughter often acted as her father's hostess at Monticello and as the voice of authority during his political absences. In this letter, she covers a wide range of plantation-related issues.

Edgehill Nov 30, 1804

My Dearest Father

Lilly was here a fortnight ago to beg I would write to you immediately about some business of his, but a change in the post day disappointed me in sending the letters written to have gone by it. he says you desired him to part with 100 barrils of corn as more than you required, but he say he has got it on very good terms 16 and 16, 6 a barril and that there is not one bushell too much, on account of the heavy hauling he has to do. he says if the horses are not highly fed they will not be able to do the work and he thinks Anderson from whom some of it was purchased will wait till the first of February for his money. after recieving your letter he went to see Moran about the double payment that had been made, he pretended he knew nothing about it but that he would see Irving and it should be rectified, and that Lilly should hear from him in a fortnight. the time has past without hearing from him and he fears he is gone to Kentucky. he is obliged to give up K. Smiths negros' tomorrow as he wished to get all the work possible out of them before they went. he defered going after Irving till their time was out, when he will immediately see him. the man that run away the first of August has never been recovered. he begged me also to speak particularly about John. he is utterly averse to the idea of having any thing to say to him another year. his conduct is such that there can be nothing like honesty or subordination where he is. his wish is that he should be sent off the plantation and indeed the instances of depravity that he mentioned in him, his art in throwing every thing into confusion, encouraging the hands to rebellion and idleness and then telling upon them so as to put Lilly out of his senses allmost, are beyond conception. he says that John has frequently created such confusion by his art as to render it impossible to punish the very hands of whom he complained most, and pieces of ill will and mischief to himself inumerable, such as cutting up his garden destroying his things and one he suspects him of having attempted to poison him. he thinks it necessary for him to be allways upon his guard against his malice. he says giving up his labour is giving up nothing for he loses ten times more labour by his presence than ten such would do. thus far I believe I have mentioned every thing necessary, for the story of John's conduct would extend beyond the limit of any letter. I really believe him to be a most determined villain equal to any crime on earth. we received the most flattering accounts from Jeffersons Master as a boy of uncommon industry and application. the others are all going on pretty well and are all remarkably healthy. Adieu My Dearest Father. Lilly's business has taken up so much of my time and paper that I have only room to subscribe my self with inexpressible tenderness. Your affectionate Daughter,

M.R.

JOHN TYLER
TO
MARY TYLER

---

*T*yler wrote this letter to his daughter during a major remodeling of the plantation house at Sherwood Forest in Virginia.

Washington June 4. 1844

My Dear Daughter
I have been so extremely annoyd of late by the constant calls made upon me and the pressure of public matters that I have not had

leizure to write. In truth I had nothing to write about which would be of any interest to you. My hope is that you are now comfortable in your chamber and that the bricklayers, having finished the brick work are actively inguaged in lathing and plaistering. You do not tell what the carpenters have done. Except that the house is all coverd in. Are the floors laid or are they now about them? When that is done their work to the House will be nearly finished. The sash and some other things are made in Philadelphia and will immediately be ordered around. When they are put in you will see that not much work will remain to be done. The porch will be the principal job. If possible I shall visit you the last of June or in July, but if prevented from doing so I will let you know.

How much corn did Harry deliver and what did he get for it? I hope he had not sold too close. How does the wheat and corn look? The oats I take it for granted are ruined by the drought.

I hope you will have an agreeable neighbour in Mrs. Gay. They staid with us when on their way home. The Doctor seemed delighted with his match and she was no less pleased. Letty plays the Queen in some style, but is pretty full of flirtation.

As to politics they go helter skelter. The Democrats are terribly alarmed at their own doings and are now looking to me for help. Clays election over Polk is nearly certain and they, or many of them anxiously desire to run a Union ticket with me and Polk. They universally admit now that I would beat Clay. I have no cause to regret what has transpired. All others are ...[one word erased] but myself, and I can either continue the contest or abandon it with honor. By not going into their convention I am savd from the fate which has killd off so many others.

I may write you again next week. What else I may do on any subject be assured my dear daughter that your happiness will ever be near to the heart of your Father, John Tyler

MARY GARFIELD
TO
JAMES GARFIELD

$\mathcal{M}$ary was just ten years old when she wrote this cute but informative letter to her father, reflecting her view of life on the family farm. From the minute details about newborn chicks to the construction of a new barn, young Mary happily updates Garfield, who was in Washington, D.C., serving as a U.S. representative from Ohio.

Mentor May 28th 1877

My dear Papa.

I was very sorry to have you go away but of course, you had to.
Papa the old white hen has hatched some of the little chickens

PRESIDENT AND MRS. JAMES GARFIELD AND THEIR FAMILY, HARRY,
ABRAM, MARY (MOLLIE), IRVIN, AND JAMES.

but I saw an egg which had some of the shell broken off and I guess she will come off all right. Miss mays is not feeling well a bit she was laying down almost all day. Irvin went to Hiram today, with Grandpa and Grandma. Hal took the grey horses to be shod in Painsville this morning. The men are going to begin the barn tomorrow, Mamma says that you will have a good large barnyard and I think so too. I want you to come home just as soon as you can. I am so glad you rented the piano for I like to play on it very much. It has been a very pleasant today.

Abe was reading to mamma and, he said about the ox. he said, "The boy is after the ox."only he pronounces after just as Miss Mays does, it sounds so funny to hear him. Papa I always liked to write to you and Mamma did you know that?

I am all the time thinking that your desk (which is in the bedroom) is in the parlour and get fooled that way. I am real well as I always am. Mr. Sumner wrote us children a long letter five big sheets of paper and he sent me a handkerchief with some words at the corner I forget what it was, I must answer his letter when Sunday comes around again. I take your place in sleeping with Mamma when you are gone. I must stop now write and answer this small letter.

Good bye from your loving daughter Molly

P.S. I must send you a kiss and a hug. M.G.

ULYSSES S. GRANT
TO
ELLEN GRANT

---

*P*ostpresidency, Grant clearly hoped to entice his daughter to make the long journey to New York City by describing how his new house would appeal to the happiness and comfort of his grandchildren. Although Ellen and her family lived in England, she and her children enjoyed many long visits with her parents.

New York City Aug. 2nd 1881

My Dear Daughter:

I did not see your Ma's letter to you which you do not quite under-stand. But what she meant to say is about this. When she wrote we had no house, and if we did not succeed in making a purchase we would be boarding at a hotel. In that case she wanted a visit. But now we have bought a beautiful house up by the Park. We will commence furnishing it about the middle of September and will no doubt have every thing comfortable by the 10th of Oct. We will want you, Algy and all the children to come so as to be here at that time or as soon after as possible. Fred & Ida and you and your children will have all of the 3rd floor. In that there are four large bed rooms. The picture of your little girl is beautiful. I have no doubt but she & little Algi will be so much spoiled that they will not want to go back to Eng-land. They will be much pleased too with their little cousin Julia. The park is so handy that the children will be able to walk out there with their nurses to play when ever the weather is good.

All are very well and send much love to you, Algi and all the children.

Affectionately yours, U. S. Grant

THE WHITE HOUSE WEDDING OF ELLEN (NELLIE) GRANT,
DAUGHTER OF ULYSSES S. GRANT, TO ALGERNON C. F. SARTORIS, AS
SHOWN IN FRANK LESLIE'S ILLUSTRATED NEWSPAPER IN 1874.

ULYSSES S. GRANT
TO
ELLEN GRANT

New York City. Sept. 29th 1881

My Dear Daughter:

Your nice long letter of Sept. 14th is received. Your Ma & I will be glad to see you as soon as you can come. We go into our house to-day, but with but little furniture. It will be two or three weeks before the furniture is all in. With all the pretty things we picked up on our trip around the world I think it will look very pretty.

MARY SCOTT HARRISON (STANDING); HER CHILDREN, BENJAMIN AND MARY; HER MOTHER, MRS. HARRISON; AND GRANDFATHER, REVEREND SCOTT.

Your Ma said something about what I was to say in refference to your proposition to bring over certain bed linens and your silver ware. I am sure if I attempt to tell you what I will make a mistake. However we have much to purchase in the way of the articles. If you bring over what you do not want in the way of linen in hand we can use it to advantage, and will pay you for it what we would have to pay elsewhere. If you will bring over a Silver Basin, Ice pitcher, slop bowl, in fact pretty complete set for 24 people, including Knives & forks, we will take them. I will tell your Ma as near as I can what I have written here and if it is not correct she must write. One thing I am sure I am right in saying. Your ma says to bring over but one girl with you. Our difficulty is more for servants rooms than anything else. Ida has but one girl who nurses the babe and does all she has to do. You will find your Ma's Maid always ready and then little Algie & I will take care of ourselves and help greatly in looking after the balance of the family.

With Kind regards to Mr. Sartoris, Sr. and love to all the balance of you, Affectionately

---

BENJAMIN HARRISON
TO
MARY HARRISON

---

*H*arrison eagerly told his daughter about the extensive improvements to his house in Indianapolis, Indiana, following his defeat by Grover Cleveland in 1892.

674 North Delaware Street, Indianapolis, Ind.
Sept 29 1895

My dear Daughter
I should have written you yesterday, but did not find time during the day and was too tired in the Evening. I am not sure

whether I have told you that I have taken an employment to argue a case in the Supreme Court of the United States on Oct. 21st-22d. It is a case involving the Constitutionality of the irrigation laws of California.

I am to meet the other counsel in the case in New York a few days before the time named, for consultation. They are to send me $2000 for a retainer and to agree upon the further fee when we meet. Mr. Choate of N.Y. is on the other side and I have already set in to make thorough preparation & will put in most of the time from now on. I have been retained in two other cases since I came home in which the retainer is 1000 & the fee not less that $5000.

The carpenters have put in a new door with a transom between the back hall & the rear bathroom, but the problem of getting furnace heat into the little back room is unsolved. They have been trying to get it up the chimney flue & have torn out the wall in the room & in the cellar, making the most intolerable mess & filling the house with lime dust while they were at work in the cellar the dust poured the windows like a white smoke. Josie is fairly sick over it, as she had just cleaned the house. And the worst of it is that it don't seem that they can now get the pipe in that way. I may have to put a little grate in the room but to get the natural gas to it will require tearing up floors. I fear the pipe to the bath room will prove too small for heating it properly.

Mrs. Miller has been reduced by her Drs. to the use of milk alone. They all say it was indigestion, but it seems to be a very peculiar & serious case. I was sorry to hear of Ben's sickness and mistake was free from side attacks. It might be well to see if some treatment or diet now would not eradicate this tendency before it becomes chronic. It will be a great drawback to him in life, if it cannot be cured. Tell him I am expecting a letter from him. If Mary wants that little knife I will send it to her.

I must go out for a little exercise & expect to mail this for the Evening collection.

A recent letter from Bettie Eaton says she & Arch came to Pueblo Col. for a little vacation & that she was taken with an acute inflamation of the eyes and lay for three weeks in a dark room.

She was able when she wrote to use her eyes a little. Arch too has a bad throat & they have had a doleful time.

Kiss the dear children for me. I will come up to see you when I go to N.Y. next month & before I go to Washington. With very very much love, Your Father Benj Harrison

---

THEODORE ROOSEVELT
TO
ETHEL CAROW ROOSEVELT

---

*T*welve-year-old Ethel was at Oyster Bay, Long Island, helping to take care of her siblings when Roosevelt wrote to her expressing his thanks, in words and pictures, for her efforts in maintaining the family. The jovial tone of these amusing letters reveals the close, personal relationship that the president had with his younger daughter.

ETHEL, DAUGHTER OF THEODORE ROOSEVELT,
AND HER MOTHER EDITH ROOSEVELT.

Dearest Ethel:
I think you are a little trump and I love your letter, and the way you take care of the children and keep down the expenses and cook bread and are just your own blessed busy cunning self. You would have enjoyed being at Valley Forge with us on Sunday. It is a beautiful place, and, of course, full of historic associations. The garden here is lovely. A pair of warbling vireos have built in a linden and sing all the time. The lindens, by the way, are in bloom, and Massachusetts Avenue is fragrant with them. The magnolias are all in bloom, too, and the jasmine on the porch.

THEODORE ROOSEVELT
TO
ETHEL CAROW ROOSEVELT

White House, Washington. June 22d 1904

Darling Ethel,
Here goes for the picture letter!

Ethel administers necessary discipline to Archie and Quentin.
Ethel gives sick Yagent a bottle of medicine.

Father plays tennis with Mr. Cooley. Father's shape & spectacles are reproduced with photographic fidelity; also Mr. Cooley's smile.

Leo chases a squirrel which fortunately he can't catch.

A nice policeman feeding a squirrel with bread; I fed two with bread this afternoon.

There! My invention has given out. Mother & Aunt Emily have been on a picnic down the river with General Crozier. We have been sitting on the portico in the moonlight. Sister is very good.

Your loving, father

LYNDON B. JOHNSON
TO
LYNDA BIRD JOHNSON

*J*ohnson is seen in his most cherished family mode in this charming letter to Lynda, written shortly after he left the White House. His Texas ranch and his grandchildren seemed to provide him with the greatest joys of his life following his presidency.

September 19, 1969

My dearest Lynda:

I have Lucinda on my calendar and I am really going to try to come up there for that little one's first birthday. We will let you know a day or two ahead of time.

The ranch machinery continues to break down and we can't seem to keep two machines going at once, but we do have some of the planting done and all the land is as beautiful as I can ever remember. I continue to spend most of my time on ranch matters.

Chuck is getting ahead of me in golf, but I will practice up on that later.

We love the colored photographs of Lucinda trying cheerfully to get her whole hand in her mouth. They are on the little table in my desk which is pretty much littered with chapters for the book and other paper work.

Much love to each of you.
Devotedly, your father Lbj

*L*uci became very involved in running the family communications businesses in Texas, including serving as chair of the LBJ Holding Company.

October 11, 1971

Daddy:

Mother and I met with Tom Johnson on Monday, October 11, to discuss the general refurbishing needs of KTBC. Tom indicated there was a general consensus between him and Elmo Brown that the AM and FM control room, plus the TV control room and the film room, needed carpeting for two reasons: (1) functionally, it would help acoustics (2) it would improve the looks.

At this time, Tom indicated that Mr. Kellam also had suggested that Jim Uzzell (the chief accountant) might be designated a separate office. The reason: Mr. Uzzell needs his privacy for obvious reasons. Many people pass by his desk, since all payrolls and accounting are done in his area. Also, the copying machine is located adjacent to him.

Tom also suggested that we might explore a more efficient use of the auditorium space on the fourth floor. It presently is used for only two profit-sharing meetings during the year, with the possible exception of some larger group meeting than could be handled by the conference room. Possibly this might be broken up into more efficient office space.

The large auditorium and a standard-size office adjacent to John Barr on the fourth floor are the only two areas which could be used for expansion into more efficient office space.

Luci Nugent

STANDING ON THE SOUTH PORTICO OF THE WHITE HOUSE
ON AUGUST 6, 1966, ARE MRS. LYNDON JOHNSON, LYNDON JOHNSON,
LUCI JOHNSON (BRIDE) AND PATRICK NUGENT (GROOM),
AND MRS. AND MRS. GERARD NUGENT.

SOURCES

Letters Sources

JOHN ADAMS

Adams Family Papers, Massachusetts Historical Society.

Abigail Adams Smith House, Colonial Dames of America, New York.

Lyman Butterfield, ed., *Adams Family Correspondence.*
Cambridge, Massachusetts: Belknap Press, 1961–1993.

Abigail Adams Smith, ed., *Journal and Correspondence of Miss Adams,*
Daughter of John Adams, Second President of the United States. New York:
Wiley and Putnam, 1841–1842.

GEORGE H. W. BUSH

George H. W. Bush, Family Papers.

George H. W. Bush, *All the Best: George Bush, My Life in Letters and Other*
Writings. New York: Scribner, 1999.

GROVER CLEVELAND

Grover Cleveland Papers, Library of Congress.

GERALD R. FORD

Gerald Ford Presidential Library, Ann Arbor, Michigan.
Susan Elizabeth Ford, Private Personal Collection.

JAMES GARFIELD

James Garfield Papers, Manuscript Division, Library of Congress.

ULYSSES S. GRANT

Ellen Grant Collection, Chicago Historical Society.

John Y. Simon, ed., *The Papers of Ulysses S. Grant*. Carbondale: Southern
Illinois University Press, 1967–.

BENJAMIN HARRISON

Benjamin Harrison Home, Indianapolis, Indiana.

Benjamin Harrison Papers, Library of Congress.

RUTHERFORD B. HAYES

Rutherford B. Hayes Memorial Library, Rutherford B. Hayes Presidential
Center, Fremont, Ohio.

THOMAS JEFFERSON

Thomas Jefferson Papers, Alderman Library, University of Virginia.

Thomas Jefferson Papers, Manuscript Division, Library of Congress.

Thomas Jefferson Papers, New York Public Library.

Thomas Jefferson Papers, University of California at Los Angeles.

Jefferson/Coolidge Papers, Massachusetts Historical Society.

Edwin M. Betts and James A. Bear, Jr., eds., *The Family Letters of Thomas
Jefferson*. Columbia: University of Missouri Press, 1966.

Julian Boyd et al., eds., *The Papers of Thomas Jefferson*, 28 vols. Princeton, New Jersey: Princeton University Press, 1950–.

Sarah N. Randolph, *The Domestic Life of Thomas Jefferson*. Cambridge, Massachusetts: Harvard University Press, 1939.

ANDREW JOHNSON

Andrew Johnson Papers, Manuscript Division, Library of Congress.

LYNDON B. JOHNSON

Lyndon Baines Johnson Presidential Library, Austin, Texas.

JAMES MONROE

James Monroe Papers, James Monroe Museum and Memorial Library, Fredericksburg, Virginia.

RICHARD M. NIXON

Richard M. Nixon, *The Memoirs of Richard Nixon*. New York: Simon & Schuster Inc., 1978.

RONALD REAGAN

Ronald Reagan, Kiron K. Skinner et al., eds., *Reagan: A Life in Letters*. New York: Free Press, Simon & Schuster, 2003.

FRANKLIN D. ROOSEVELT

Franklin D. Roosevelt Presidential Library, Hyde Park, New York.

Elliott Roosevelt, ed., *F.D.R.: His Personal Letters, 1928–1945*, 2 vols. New York: Duell, Sloan and Pearce, 1950.

THEODORE ROOSEVELT

Theodore Roosevelt Memorial Association Collection, Houghton Library, Harvard University.

Theodore Roosevelt Papers, Manuscript Division, Library of Congress.
Alice Roosevelt Longworth Papers, Library of Congress.

Elting Morison et al., eds., *The Letters of Theodore Roosevelt*, 8 vols. Cambridge, Massachusetts: Harvard University Press, 1951–1954.

Joseph B. Bishop, eds., *Theodore Roosevelt's Letters to His Children*. New York: Charles Scribners, 1919.

WILLIAM HOWARD TAFT

William Howard Taft Papers, Manuscript Division, Library of Congress.

Helen Taft Manning Papers, Manuscript Division, Library of Congress.

HARRY S. TRUMAN

Harry S. Truman Presidential Library, Independence, Missouri.

Margaret Truman, *Letters from Father: The Truman Family's Personal Correspondence*. New York: Arbor House, 1981.

JOHN TYLER

John Tyler Papers, Manuscript Division, Library of Congress.

Lyon G. Tyler, *The Letters and Times of the Tylers*, 3 vols. Richmond, Virginia: Whittet & Shepperson, 1884–1885 and Williamsburg, Virginia: [William and Mary College], 1896.

GEORGE WASHINGTON

George Washington Letters, Chapin Library, Williamstown, Massachusetts.

George Washington Letters, J. P. Morgan Library, New York.

George Washington Letters, Mount Vernon Ladies Aid Society, Mount Vernon, Virginia.

John C. Fitzpatrick, ed., *The Writings of George Washington*, 40 vols. Washington, D.C.: Library of Congress, 1931–1944.

"From the Collection of Edmund Law Rogers," Century Magazine, vol. 40 (1890), pp. 22–25.

WOODROW WILSON

Woodrow Wilson Papers, Manuscript Division, Library of Congress.

Woodrow Wilson Collection, Princeton University, Princeton, New Jersey.

Ray Stannard Baker Collection of Wilsoniana, Manuscript Division, Library of Congress.

William G. McAdoo Papers, Manuscript Division, Library of Congress.

Arthur S. Link et al., eds., *The Papers of Woodrow Wilson*, 69 vols. Princeton, New Jersey: Princeton University Press, 1964–1994.

Secondary Sources

Carl S. Anthony, *America's First Families*. New York: Simon and Schuster, 2000.

Patricia Brady, ed., George Washington's *Beautiful Nelly: The Letters of Eleanor Parke Custis Lewis to Elizabeth Bordley Gibson, 1794–1851.* Columbia: University of South Carolina Press, 1991.

H. W. Brands, ed., *The Selected Letters of Theodore Roosevelt.* New York: Cooper Square Press, 2001.

Robert A. Caro, *The Years of Lyndon Johnson: The Path to Power.* New York: Alfred A. Knopf, 1982.

Robert A. Caro, *The Years of Lyndon B. Johnson: Means of Ascent.* New York: Alfred A. Knopf, 1990.

Robert A. Caro, *The Years of Lyndon Johnson: Master of the Senate.* New York, Alfred A. Knopf, 2002.

Betty Boyd Caroli, *The Roosevelt Women.* New York: Basic Books, 1998.

Thomas L. Connelly and Michael D. Senecal, *Almanac of American Presidents from 1789 to the Present*. New York: Oxford, 1991.

Frank Cormier, *LBJ: The Way He Was*. New York: Doubleday & Co., 1977.

W. H. Crook, *Memories of the White House*. Boston, Massachusetts: Little, Brown & Company, 1911.

Kathleen Dalton, Theodore Roosevelt: *A Strenuous Life*. New York: Alfred A. Knopf, 2002.

William A. DeGregorio, *The Complete Book of Presidents*, 2nd ed. New York: Dembner Books, 1989.

Joseph E. Fields, *"Worthy Partner": The Papers of Martha Washington*. Westport, Connecticut: Greenwood Press, 1994.

Doris Kearns Goodwin, *Lyndon Johnson and the American Dream*. New York: St. Martin's Press, 1991.

Doris Kearns Goodwin, *No Ordinary Time: Franklin and Eleanor Roosevelt, The Home Front in World War II*. New York: Simon & Schuster, 1994.

Joseph N. Kane, *Facts about the Presidents*. New York: H.W. Wilson Co., 1989.

Margaret Leech and Harry J. Brown, *The Garfield Orbit*. New York: Harper & Row, 1978.

Eleanor Wilson McAdoo, *The Woodrow Wilsons*. New York: Macmillan Company, 1937.

David McCullough, *John Adams*. New York: Simon & Schuster, 2001.

David McCullough, *Truman*. New York: Simon and Schuster, 1992.

Edmund Morris, *The Rise of Theodore Roosevelt*. New York: Coward, McCann & Geoghegan, 1979.

Geoffrey Perret, *Ulysses S. Grant: Soldier and President*. New York: Random House, 1997.

Monte M. Poen, ed., *Letters Home by Harry Truman*. New York: G. P. Putnam's Sons, 1984.

Sandra L. Quinn and Sanford Kanter, *America's Royalty: All the Presidents' Children*. Westport, Connecticut: Greenwood Press, 1983.

Ishbel Ross, *An American Family: The Tafts—1678 to 1964.* New York: World Publishing Company,1964.

Frances W. Saunders, *Ellen Axson Wilson.* Chapel Hill, North Carolina: University of North Carolina Press, 1985.

Robert Seager II, *And Tyler Too: A Biography of John and Julia Gardiner Tyler.* New York: McGraw Hill Book Company, 1963.

William Seale, *The President's House: A History*, 2 vols. Washington, D.C.: White House Historical Association, 1986.

Harry J. Sievers, *Benjamin Harrison: Hoosier President White House and After.* New York: Bobbs-Merrill Company, 1968.

John Y. Simon, ed., *The Personal Memoirs of Julia Dent Grant.* New York: G. P. Putnam's Sons, 1975.

Marie Smith and Louise Durbin, *White House Brides.* Washington, D.C.: Acropolis Books, 1966.

Hans L. Trefousse, *Andrew Johnson: A Biography.* New York: W. W. Norton & Co., 1989.

T. Harry Williams, ed., *Hayes: The Diary of a President, 1875–1881.* New York: David McKay Company, 1964.

ACKNOWLEDGMENTS

A special thanks to those people who generously donated their time and effort to locate letters and photographs and provide valuable information—

First, to Susan Ford Bates who made a great personal effort to provide letters from her father, Gerald Ford; to George H. W. Bush for providing personal correspondence with his daughter, Dorothy; and Dennis Revell, who made a special effort to locate letters between his late wife, Maureen, and Ronald Reagan.

Then to those staff members in the libraries and the offices of presidents for their extra assistance: Nancy Lisenby and Linda Casey Poepsel, the Office of George H. W. Bush; Joanne Drake, Office of Ronald Reagan; Debbie Carter and Mary Finch, George Bush Presidential Library; Linda Seelke, Lyndon Johnson Presidential Library; Anne Moore and Jennifer E. Capps, President Benjamin Harrison Home; Nan Card, Rutherford B. Hayes Presidential Center; Leigh A. Gavin, Chicago Historical Society; Alycia Vivona, Franklin D. Roosevelt Presidential Library; Kenneth G. Hafeli and Donna Lehman, Gerald Ford Presidential Library; Pat Virgil, Buffalo and Erie County Historical Society; Daniel Preston of the Papers of James Monroe; David Voelkel of the James Monroe Museum and Memorial Library; the anonymous staff members who processed for public use the collections utilized in the compilation of this work at the Library of Congress; the presidential libraries of George H. W. Bush, Lyndon Johnson, Harry S. Truman, Richard Nixon, Ronald Reagan, and

Rutherford B. Hayes; Harvard University; the University of Virginia; George Washington's Mount Vernon; Benjamin Harrison Home; and the James Monroe Museum and Memorial Library.

Heartfelt thanks to Iris Bodin Newsom of the Library of Congress Publishing Office, without whom this book would not have been completed in such a professional and timely fashion; W. Ralph Eubanks, Director of Publishing, for his critical support in bringing this project to fruition and completion; and Laura Ross, our New York editor.

PERSONAL ACKNOWLEDGMENTS

Gerard W. Gawalt extends his thanks and sympathy to his wife and friend, Jane Cavanaugh Gawalt, for her help in completing "one last project."

Special thanks go to my daughters, Susan, Ann, and Ellen, for growing with me into our own special father-daughter friendships.

Ann G. Gawalt extends her thanks and special recognition: First, I owe a great deal of gratitude to my husband, Brian Rushforth, my partner in all things great and small, who has allowed me space and time to work on this project. My mother, Jane, the ultimate Daddy's girl, listened patiently to the two collaborators of this project over Saturday dinners and walks in Maine. Her measured words and faithful encouragement helped spur the work. My two sisters, Susan and Ellen, exceptional and accomplished women, also lent their wisdom. I would also like to acknowledge these individuals who shared their thoughts and advice: Sharon Donovan, Molly Newman, Becky Cocolis, and Tom Herlihy. Finally, I would like to thank my father for sharing a part of his life's work with me. I am honored to have this opportunity to work with him and be the beneficiary of his sage advice.

Permission to publish letters was granted by the following institutions and people: Eleanor R. Seagraves; Office of Ronald Reagan; James Monroe Law Library and Museum; Harvard

University Press; Harvard College Library; New York Public Library; Astor; Lenox and Tilden Foundations; University of Virginia Library; Office of George H. W. Bush; Mount Vernon Hotel Museum and Garden; Mount Vernon Ladies' Association; Chicago Historical Society; University of California at Los Angeles; President Benjamin Harrison Home; Rutherford B. Hayes Presidential Center; and Harry S. Truman Library.

INDEX

Abbaye Royale de Panthemont, 98
Adams, Abigail (Amelia, Emmy, Nabby), 18, 38-39, 73-74, 94-96, 132-133, 177-181, 194, 221, 222-228, 233-234, 265-268
Adams, John, 17, 38-39, 73-74, 94-96, 132-133, 177-181, 194, 221, 222-226, 227-228, 229, 233-234, 265-268
Advice, 72-91
Annapolis, 75, 96
Aranjuez, Spain, 102
Atlee, Clement, 284-285
Austin, TX, 216

Baby Ruth. See Cleveland, Ruth.
Baldwin School, 120
Berlin, Germany, 284
Billington, James H., 8
Birthdays, 69
Boating, 57
Boettiger, Clarence John, 253, 257
Bonnie and Clyde, 128
Braintree, MA, 178, 223
Budapest, 277
Bermuda, 87, 229
Burr, Aaron, 228, 229
Bush, Dorothy (Doro) W., 35, 64-65, 66-68, 71, 174-175, 191
Bush, George H. W., 35, 64-65, 66-68, 71, 174-175, 191

Caldicott, Helen, 262
Camp, 63-65
Camp David, 191
Camp Ripley, Minn., 84

Campan, Madame, 101-102
Cancer, 203, 215
Cathedral School, 119
Cattle Queen of Montana, 61
Charles XII, 106
Chase, Mrs. Irving, 251
Childbirth, 156-175
Christmas, 45, 71
Civil War, 106, 109
Clay, Henry, 234-235, 294
Cleveland, Esther, 25, 45, 165
Cleveland, Frances Folsom, 149
Cleveland, Grover (B. Stephen Grover), 25, 45, 149, 204, 299
Cleveland, Ruth, 25, 45, 149
Cleveland, OH, 110, 115
Cold Harbor, VA, 108
Communism, 285-286
Consolation, 192-219
Coolidge, Calvin, 11, 211, 250, 252-253, 283
Cornish, NH, 144
Count Apponyi, 277
Cox, Edward, 154
Custis, Eleanor (Nelly) Parke, 16-17, 78-81
Custis, Elizabeth Parke, 16-17, 136-138, 139-140, 195
Custis, Martha Parke, 16-17

Davis, John W., 250
Declaration of Independence, 38
Derby, Richard, 141-142, 185-186
Derby, Richard, Jr., 185-186
Diet, 210, 214

Dimmick, Mary Scott Lord, 204
Driving, 187

East Chester, 228
Edgehill, 160, 292
Education, 92-129
Encouragement, 176-191
Eppes, Mr., 160-162, 229-232
Eppington, 76

Farmington, CT, 116
Filmore, Millard, 11
Fishing, 258
Football, 118
Ford, Gerald R., Jr., 33-34, 69-70, 90-91
Ford, Susan Elizabeth, 34, 69-70, 90-91
Fort Riley, 58
Friendship, 36-71

Galena, IL, 238
Galt, Edith Bolling, 144-147
Gardiner, Julia, 142
Garfield, James A., 10, 25, 36, 41, 42-43, 44, 92-93, 110-111, 111-112, 176, 177, 183-184, 185, 238, 290-291, 295-296
Garfield, Lucretia, 184
Garfield, Mary (Molly, Mollie), 25, 36, 41-43, 44, 92-93, 110-111, 111-112, 176, 177, 183-184, 185, 290-291, 295-296
Genet, Edmond Charles, 265-266
George, Lloyd, 282-283
German Town, 137
Golden Gate Bridge, 255
Gouverneur, Samuel L., 162
Grand Tour, 271
Grant, Ellen (B. Julia) Wrenshall, 23, 40-41, 108-109, 193, 203-204, 238-239, 240-241, 269-270, 296-297, 298-299
Grant, Julia Dent, 270
Grant, Ulysses S., 12, 23, 40-41, 108-109, 193, 203-204, 235, 269-270
Greeneville, TN, 202, 236, 237
Griffin, Merv, 65

Hamilton, Alexander, 224
Harrison, Benjamin, 14, 26, 204-207,

299-301
Harrison, Caroline L. Scott, 204
Harrison, Marthena, 206
Harrison, Mary (Mamie) Scott, 26, 204-206, 207, 298, 299-301
Harrison, Mrs. Russell, 206
Harrison Walker, Elizabeth, 26
Harvard College, 180
Hay, George, 197
Hayes, Frances (Fanny), 24, 82-83, 93, 112-114, 115-116, 117-118
Hayes, Rutherford B., 10, 24, 82-83, 93, 112-118
Health, 192-219
Helsinki, 287
Home life, 290-306
Hope Park, 136
Hunting, 48

Indianapolis, IN, 299

Jamaica, Long Island, 225
Japan, 269
Jay, John, 267
Jefferson Eppes, Maria, 158
Jefferson, Martha, 12, 14, 19, 72, 74-75, 96-98, 99-101, 133-135, 292-293
Jefferson, Mary (Maria), 14, 19, 73, 76-77, 156-157, 158-162, 181-183, 228-232
Jefferson, Thomas, 7, 12, 14, 18-19, 72, 73, 74-75, 76-77, 96-101, 133-135, 156-157, 158-162, 181-183, 224, 227, 228-230, 231-232, 292-293
Johnson, Andrew, 22, 192-193, 201-203, 221, 235-237
Johnson, Eliza McCardle, 202
Johnson, Lucy (Luci) Baines, 32, 65-66, 124-125, 216-218, 305-306
Johnson, Lynda Bird, 32, 63-64, 124-125, 126-128, 174, 189, 215-216, 260-261, 304
Johnson, Lyndon B., 10, 13, 31-32, 63-64, 65-66, 124-128, 174, 189, 215-218, 260-261, 304-306
Johnson, Martha, 22, 192-193, 201-203, 221, 235-237
Johnson, Rebekah Baines, 215-216
July 4th, 38

Kennedy, John F., 259
Kennedy, Robert F., 218
Key West, FL, 285
Keystone Ranch, 48

Law, Thomas, 136, 139, 195
LBJ Holding Company, 305
League of Nations, 249, 280, 282
Library of Congress, 7, 11, 12
Lincoln, Abraham, 7, 193, 201, 235
Lodge, Henry Cabot, 249-250
London, 103
Longworth, Nicholas, 242-243, 245, 246, 277
Loon Lake, 205

Madison, James, 7, 19, 224
Malaoañan Palace, Philippines, 272
Manning, Frederick J., 148, 170
Marlborough, Duke of, 105
Marriage, 130-155
McKee, Benjamin Harrison, 206
McKee, Mary Lodge, 206
McKinley, William, 245
Mentor, OH, 41, 112, 295
Mittleberger (Augusta) School, 112
Monroe, Eliza Kortright, 20, 101-102, 103-105, 162-163, 164, 196
Monroe, Elizabeth Kortright, 197
Monroe, James, 12, 19, 101-103, 104-105, 162-164, 196-198
Monroe, Maria Hester, 20, 197-198
Monticello, 160, 292-293
Music, 59, 84-87

Nashville, TN, 201
National Archives, 12
New Haven, CT, 151, 153
New York City, 56, 77, 133, 240, 267, 296, 297, 298
Nixon, Julie, 33, 153-154, 190, 289
Nixon, Patricia (Tricia), 33, 155
Nixon, Richard M., 32-33, 153-154, 155, 190, 289
Nobel Peace Prize, 274
Nugent, Patrick, 65, 306

Oak Hill, 196, 197
Orme School, 88, 128, 218

Oslo, 287
Overseas travel, 264-289
Oxford, England, 52
Oyster Bay. See Sagamore Hill.

Paris, 40, 132, 180, 182
Passy, France, 95
Patterson, David Trotter, 235
Pen-Y-Groes, Bryn Mawr, PA, 148
Philadelphia, 38, 74, 78, 94, 139, 195, 266
Philippines, 271-273
Polio, 213
Politics, 220-263
Polk, James K., 234-235, 294
Porter (Sarah) School, 112, 116

Quincy, MA, 233

Rachmaninoff, 59
Randolph, Thomas Mann, 133, 135
Reagan, Nancy Davis, 61
Reagan, Patricia (Patti) Ann, 34-35, 61-62, 62-63, 88-90, 128-129, 218-219, 262-263
Reagan, Ronald Wilson, 34, 61-62, 62-63, 88-90, 128-129, 174, 218-219, 262-263
Richmond, VA, 135
Robb, Catherine Lewis, 174
Robb, Charles, 125, 126-127, 189
Rogers, Nicolas Lloyd, 197
Roosevelt, Alice Lee, 14, 27, 45-46, 83-84, 118-119, 220, 242-243, 243-244, 245-246, 247, 265, 274-278
Roosevelt, Anna (Sis) Eleanor, 30, 56-58, 172-173, 213-215, 221, 253-257, 258-259
Roosevelt, Edith, 301
Roosevelt, Ethel Carow, 7, 13, 14, 27, 47-52, 119, 141-143, 185-186, 291, 301-303
Roosevelt, Franklin Delano, 10, 30, 56-58, 172-173, 213-215, 221, 253-257, 258-259
Roosevelt, James, 257
Roosevelt, Quentin, 208-209, 302
Roosevelt, Theodore, 7, 10, 13, 14, 27, 45-46, 47-52, 83-84, 118-119, 141-

143, 185-186, 208-209, 220, 242-246, 247, 265, 274-278, 291, 301-303
Russo-Japanese War, 274-276

Sagamore Hill, Oyster Bay, Long Island, 51, 141, 142, 185, 208, 301
Salzburg, Austria, 271
Santiago, Cuba, 47
Santo Domingo, 233-234
Sartoris, Algernon, 240-241, 297, 299
Sayre, Francis B., 143, 164
Sayre, Francis Woodrow Wilson, 164
Scandinavia, 287-288
Seattle, WA, 214, 254, 255
Shennondale, 163
Sherwood Forest, 199, 293-294
Smith, Elizabeth Quincy, 194
Smith, William S., 132, 222-223, 224
Smoking, 85, 89
Sources, 307-313
Spanish American War, 47
Spiegel Grove Fremont, OH, 82, 117
Supreme Court of the United States, 121, 170, 210, 251, 282
Swedish Hospital, Seattle, WA, 173

Taft, Charles, 211
Taft, Helen Herron, 28, 52-53, 120-121, 122-123, 130-131, 148-153, 157, 170-172, 210-211, 212, 250-252, 253, 264, 271-274, 282-283
Taft, Robert, 211
Taft, William Howard, 10, 13, 28, 52-53, 120-121, 122-123, 130-131, 148-153, 157, 170-172, 210-211, 212, 245, 250-252, 253, 264, 271-274, 282-283
Thomas Jefferson: Genius of Liberty, 7
Time to Heal, 90
Tokyo, 269
Toulon, France, 100
Travel, 103, 264-289
Treaty of Portsmouth, 274
Truman, Bess, 188
Truman, Harry S., 10, 13, 31, 37, 58-61, 73, 84-86, 87-88, 123-124, 187-188, 259-260, 284-286, 287-289
Truman, Mary Margaret (Margie), 9,

31, 37, 58-61, 73, 84-86, 87-88, 123-124, 187-188, 259-260, 284-286, 287-289
Tyler, Elizabeth (Lizzie), 21
Tyler, John, 14, 21, 105-106, 107-108, 131, 140-141, 198-200, 234-235, 293-294
Tyler, Letitia, 198
Tyler, Royall, 132, 178
Tyler Jones, Mary, 21, 105-108, 131, 140-141, 198-200, 234-235, 293-294

Vietnam, 289

Waller, William N., 234-235
Washington, George, 7, 10, 11, 13, 16-17, 18, 78-81, 136-140, 195, 224, 265, 267
Washington Lear, Frances Bassett, 195
Washington, D.C., 44, 45, 49, 59, 60, 105, 110, 118, 123, 140, 158, 159, 161, 162, 187, 198, 230, 232, 243, 245, 250, 277, 293
Watergate, 190
Whig Party, 234
White House, 53, 57, 143, 147, 155, 166, 258, 278, 302
Williams College, 164
Williamstown, MA, 145, 164, 183
Wilson, Eleanor (Nell) Randolph, 14, 29, 54, 55-56, 146, 168, 249, 279
Wilson, Ellen Axson, 146, 166, 207
Wilson, Jessie Woodrow, 14, 29, 37, 53-54, 55, 143-144, 145-146, 147-148, 164-167, 168-169, 207-208, 247-248, 250, 265, 278-279, 280-281
Wilson, Margaret Woodrow, 14, 29, 54, 144-145, 146, 265, 279
Wilson, Woodrow, 10, 14, 28-29, 27, 53-54, 55-56, 143-148, 164-169, 207-208, 247-250, 265, 278-279, 280-281
Women's Suffrage, 248
World War I, 53, 165, 247-248, 249, 278-279
World War II, 60, 258, 284

Yale University, 121, 250, 282